Fine
Print
On
Type

The Best of
Fine Print Magazine
on
Type and
Typography

Edited by
Charles Bigelow
Paul Hayden Duensing
Linnea Gentry

Fine Print

Bedford Arts

San Francisco 1989

Published by:
Fine Print
P.O. Box 3394
San Francisco, California 94119

Bedford Arts
250 Sutter Street, Suite 550
San Francisco, California 94108

Acknowledgments:
"The Types of Jan Van Krimpen," originally published in
Fine Print, April and July 1981, is included in *Letters of Credit*
(London: Gordon Fraser; and Boston: David R. Godine,
1986), and is here reprinted by permission.

"After All, What Does Functional Typography Mean?"
by G. W. Ovink was originally published in *Printing and
Graphic Arts*, 1953, and is reprinted with permission of
Roderick Stinehour.

The illustrations for "A New Civilité" are reproduced by permission of Hermann Zapf. Other essays published by permission of the authors include "Eric Gill's Perpetua Type" by
James Mosley; "The Dante Types," and "Rejoinder and
Extension to Herbert Johnson's 'Notes on Frederic Warde
and the True Story of His Arrighi Type.'" by John Dreyfus; as
well as "The Stone Family of Typefaces: New Voices for the
Electronic Age" by Sumner Stone.

E. M. Ginger, Editorial Direction

Library of Congress Cataloging-in-Publication Data

Fine print on type: the best of Fine print magazine on type
and typography / edited by Charles Bigelow, Paul Hayden
Duensing, Linnea Gentry.
     160 pp.
     Includes index.
ISBN 0-9607290-1-1 : $39.95. ISBN 0-9607290-2-X (soft):
$19.95. ISBN 0-938491-16-4 (Bedford Arts) : $39.95. ISBN
0-938491-17-2 (Bedford Arts : soft) : $19.95

     1.Type and type-founding. 2. Printing, Practical—
Layout. I. Bigelow, Charles A., 1945– II. Duensing, Paul Hayden,
1929– . III. Gentry, Linnea, 1948– . IV. Fine print.

Z250.F483 1988   88-17729
686.2'2—dc19   CIP

Contents

Introductions

The art of typography is based on the relationships between forms of letters and their meaning as signs. As images, the letters are grouped into words, the words are strung into lines, the lines are ranked into columns, the columns are divided into pages, and the pages are gathered into books – visual objects with multiple layers of organization. As signs, the letters form words, the words make up sentences, the sentences assemble into paragraphs, and the paragraphs become texts – conceptual objects with manifold levels of meaning.

The profusion of typographic signs, the intricacy of their construction, and the complexity of their interrelationships often captivate the literate mind that strays from concentration on letter meanings to contemplation of letterforms. As a cultural phenomenon, the shift of attention from meaning to form often indicates a change in either the technology or the usage of literacy. In the history of our own alphabet, the epigraphic experiments of archaic Greece, the writing manuals and geometric letter constructions of Renaissance Italy, the florescence of typefounders' fantasies in Industrial England, and the font fascination of present-day desktop publishers are all indicators of changing perceptions of literacy.

Such times of transition engender serious thought about the state of the literate art. The present era of digital typography, which has transformed many of the basic tools of writing, is no exception. This collection of essays from *Fine Print*, some of which I was fortunate to edit and a few of which I was privileged to write, examine an art in transition. What has been noteworthy about the transition is that typography has remained an art, whether based on the casting of intricate sculptures by methods essentially unchanged since their invention or perfection by Gutenberg, or based on the painting of pixel patterns by beams of laser light controlled by algorithms of computer graphics.

Why is typography an art? Its purpose is, after all, utilitarian – the conveyance of linguistic information between persons so separated in space, time, or culture that the spoken word cannot communicate without intermediation. Although work of minimal functionalism is commonly found in all eras of literacy, there is often refined work whose execution rivals that found in any other artistic medium. Why does typography so often demand great subtlety of design, exquisite refinement of detail, and exacting precision of execution, all seemingly disproportionate to the mundane task of marking down signs that have no apparent value in themselves, but exist only to represent the elements of speech and language?

Franz Boas, a pioneer in the study of non-literate cultures, observed in his influential study, *Primitive Art*, that careful attention to formal elements like regularity and symmetry, and emphasis on virtuosity and mastery of technique are found throughout the so-called primitive arts of the world – in the weaving of baskets, in the painting of pottery, in the carving of wooden implements, in the flaking of stone arrowheads. It should not surprise us to find the same artistic qualities in typography, if we accept that typography is an industrialized form of writing and that the ancient sages who so brilliantly invented the art of writing were themselves primitives and, indeed, illiterates, at least at first.

When we view writing in the city-states of Mesopotamia at the end of the Neolithic era, or in the Mayan temple cities of Meso-America, it shows even in its early days a high degree of regulation and graphic sophistication. Such qualities taken over from primitive art have changed but little in the intervening five millennia of literacy. The more we learn about the origins of writing, the more we may come to consider it less as the first signal invention of civilization and more as the last great intellectual achievement of the stone age.

If the revolutionary art of literacy was developed according to the high standards of pre-literate traditional arts, and if those standards have endured as the art has evolved, then we must re-examine Stanley Morison's claim that "the enjoyment of patterns is rarely the reader's chief aim." While he is right that such enjoyment may not be the chief aim of the *reader*, the making and enjoyment of literate patterns has undoubtedly been one of the principal aims and pleasures of the *scribe* since the very beginning of literacy. As the proliferation of inexpensive, computerized typographic tools threatens to make every author a potential typographer, the creation and enjoyment of typographic patterns may assume an even greater role in the fabrication of texts.

Moreover, like the ancient inventors of writing, the modern typographer still labors at the semiological foundations of literacy. In approaching each work, each design task, the typographer must examine basic principles. How shall the structure of a particular text be manifested? What are the relevant elements of language to be displayed? Which elements should be displayed iconically, which indexically, which symbolically? In this way, the typographer continually faces fundamental problems not unlike those familiar to the primitive artists discussed by Boas. How do the shapes convey meanings? How can the message be brought to life? What techniques are efficient and pleasurable for the fabricator and user both? The typographer also faces questions of the continuity of culture. How much of a design should be based on conventional wisdom? How much opportunity is there for innovation? How much for personal expression?

These questions are important not only when author and typographer are separate people, as has usually been the case, but also when the roles are combined in the same person, as will more and more be the case. "Typographic literacy" will become one more flavor of literacy that the modern author à la mode is expected to master. But of course as readers we are already typographically literate – we recognize the difference between capitals and lower case, roman and italic, normal and bold, seriffed and sans serif styles, and so on, and we understand the significance of such graphic variations in the particular texts. But this is mostly a passive understanding. Like a passive vocabulary, we read it but don't write it.

What we can anticipate in the immediate future of writing is an expansion of the active typographic vocabulary. The choice of styles and arrangements of typefaces in a text will be up to the author. Which shall it be? Galliard or Syntax? Century Schoolbook or Zapf Chancery? Isadora or Lucida? Will 10-point Times Roman be better set solid or with 2 points of leading? In a 20-pica column or a 30? Is seriffed type more legible than sans serif? Is legibility just familiarity?

Of the asking of such questions, both trivial and profound, there will be no end, and the task of typographic criticism will be to elucidate, to educate, to inquire, and to inform, as literacy moves into its sixth millennium. The collection of essays gathered here will help to point the way.

Charles Bigelow

One of the distinctive features of the human race is the ability to understand the notion of time and to conceive of past, present, and future (every human language embodies these three basic verb forms, whether it is considered an "advanced" language or one of the supposedly "primitive" speech systems). Bound up in this awareness is the need to record, first as writing, and in a more refined – and mechanical – sense as printing. The purpose of recording our thoughts, discoveries, skills, and experience is to share these with others with whom we can have no immediate contact across space or time.

In the series of essays which follow, the authors offer up their observations and opinions to their readers as a form of sharing the best of which they are capable with an unknown, unseen audience. It is the corpus of this legacy, given by one generation to the next, which constitutes the literature of our art and craft. Although the range of topics and viewpoints is wide, the unifying element – type – is the agent which is the core of this volume.

In the years during which *Fine Print* has surveyed and recorded the graphic field, we have seen a bewildering panorama of trends, eddies, crosscurrents, and upheavals. The photographic revolution in typesetting has itself been supplanted by electronics and digitization, and surely the next step is only months, or milliseconds, away.

For the letterpress printer, the demise of the great traditional sources of metal type has, at times, seemed to spell the beginning of the end, the *Schriftendämmerung*, the Twilight of Type. Yet the reduction of new metal faces has brought a close re-evaluation of the type designs we have. We begin to see typefaces being used with verve and ingenuity and taste, in ways unimaginable a decade ago. And as the production of new designs moves ahead in the electronic media, the use of contemporary technology in the service of fine printing cannot be far off. It seems fitting, then, that *Fine Print* should offer a collection of the published articles as a sort of summing up, a state-of-the-art report on where we have been and where we (think we) are. For we cannot adequately measure progress without some finite standard or, as I put it in an essay some years ago, "What we need is not so much the design for a new type, as a set of standards by which to judge the faces we have created and inherited." We at *Fine Print* hope that this collection will provide the infrastructure for those standards.

Paul Hayden Duensing

The essays gathered in this volume comprise a remarkable analysis of the many facets of the typographic arts. Their topics are both broad in scope, as in the surveys of Van Krimpen's and Menhart's entire works or the overview of wood types; and deep, as in the technicalities of matrix production, the applications of METAFONT, or the ongoing controversy of the Warde/Morison debate. Some of the authors within these pages look to the past for their standards of aesthetic and practical typography. Some reach out to the possibilities offered by pixels and lasers in order to endow the future with the standards born in the past. The eclecticism of their essays, in subject and stance, reveal a marvelous dynamism, a wealth of resources available for the continuing alliance of practical and aesthetic applications.

When we started the "On Type" column in the pages of *Fine Print* almost a dozen years ago, this dynamic analysis was our goal. To review the foundations of our typographic heritage, to scrutinize the successes and failures of our current efforts, and to investigate the wide array of potential tools with which to carry our standards of a "fine" typography into a technologically biased future. No other non-commercial publication was (or is now) examining the art of typography with the consistency, scope, diversity, and depth seen here.

True fine typography and printing never stand alone outside of the mainstream of human endeavor. They both nourish and are nourished by the issues, ideas, and media practices within the common marketplace of their time. When typography and design do isolate themselves from that mainstream, they become mere novelty items, soon to become relics of stagnation. Fine typography and fine printing are at the heart of mankind's investigative and determined effort to understand ourselves and our world. As typographers, we are linked with the philosophers, scientists, poets, theologians, artists, and humanitarians who search for our proper place in the universe. We take all the ideas, discoveries, talents, and tools amassed over the centuries and attempt to give them back in a fitting format.

That is our task as typographers; these essays are the ongoing analysis of that task. They speak for themselves.

Linnea Gentry

GOUDY SCRIPPS OLDSTYLE

A B C D E F G H I J K L M N O P Q R S T U V W X Y Z
a b c d e f g h i j k l m n o p q r s t u v w x y z
1 2 3 4 5 6 7 8 9 0 & fi ff fl ffi ffl ct

The type itself is a straightforward, simple design that
displays no freakish qualities. It is not "fool-proof"--it
requires careful handling to bring out its best.   F.W.G.

A "forgotten" Goudy type, especially commissioned in 1941 to serve as the proprietary type of Scripps College in Claremont, California, will soon be revived by the College. Scripps Old Style was an outgrowth of Frederic Goudy's visits to the college campus in 1938 and 1939 when he delivered a convocation speech on the subjects of letter design and printing. He was captivated by the Mediterranean architecture and the quiet beauty of the campus and mentioned that his love for Scripps had inspired him to create a variation of the letter S as a symbol of the college.

Over the next few years, interest in books and book design continued to grow among students at Scripps, an interest that was fostered by Dorothy Drake, librarian of the then new Denison Library. This enthusiasm culminated in 1941 when the graduating class decided that the establishment of a college press would be their gift to the school. They raised a modest sum of money and this was augmented by a benefactress of the college, Catherine Coffin Phillips, who agreed to underwrite the cost of a commission to Frederic Goudy for the design of a Scripps College type.

By the end of summer, 1941, Goudy had completed the designs and preliminary proofs and they were sent to Scripps for approval. Part of the unique character of Scripps Old Style lay in the distinctive tail on the lower-case s, developed from Goudy's personal conception of the letter for Scripps.

However, Goudy encountered difficulties in completing the type. The Scripps type was the first matrix cutting he had attempted following the disastrous fire in his own workshop. He had made his large master patterns as usual, but had no suitable engraving machine for reducing them to the smaller metal-working patterns. Finally the University of Syracuse

School of Journalism generously allowed him to use their equipment, and he was able to cut 106 16 pt. matrices which were cast onto an 18 pt. body by Mackenzie & Harris of San Francisco.

Scripps College still holds a small quantity of the 16 pt. roman, displayed above, and Goudy continued to work on other roman sizes and an italic face until his death in 1947. In fact, there are drawings, patterns, and matrices for 12 and 14 pt. roman; 12, 14, and 16 pt. italic; 16 pt. small caps, and 24 pt. roman caps, but these sizes require justifying of the matrices and casting. Typefounder Paul H. Duensing and typophile Muir Dawson met in December 1976 with Scripps College President John H. Chandler to inspect these holdings. They found all in order for the final justification to be made and the College was encouraged to complete the casting of the various sizes and styles of the type. Recently a further impetus has been lent to the project by the generous offer of financial assistance from Mrs. Lucille Morrison, daughter of Catherine Coffin Phillips and longtime friend of the College.

From its inception in 1941, the Scripps College Press has been instructional press. The first projects were printed on a Washington hand press provided by Ward Ritchie. Later, instruction was offered in book design and printing using Chandler and Price pilot and platen presses and a Vandercook No. 1 proof press. From 1946 until his retirement in 1971, Joseph Arnold Foster continued to develop printing as a serious academic pursuit, and he established a formal printing room which included a collection of some fifty different type faces. Since 1971, the press has been utilized for private printing projects of the College, including broadsides and programs.

Fleischmann Antiqua

Linnea Gentry

One of the most interesting aspects of Dante's *Die Hölle* (The Inferno) published in Berlin in 1923 is the use of Fleischmann Antiqua for the text face. The type was called Augustin Roman Number 2 when Joan Michal Fleischman first cut the punches for the Wetstein and Enschedé foundries in Haarlem in 1732.

Fleischman was originally from Nuremberg but spent most of his adult life working in Holland for Dutch foundries (hence the difference in the spelling of his name). He worked in a close and friendly association with Johannes Enschedé for thirty-three years and produced a wide variety of types: romans, italics, blackletter, a script, Greek, Arabic, Armenian, and musical characters. Because he was extremely skilled in precision cutting, his letters enjoyed a wide popularity on the Continent until the last quarter of the eighteenth century. His smaller sizes were in demand for setting newspapers and bibles.

His work continued to be held in high esteem by the succeeding owners of the Enschedé foundry even after Fleischman's death in 1768. The introduction to *The House of Enschedé 1703–1953* (Enschedé, 1953) states: "They have taken every opportunity of acquiring the types cut by Fleischman for other typefounders, so that virtually the whole of the master's work is now reverently preserved at Haarlem. In recent years—for a century or more—none of the type from Fleischman's matrices has been sold: it is reserved for finely printed editions from Enschedé's presses." Nevertheless, Georg Belwe designed a modern recutting of Fleischman's Roman for the Ludwig Wagner typefoundry of Leipzig in 1927. Recently, Typoart in Dresden handled that recutting. The Fleischman in *Die Hölle* is the original Enschedé cutting. But the supposed restrictions on Fleischman's types by Enschedé

brings into question how the publisher of the Dante, Hans Heinrich Tillgner, or its printer, Jakob Hegner of Hellerau bei Dresden, acquired the face for their 1923 edition. Unfortunately there appears to be no information on this matter.

The typeface bears little resemblance to the Dutch face of Van Dijck cut in the previous century. When compared with his contemporaries in England, Caslon and Baskerville, Fleischman's Augustin Number 2 reveals a surprisingly modern quality. It lacks the comfortable readability of Caslon but is more sophisticated in line. It does not have the measured grace of Baskerville, but the eclectic spirit of its individual characters gives it strength and vivacity.

The face named (confusingly) Augustin Roman Number 1 by the Enschedé foundry was cut six years after Number 2 in 1738. The capitals of this face bear a striking resemblance to Bodoni's type of the 1780s in the joining of the thick and thin strokes, though not in the slant of his serifs. Any further similarity is lost in the lowercase.

The response to Fleischman's types has varied considerably. Updike in his *Printing Types* has this to say: "His types are singularly devoid of style, and usually show a drift toward the thinner, weaker typography which was coming in Holland as everywhere else." He goes on to describe them as: "capital letters in roman and italic of a very Dutch and ugly cut. . . . He uniformly extracted all interest from his fonts, partly through tightening the cut, which gave monotony of colour, and partly by his large, round lowercase letters, made more rolling in effect by shortening the descenders in a very modern way." Perhaps Updike's public prejudice against Fleischman's types contributed to the lack of interest by American printers in his work.

But the praise accorded him in Holland lasted for centuries. Charles Enschedé in his *Fonderies de caractères et leur materiél dans les Pays-Bas du XVe au XIXe siècle* of 1908 calls him "the greatest punchcutter that ever lived and that will probably ever live." And surely the use of Fleischman's Augustin Roman Number 2 in this superb Expressionist edition of Dante's *Die Hölle* is a testament to its lasting appeal. The vigor and strength of this face remain a distinctive yet integral part of the book.

Auguſtyn Romein No. 2.

Commentateurs d'Ariſtote auroit tout autrement répondu à la queſtion de l'Impératrice, que ne fît Pierre. Il auroit ſoutenu que le bien public demande & qu'en cette action là, autant & plus qu'en aucune autre. 13467890℞ѵ[†]*¶?) ABCDEFGHJ KLMNOPQRSTUVWXYZÆ

Civilité

D. Steven Corey

Type designs have generally been more successful when they follow the more static creations of the human hand: the formal book hands, the uncials and the gothics, the clean incised lines of inscriptional Roman capitals. Type has seldom captured successfully the actual movement of the hand in writing, the running quality of the more informal, cursive hands. In fact, leaving aside the italics, few so-called "script types" are truly pleasing when presented in quantities of more than a few lines.

The types called Civilité represent an early attempt "to render a cursive hand of the sixteenth century, known as batarde, in a calligraphic form."[1] Ultimately, both the hand and the type dropped from use, but they continue to present an interesting curiosity to the eye today. Stanley Morison, in his article "On Script Types" (*The Fleuron*, 1925), states that "the term bastarda, bastarde, batarde and bastard was used in the fifteenth century somewhat arbitrarily to designate a current or cursive variety of a formal or text letter."

A French cursive hand; manuscript leaf, 1494. 29 x 20 cm. (The Bancroft Library, University of California. Selected by Georgianna Greenwood.)

1. Harry Carter and H.D.L. Vervliet. *Civilité Types*. Oxford: Oxford University Press, 1966. Unless otherwise noted, all quotes in this article are taken from this definitive work.

Special characteristics of this batarde, sloped, rather long descenders, and an *r* whose first stroke leans backwards, appear in French documents in the late fourteenth century. Before the middle of the fifteenth century a recognizable style of writing had developed in France in which the letterforms were adapted to make the pen's passage from one letter to the next easier than it had been in earlier Latin scripts. French scribes used the hand for correspondence and notes and for the less elaborate kinds of books, and they knew, or invented a good many slightly different forms with such names as: *Carrée, Ancienne, Commune* or *Courante d'Estat, Ronde, de Comptes*, and *Secretarienne*.

Carter and Vervliet date the spread of this hand to the Burgundian Low Countries and to England roughly in the last quarter of the fifteenth century and they credit John Baildon with having first published the name "Secretary" for the corresponding English style of writing, thus providing a label for the types derived from it.

In 1557 Robert Granjon in Lyon cut a typeface based on a current French batarde and called it *lettre françoise*, hoping to create a kind of French national typeface. The name Civilité eventually came to be applied to Granjon's *lettre françoise* because of its frequent use for such books as Erasmus' *De Civilitate Morum Puerorum Libellus*, a popular etiquette book for children. The work was translated into many languages, including French, in which the title becomes *La Civilité Puerile*.

Granjon's Civilité found favor when it first appeared.

> It is not surprising that a type imitating handwriting was welcomed for certain purposes for reasons quite other than those advanced by Granjon in its favor. To be addressed in manuscript is a compliment, and pseudo manuscript had about it an allusion to the handwritten books presented to the most eminent patrons. Printers, for their part, have a need for a distinguishing type: it seems to mark the separateness of forewords and dedications and to add grace and variety to headings and titles.

Civilité was first used for Innocenzio Ringhieri's *Dialogues de la Vie et de la Mort*, printed by Granjon at Lyon in 1557. Christophe Plantin bought matrices within a few months, as did William Silvius. The St. Augustin size (approximately 14 pt.) cut for Plantin by Granjon became the favorite Civilité type. A second Civilité appeared at Paris in 1558 in books published by Philippe Danfrie and Richard Breton.

Like Granjon's, Breton's publications in Civilité type resolve themselves into belles-lettres, Protestant piety, children's lessons, and music. Breton's death in 1571 marks the end of the attempt to introduce the Civilité as a type for texts of literary pretensions.

A third Civilité was cut by Ameet Tavernier at Antwerp. Throughout the Low Countries, Civilité types enjoyed a wider and longer use than their French counterparts.

However, Civilité fought a losing battle for popularity with roman and especially italic type which by that time "had established itself too firmly in the favor of printers and readers to admit any rival as the subsidiary antiqua fount."[2] Not only that, the first Civilité had at least 138 sorts, as compared with some 120 usual at the time for roman or italic.

The thirty ligatures of Civilité compare with about twenty normally supplied for the roman, and in addition it requires two dozen extra sorts for the initial, final, and other alternative forms of the lower-case letters. These last were a tax on the time of the punchcutter, typefounder, and compositor. Like all Gothic scripts made into type, this one suffered from having fine minims projecting from the letters on either side, making the type difficult to cast and to rub, and quick to show wear. More than all this, it was poor value in legibility for the space it occupied.

Evidently, too, the rise and decline of Civilité in France was linked to the fortunes of French Protestantism as it was the face used for many Protestant tracts.

As the tolerant phase passed and printers were increasingly troubled for their heterodoxy, from 1562 onward, the use of the type by French printers became infrequent, and with the Massacre of St. Bartholomew in 1572 it ceased for a time.

Although the bibliography of books using Civilité at the back of Carter and Vervliet's volume lists 636 titles printed from 1557 to 1874, the last book largely in Civilité was printed in 1767. Stanley Morison considered that revisions and recuttings of Civilité, whether by Louis Perrin or the American Typefounders Company, were too archaic for modern use. Nonetheless, Civilité was used to good effect in the 1930s, when the Limited Editions Club used it for the title pages of their editions of *The Kasidah* and *The 1001 Nights*, both illustrated by Valenti Angelo. Mr. Angelo recalls that the use of Civilité was recommended by Frederic Warde, who was then at the Rudge firm, and who worked on these books in con-

2. S.H. Steinberg. *Five Hundred Years of Printing.* New York: Penguin Books, 1974.

junction with Bruce Rogers. Currently, Anthony Baker's Gruffyground Press of Somerset, England will soon issue an edition of Shakespeare's *The Phoenix and the Turtle* printed in Civilité and harking back to the "Secretary" hand prevalent in Elizabethan England.

Shown are three specimens of Civilité. The first is the Civilité cut by Robert Granjon for Christophe Plantin in 1557 and now in the possession of the firm of Joh. Enschedé en Zonen in Haarlem, Holland. Although the firm no longer casts fonts of the type due to the difficulties of casting such spiky, delicate forms, a font was most generously provided to *Fine Print* by Mr. Sem Hartz, General Art Director of the firm, from his private collection. The second is a specimen of the Deberny & Peignot Civilité, descended from the Danfrie cutting of 1558. This font is from the extensive collection of historic types originally formed by the Grabhorn brothers of San Francisco, and kindly loaned by printer Andrew Hoyem of the Arion Press (formerly Grabhorn-Hoyem). The third specimen, sent to us by Mr. Paul Hayden Duensing of Kalamazoo, Michigan, is a type called Circular Script, cut by the defunct Hanson Foundry of Boston, Massachusetts. Mr. Duensing has a partial set of experimental mats made from this type. This Hanson cutting is shown in a few editions of the specimen book of the American Typefounders early in this century, after which it disappears from view.

Private Type Faces

Paul Hayden Duensing

Throughout the history of the private press movement, and especially in that rarified atmosphere we call "fine presses," much has been made of the fact that some have had proprietary type faces, used exclusively by a single press or individual. When private presses were less common and were owned by those of considerable wealth, such private types were a feasible and logical extension of the aims, the images, and the philosophies of the presses. Thus William Morris's private faces, the Golden, Chaucer, and Troy types, all reflected the obsessive medievalism of the owner. Similarly, the faces associated with the Vale, Doves, Zilverdistel, Eragny, and other presses all reflected their owners' affinities for history, usually using as models early incunabular romans or gotico-antiqua transitional forms. Closer to our own times, Eric Gill created designs which were at first used as his private type and later were produced by The Monotype Corporation Limited as Joanna. Will Carter's Octavian has had somewhat the same history.

There can be no denying the desirability of owning one's exclusive design, giving to all one's productions a consistency and continuity, reinforced with a strong quality which makes all productions instantly recognizable. But, as with most things which are custommade, private type faces are expensive.

Even in Morris's time, the production of a private design was no light undertaking, and even given the greater number of typefounders at that time, the costs were very high. In today's inflationary world, the cost is best described as staggering. It is nevertheless possible to design and produce a private type exclusive to a single press; the cost revolves to a considerable extent around how much the individual can or will do, and how much must be hired to be done by others.

Added to the basic consideration of whether to do a design in the first place, is the consideration of how extensive the project should be. Will there be only a new lowercase added to existing capitals of another font, or an uncial or common-case design which needs no capitals; and will there be italic, accented, and swash characters, or harmonizing ornaments? Obviously the ideal situation would be to have a complete series, but in an attempt to deal realistically with a balance between what is affordable and what is necessary, I would like to submit some possibilities for consideration, beginning with the least investment of time and money, and progressing to more complex and expensive ventures.

Most private presses today have settled on one or two favorite type designs as "house faces" which they use frequently and with which they feel comfortable. One way of adding a bit of distinction to the productions of a press is to design and produce a few swash or special characters which harmonize with the existing font, perhaps usable in the press name, such as flourished caps and a swash final letter. Depending upon the font, one may sometimes redesign only the high frequency letters, such as the vowels and *d, h, r, s, t*, which, if well done, may impart a much different look to the printed page. Beyond these possibilities are of course infinite degrees of involvement: an entire lowercase, an entire font, perhaps with italic, etc. Before one goes too far, however, it might be wise to investigate the possibility that some special characters already exist for the font in question, by writing to the manufacturer. The next possibility is to examine the specimen books of The Monotype Corporation Limited, who have in their matrix library a huge number of special and swash mats for their more popular faces, which often may be adapted to one's present type for a minimal outlay of effort and money. Many of these "specials" are not in the regular catalog, and it often pays to inquire about them. For example, there are unpublished swashes for Blado and Times Roman, and a huge number of swash variants for their Garamond series, as well as Lutetia, Bembo, and others.

Assuming that these possibilities have been examined and found wanting, the next step is to consider designing the custom characters oneself. It may be well to interject here a few remarks on aesthetics in type design, although the final decisions must always rest, in the end, with the proprietors. First, there is the need to avoid very bizarre forms. While these do indeed advertise the individuality of the press, they often become tiresome and difficult to use. The best approach, it seems to me, is to base the design on an existing letterform, perhaps picking a type such as Baskerville, Garamond, Bembo, Palatino, or any of a number of other well-designed and well-proportioned fonts, as a point of departure. Conservative designs wear well, and are adaptable to a wider variety of texts; fonts that are wild and grotesque have a shorter typographic half-life. A good criterion for arriving at a design motif is to consider the kinds of things printed in the past at one's press and those contemplated for the future, and to attempt to produce a design which will reflect and be compatible with those trends. In conjunction with choosing the design, one must determine the size or sizes at this point, for, as we shall later discover, size influences design. Obviously the size of page generally printed, influenced by the capacity of the press equipment, will largely determine the basic text size to be made. Depending on the design, a size of 12˙ to 16˙ is often the most useful range. Below 12˙ much of the individuality of the design will be lost, and above 16˙ one must be confined to elephant folio formats. Although it is not a common type size, I rather favor 16˙ as one which allows the design of the type to show, sets well, and yet may be used in octavo as well as quarto books. Beyond that size, a set of titling caps in 24˙ will often be found most useful.

Although I have warned above of the dangers of becoming too heavily committed to production of a variety of fonts at the outset, let me now suggest that it is wise, however, to at least *design* a complete font at the outset. By this I mean that if there is a thought of perhaps doing an italic eventually, plus some swashes, reference marks, paragraph indicators, or harmonizing ornaments, they should be designed at the same time as the basic alphabets. Once the design is produced and used, and the original feel and momentum of the basic design has been lost, it is extremely difficult to recapture the same essence. Design it all, then, and produce what you can afford, incrementally.

With these preliminaries in mind, then, let us consider the actual design process. If the project is to add a few significant swashes to an existing font, the first order of business is to acquire a sharp proof of the model type *in the same size* as the characters you wish to cut. This is very important, as the design of a type varies from one size to another, in terms of width as well as weight (a given letter being wider, heavier, and having more open counters in the smaller sizes, and becoming narrower, lighter, and having greater contrast between thick and thin strokes as it goes up in point size). This sample should now be photographically enlarged to a size comfortable for working. I prefer five times up in size, but it also depends on the design. Let us assume that the project is to cut a swash *F*, *P*, and *t* for 36˙ Janson Italic. (See Figure 1.) These characters

Figure 1.

from the original font are enlarged to a 180˙ size as a photostat, and slipped under a piece of tracing paper. Various trials are made in pencil, tracing appropriate parts of the original

Figure 2.

Figure 3.

letter and adding original touches where desirable. (See Figure 2.) When a good candidate is finally produced, the tracing is transferred to a piece of smooth, ink-receptive card stock and carefully inked in, with some appropriate reference marks for alignment, set width, and inclination.

Next, I have a film positive made of the drawing reduced to the final (36˙) size, and I place this over the proof of the original, checking for weight, stress, and harmony. (See Figure 3.) Whether the project is only a few characters or a complete font, it is of the utmost importance to see that there is consistency in the weight of strokes, bracketing (where the heavy and light strokes curve either into each other or into serifs), the length and thickness of serifs, and—in the case of italics—inclination. It will often be found, when making a large number of characters, that the design develops and evolves. It is then necessary to go back to some of the earliest characters and redraw them, because the font has departed from, or enlarged upon, the original design premise.

Once the drawing seems to satisfy all the criteria, it is ready for production. If the matrices are to be produced commercially, the drawing is shipped off and eventually the matrices are returned, type is cast, and the project is over. There are several firms in the United States which will engrave matrices to order, such as Service Engravers of New York. For small composition sizes, Hartzell Machine Works can prepare punched matrices for Monotype composition at their Chester, Pennsylvania plant. Intertype and Linotype are also able to prepare special matrices for their respective machines. In addition there are excellent matrix facilities in Japan (e.g., Eiko Company Ltd., near Tokyo), in Germany, Israel, England, and elsewhere. Costs are based on the number of characters submitted for a given size, the complexity of the design, point size, and process by which the matrices are made. It is wise to confer with the matrix makers as to the form in which they prefer the design (some like two-inch film, others want only the drawings), as well as to confer with the person who will cast the type as to the requirements for matrices on the specific casting equipment available.

Basically there are three ways of producing matrices for the casting of single types, and each of these has both advantages and drawbacks. The first and most direct method is to engrave the character in brass by means of a pantograph. The second is to engrave a punch, either by hand or machine, harden it, and drive it into a piece of copper, which is then machined flat and true as a matrix. The third method is to engrave the character in lead or acid-resisting aluminum alloy (either by hand or machine), place it in an electrolytic bath, and electrodeposit copper over the face, creating an intaglio matrix of the relief original. In the concluding installment of this article, to follow in the next issue, we will consider briefly the work involved in each of these procedures and what advantages and disadvantages may be expected from each.

In the first installment of this article, an overview was given of the various ways in which the effect of a private typeface can be achieved, ranging from adding a few modified characters to an existing font to the design of a complete and original font. Let us now consider briefly the work involved in each of the procedures for producing matrices and what advantages and disadvantages may be expected from each.

ENGRAVED MATRICES

The equipment for engraving matrices consists essentially of some kind of reducing pantograph capable of accurately engraving to a constant depth in brass; of a means of sharpening the engraving cutters; of a device for accurately determining the depth of cut; and a fixture for holding the matrix blank on the work table. In my own case, I have found the Panto-Utility Engraver UE2 from H. P. Preis Company, Hillside, New Jersey, a splendid machine. A Mico cutter grinder, manufactured by Mico Instrument Company of Cambridge, Massachusetts, and a needle depth-micrometer complete the major items.

For the pattern, a Kodalith film positive is made in the same size as the drawing. Next I order a Nylaprint or Dycril unmounted plate (with the letter reading correctly left-to-right, and not flopped, as in a letterpress printing plate). This positive film produces a plate in which the image of the letter is recessed, providing the guide for the pantograph stylus. (See Figure 4.)

Figure 4. The pattern plate for engraved mats is a right-reading sunken image guide for the pantograph stylus.

A matrix blank of either free-machining brass or aluminum is placed into the holding fixture, the proper ratio (5:1 reduction) is set, a cutter size selected (say .003″) and stylus size selected. (If the cutter is .003″ and the ratio is 5:1, then the stylus must be .003″ x 5 =

.015″ in order to accurately portray the design in the finished matrix). The pattern is now adjusted so that the body area of the cast type will rest 8 points from the left edge of the matrix and 24 points from the top. The pattern and matrix blank are secured firmly and the depth gauge of the pantograph is adjusted so that it will make its first cut .015″ deep. A drop of oil (or kerosene for aluminum) is spread over the work area, the cutting head lowered, the stylus moved about inside the pattern and the cutting begins. When the first cut is finished, the motor is stopped and the chips are removed. The cutter depth is reset for the second cut to .030″ and for the third cut to .045″. Now the cutter is removed and inspected for wear, flatness, and width, since the final cut will actually be the face of the letter, and a broken or undersized cutter will not produce a proper printing surface. The depth is now set to .051″ and there is much methodical traversing of the pattern in a circular motion. When the cutting is thought to be finished, the chips are brushed out and a bit of sealing wax is dripped into the cavity. The shank of the stick of wax is then quickly jammed into the cooling puddle of wax and the lump in the letter cavity is pulled out. With it come any chips not caught with the brush. The depth is now checked with the needle depth-micrometer to be certain that the cut is at least .050″ and then scanned with a strong (40x) magnifier under a Tensor light to check for places missed by the cutter.

When the matrix appears smooth and without blemishes on the face, it is placed face down on a large, smooth, flat file and rubbed, being frequently checked with the depth-micrometer until the letter cavity measures exactly .050″ deep everywhere over its surface. (Alternatively, the matrix may be placed in a small milling machine and the depth adjusted to .050″ by surface milling.) (See Figure 5.)

The matrix is now finished and ready for casting. The greatest disadvantage of engraved matrices is that the engraving must be done with a revolving cutting tool which, for strength, is pyramidal in shape. Thus the hole at the surface of the matrix is larger than the size of the face of the letter. When the type is cast, the base of the letter, resting on the shoulder of the type, is wider than the body and the type must be rubbed on a file ("dressed") in order to fit closely to the next letter

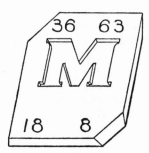

Figure 5. The finished engraved matrix ready for final checking and casting. Champfered corners permit locking the matrix on a Monotype Sorts Caster. (After Legros and Grant.)

(See Figure 6.) Engraved matrices take from 45 minutes to two hours to make, depending on point size and design complexity.

Figure 6. The unrubbed type from an engraved matrix overhangs the body, setwise. Dressing the type on a file allows tight fitting of the letters. (After Legros and Grant.)

HAND-CUT PUNCHES

Cutting punches by hand is the older, more traditional way, but it demands a great deal of patience and manual dexterity. A punch is really a piece of type (but with a much larger body) engraved on the end of a two-inch-long bar of steel (See Figure 7.) When the cutting is completed, the punch is hardened, tempered, or "drawn back," and driven into a piece of copper a little over the depth desired (perhaps .055″). The copper is then filed flat and true, the depth filed, and the matrix is ready for casting. (There is an excellent and detailed discussion of the process in *The Dolphin* I: 1933,

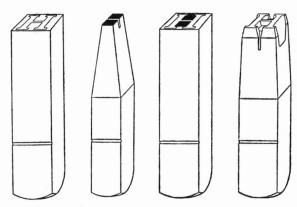

Figure 7. For handcut punches, the design is traced on the end of a steel bar. Counters of letters are counter-punched, cut with a graver or drilled out. The counter having been shaped, the outsides of the letter are filed away to the traced outlines. The hardened punch is then driven into copper to form the matrix. (After Bohadti.)

pp. 24–57, by Paul Koch.) If the overview given here makes the process seem very simple, it is because mention has been omitted of the long hours of learning to use the graver, burin, and file, and the practice necessary to the development of a steady hand and keen eye.

Handcut punches are very time consuming to make, and even mats from machine-cut punches are more expensive than making engraved matrices. Punched matrices do, however, allow very tightly fitted characters without the necessity for rubbing the type after casting. Handcut punches may require from two hours up to a full day's time per character, while machine-cut punches may demand one to two hours. To this, time for hardening, drawing, and driving the punches must be added, but this varies so widely that no meaningful figures can be given.

MACHINE-CUT PUNCHES

In cutting punches by machine, the punch blank (a square bar of good, annealed, non-deforming, oil-hardening tool steel perhaps 1/32″ larger in each dimension than the letter, and about two inches long) is carefully surfaced on what will become the typeface end, on an Arkansas white stone. Whereas the pattern for engraved matrices was a right-reading, sunken image, that for punchcutting is a wrong-reading image in relief (like an enlarged piece of type). The area of the letter is left in .055″ relief as the rest of the punch is milled away to form a shoulder. The effective size of the tracing stylus is altered according to the depth of cut, and the design of the character begins to become apparent as the cutter point comes closer and closer to the final outlines of the letter. The punch from the shoulder to the face thus has a very slight taper except in those spots where it must fit very tightly and was previously milled very close. Finally the detail of the face is finished using only the point of the cutting tool. The punch is then hardened, drawn and driven as in the case of the handcut punch.

ELECTRODEPOSITED MATRICES

Finally, it is possible to electroplate matrices by using a letter engraved like a piece of type, in lead or acid-resisting aluminum alloy. The letter is placed in a suitable holder, "waxed in" (that is, paraffin or beeswax used as a resist in areas where no deposit is desired) and placed in a small electrolytic bath (See Figure 8.) A solution of concentrated copper sulfate in distilled (but

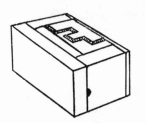
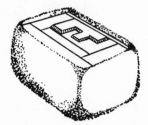

Figure 8. Type is surrounded by spaces to form matrix area. A wax resist covers all but the type face.

not de-ionized) water and additional amounts of sulfuric acid are added. The type is connected to a direct current source of very low amperage and voltage, a bar of copper is attached to the other electrode and both are submerged in the dish. The current now passes from the copper bar through the solution to the letter and, in so doing, it deposits copper ions onto the surface

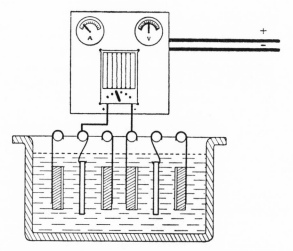

Figure 9. In the electrolytic bath, the copper ions move from the anode (copper bar) to the cathode (type) through the copper sulfate solution. (After Bohadti.)

of the letter (See Figure 9.) If the process continues undisturbed for about six to ten days, a 1/8″ deposit of copper will build up on the type and, when the two are separated and the excess on the back is removed, the result is a castable matrix, which is an exact duplicate of the pattern letter (See Figure 10.)

Figure 10. When the deposit and master are separated, the former is an exact intaglio replica of the latter. The back is ground parallel to the front side, and matrix is ready to cast.

Obviously, existing type can also be copied in this way and the pirating of designs between rival founders has been around almost as long as the process of electrolysis has been known. On balance, it is a useful way to make exact replica matrices of obsolete faces, or to replenish characters in short supply. A disadvantage of this process is, however, that the replica types can be no better than the originals: if there are broken lines and battered serifs in the originals, they will be faithfully reproduced in the replicas as well.

Unless existing type is being duplicated, electro mats need engraved originals, made either by hand or machine, which is moderately expensive. But if existing

type is used, electrodepositing is much the cheapest method of matrix production. Electro matrices, like punched matrices, provide type which also fits tightly without rubbing or dressing. About one hour is required to make each character ready for the plating bath; seven to ten days for plating and from one-half to one and one-half hours for the machining necessary to finish the matrix ready for casting.

When the matrices have been completed by whatever method, they are placed in the typecasting machine (Monotype Sorts Caster, Thompson, Giant, or Supercaster). A trial cast is made and checked for alignment, quality of face and cast, set width (both of the proper body width and the proper positioning of the character on that width), and height-to-paper. For the machines mentioned above, the depth of the letter from the surface of the matrix is usually .050″, although in sizes above 36 point it may often be .065″. Some Thompson Type Casters were made for casting single types from linecasting matrices, and mats for these machines must be .043″ deep. Thus it is important to establish in advance the requirements of the machine upon which the casting will be done.

When the type is delivered, inspect it to see that the feet are plowed clean, the body is solid and the face has not become wrinkled or frosty from incorrect casting temperature. Rub any kerns or burrs on a large flat file, brush the type clean, and pull a proof with the various letters intermixed to check alignment, fit, and compatibility. The proof will also serve as a reference for tracing future layouts and a document for pride in showing one's latest typographic triumph—for there is no thrill quite like the creation of a piece of type!

(Fine (Print

Figure 11. In a final test, new letters are proofed with the original font.

FOR FURTHER READING

For those inclined toward further reading in this subject, the following basic works (in addition to the Paul Koch article already cited) are recommended.

Fournier, P. S. *On Typefounding.* London: Soncino Press, 1923 (Translated by Harry Carter).

Goudy, F. W. *Typologia: Studies in Type Design and Type Making.* Berkeley: University of California Press, 1940. Reprinted, 1978. (See review, page 81.)

Legros, L. A., and J. C. Grant. *Typographical Printing Surfaces.* London: Longmans, Green & Co., 1916.

Moxon, Joseph. *Mechanick Exercises or the Whole Art of Printing.* London: Oxford University Press, 1958 (Edited by Harry Carter).

Pursuit of the Ideal:
The Uncial Letters of Victor Hammer

D A V I D   F A R R E L L

UNCIAL LETTERS were first cast into type in 1923. In that year, Klingspor Foundry at Offenbach, Germany, produced the Hammer Unziale, the first of five uncial alphabets cut by Victor Hammer (1882–1967). The only other uncials of this period discovered by this writer are Friar (1937) created by F. W. Goudy (who acknowledged his debt to Hammer) and Libra (1939) by S. H. DeRoos. Hammer, the Austro-American artist, printer, and typographer, modelled his letters on his own handwriting much as the great fifteenth-century typographers based their letters on contemporary manuscript hands.

The medieval uncial, one of the major bookhands of antiquity, was a majuscule letter with roots in the Roman cursive script of the second century. Although it remained in use for five centuries, it showed remarkably little development after the fourth century. A still more cursive letter, the minuscule half-uncial, evolved from the uncial and in time superseded it. The most famous example of the half-uncial appears in the *Book of Kells*, written by Irish monks in the seventh century. The derivation of "uncial" has not been precisely determined; it has the same root as the Latin words for "ounce" and "inch" and may refer to the inordinate amount of space the elegant, rounded uncials, "like a string of pearls" (to use Hammer's figure of speech), occupied on the page. Hammer's letters were based on uncial, half-uncial, and Roman models, so they cannot be considered pure, but he called them uncials because of their medieval prototypes.

Hammer's letters were the result of a conscious effort, supported by a fully articulated philosophy, to create a new letterform for modern English, French, German, and Italian, the languages with which he was conversant. Craftsmanship also set Hammer apart from his contemporaries, for he not only drew his letters, he cut and cast them himself, or directly supervised their cutting and casting. And with his uncial letters he produced some of the most beautiful books of the century at the Stamperia del Santuccio, the hand press he first established at Florence in 1929 and later moved to the United States.

Hammer's interest in typography and printing developed from his artistic vocation as a prominent portraitist and sculptor in his native Vienna and his study of calligraphy. Using a German translation of Edward Johnston's *Writing and Illuminating and Lettering*, he began to practice writing various alphabets around 1910. "Instinctively I chose my models from uncials and half-uncials," he wrote later. Here is the germ of his philosophy. He believed that ancient letters—uncials as well as Roman and black letter alphabets—had been created by the demands of ancient languages and were inadequate for the orthography, syntax, and international vocabularies of modern languages. The problem for Hammer, an artist, was chiefly visual, but it was due to linguistic circumstances. Comparing Latin with modern German written in the Roman alphabet, for example, he demonstrated that consonants tend to crowd together more in German words; hence the proliferation of their ascenders and descenders interrupts the flow of the line.

These problems are discussed in an essay sometimes called Hammer's manifesto, *Type Design in Relation to Language and the Art of the Punch Cutter* (1946). After describing his intention in creating a letter based on ancient models but wholly new, he gave his conception of the type designer's aim: "It is not the reader and his demands that I wish to satisfy, any more than it is the writer. It is my conviction that the type designer should do his work in the service of the language." Hammer's solution to one aspect of the visual and linguistic problem, then, was to design his uncial letter with ascenders and descenders curled close to the baseline. While retaining the essential features of the manuscript uncial—the elegant, shaded, sinuous stroke achieved with a broad-edged pen—the Hammer letters do not closely resemble any of the medieval prototypes. The Hammer uncials emphasize the diagonal line whereas many manuscript uncials emphasize the vertical line. This intentional feature is called the *ductus* (from the Latin "to lead"); it pulls the eye naturally from left to right. Typecasting the uncial produced letters that are uniform and allow more regular and tighter letter- and word-spacing. As a result, the typeset page looks neater, if not more beautiful, than the manuscript page. It is also important to note that Hammer introduced diacritics and modern punctuation marks as well as uncial-inspired Arabic numerals and capital letters.

The difference between the manuscript and typographic uncial is also illustrated by Hammer's use of Roman capitals. The medieval hand was a majuscule; it had no capitals. Enlarged uncials or rustic capitals were used when it seemed appropriate to a scribe. Hammer believed capitals were unnecessary and his first two alphabets—Hammer Unziale and Samson—were created without them. A larger point size was used when initial letters were needed for emphasis. By the time Hammer cut his third and fourth uncial alphabets—Pindar and American—he found that capitals could enhance their appearance and were required by others interested in using his letters. The capital Hammer created is a distinctive sans serif obviously inspired by the uncial. The familiar broad-edged pen stroke is apparent in the rounded strokes of letters such as *C*, *D*, *O*, and *S*. In place of a serif, Hammer slightly broadened the line at the end of a stroke (as in *A* and *Z*), or made a slight upturn at the end of a stroke (*E* and *T*). The result is a capital letter as graceful and austere as the noblest Roman, slightly reminiscent of Optima.

THE HISTORY OF THE HAMMER ALPHABETS

Hammer Unziale. This face was cut in 1921 by N. Schuricht, a typecutter from the Austrian Staatsdrukkerei, during a summer at Hammer's house at St. Martin im Innkreis, Austria. In 1923, Karl Klingspor, one of the first to become interested in Hammer's experimental designs, cast the Hammer Unziale at his foundry; Stempel later produced two more sizes (exact body sizes undetermined). It has been used extensively both as a text and a display face and some typographers consider it the only Hammer uncial.

Although Hammer considered Schuricht an able craftsman, he was unhappy with the alphabet that resulted from their collaboration. He never used it himself and when it was mentioned he would say, "let us forget about it." If one compares Hammer Unziale with the alphabets produced after Hammer himself learned the craft of punchcutting, one can see at a glance why Hammer regarded it as an unsuccessful if instructive experiment. The shapes of letters such as *b*, *c*, *g*, *s*, and *t*, for example, are radically different in the later alphabets, and the vertical line of the Hammer Unziale is superseded with the diagonal stress that becomes more and more pronounced in the alphabets that followed it.

Samson Uncial. Soon after the designs for Hammer Unziale were completed, Hammer moved to Florence where he established the Stamperia del Santuccio. He was still determined to produce a typeface for his own use and, in 1926, employed Paul Koch to cut a new uncial letter. Koch had learned punchcutting at Klingspor Foundry where his father, Rudolf, one of Hammer's closest friends, was artistic director. In 1928 the matrices were ready and Koch and Hammer's son, Jacob, hand cast the new type in 14˙. It was called Samson because it was first used in Milton's *Samson Agonistes* (1931), the first book from Hammer's press. Again there were no capitals with the exception of the initial *I*. A number of Greek letters were cut by Hammer and cast at the same time for an inscription in the Milton. Later, Koch

recut some of the letters. Koch's revised version of Samson Uncial was first used to print Tasso's *Sonetti* (Stamperia del Santuccio, 1933).

Following publication of the Tasso, a number of other letters (including *b*, *d*, and *f*) were redesigned and cast along with Hammer's first capitals. This transitional uncial was first used to print a fragment of *Eine Redende Blume* (about 1932).

Pindar Uncial. This was the first uncial that was cut by Hammer alone. He began work on it in 1930 and Klingspor cast it in 12˙ between 1933 and 1935. Pindar is named for the work in which it first appeared, Hoelderlin's *Fragmente des Pindar* (Stamperia del Santuccio, 1935). It was accompanied by a newly-cut capital slightly larger than the capitals used in *Eine Redende Blume*.

In 1939, unable to remain subject to the Nazis, Hammer moved to Aurora, New York. Although he left behind all his cutting and casting tools and type fonts in Austria, he was determined to continue cutting punches. He soon produced punches for a new letter and a trial casting of it was made in 1939–40 at the American Type Foundry. Twenty-five letters in 14˙ were cast and Hammer printed a specimen, *Credo in unum deum Patrem omni potentem* (1940). When the producers saw no profit in the unusual letter Hammer abandoned his plans for it.

American Uncial. While the casting of the 1939–40 letter was underway, Hammer was already at work on another uncial that was similar to, but a larger point size than, Pindar Uncial. With the assistance of R. Hunter Middleton, Norman Forgue, and members of the Society of Typographic Arts in Chicago, Hammer had the new letter cast in 14˙ (with new capitals) in 1945 by Charles Nussbaumer at Dearborn Type Foundry. In 1952 Klingspor produced it for sale

αΒcδεfghijκλμνοpqℛ₵ʃτuvwxyℤ
1234567890

αΒcᴅєfghijꞰklmnopqℛs
τuvwxyz
1234567890

abcᴅefghijklmnopqℛ
stuvwxyz
ABCDEFGHIJKLMNOP
QRSTUVWXYZ
1234567890

top, Andromaque 12˙   *center,* Samson 14˙
bottom, American 18˙

in Europe. Since 1957 Stempel has produced it under the name Neue Hammer Unziale to distinguish it from the earlier Hammer Unziale.

American Uncial was cast later in 18· (with capitals) and in 28· (without capitals). It was first used in a keepsake produced for the Society of Typographic Arts called *A Dialogue on the Uncial between a Paleographer and a Printer* (1946). Later, it was used to print Hoelderlin's *Gedichte*, generally considered to be the masterpiece from Stamperia del Santuccio.

Andromaque Uncial. The final uncial is the intriguing Andromaque, a cursive letter cut by Hammer in the mid 1950s. A trial casting of 12· was made at the Deberny-Peignot Foundry in France in 1959, and it was first used to print a specimen sheet published with Hammer's essay in *Chapters on Writing and Printing* (Anvil Press, 1963). Before his death, Hammer started cutting a 14· alphabet and completed punches for almost half the letters. R. Hunter Middleton has recently completed cutting this size of Andromaque and a trial casting is underway.

With the exception of Hammer Unziale and Andromaque, the first impression of many readers is that Hammer's uncial alphabets differ very little. The impression is not entirely mistaken, for, while there are obvious differences (*a* and *b*, for example, are unique in each alphabet), Hammer's typography was motivated by a search for an ideal, a letter representing a personal vision of unity and perfection. He was not a "designer's" typographer who creates a variety of moods in his letter designs, but an artist, philosopher, and craftsman who sought a form consonant with a philosophy of the needs of modern language.

Upon closer comparison one quickly sees that a page set in Samson, with its pronounced ductus and the distinct shapes of certain letters is markedly different from a page set in American. The letters *v* and *w*, for example, evolve from straight-line strokes in Hammer Unziale to curved-line strokes in Pindar and American. The letters *s* and *t* in the first two uncial alphabets are also quite different from the same letters in the following two.

Andromaque, on the other hand, is so remarkably different from the preceding alphabets that one may well wonder whether it represented Hammer's final statement or an entirely new departure. In view of the radical changes in letterforms—each letter in Andromaque was newly conceived—it does appear to be a departure from Hammer's previous work but it is nonetheless consistent with Hammer's philosophy of language and letterforms. Andromaque, like the others, is based on Hammer's manuscript but, unlike the others, it requires no separate capitals. The letters are shaped with the broad-edged pen, which gives them the uncial flavor, and certain letters (*a*, *e*, and *s*) are reminiscent of Greek letterforms. The result is an alphabet with a foreign yet familiar appearance that could be used equally well with various languages, the alphabet without capitals that Hammer had long sought.

AFTERWORD

It might appear from Hammer's preoccupation with the uncial letter that he had a unique but narrow view of typography. Disregarding the uncial-inspired Roman capitals, he completed only uncial alphabets (although he left unfinished a Roman alphabet and an alphabet for the typewriter). Obviously, he preferred the uncial form; he printed with nothing else at Stamperia del Santuccio. But it must be remembered that Hammer was master of several arts and crafts, that apart from his letter designing and punchcutting he was occupied for most of his life with painting, teaching, and writing. As master of the book arts, he established several hand presses and printed and bound many of his books himself. He did print and design books with Roman alphabets when the occasion demanded. During his residence at Aurora, when he was newly arrived from Austria (without his beloved uncial fonts), he accepted a number of commissions (including those from Pantheon, New Directions, and Herbert Steiner's *Aurora* and *Mesa* series) in which he used Spiral, Emerson, Garamond, and occasionally, Civilité. In fact, all but one title from Hammer's Wells College Press (1941–1949) and Hammer Press (1945–1948) were published in one of these Romans.

If Hammer's vision is considered narrow it must also be considered one of the most profound in typography. He worked slowly, to be sure, but untrammeled by the demands of commerce and fashion, always in pursuit of the ideal.

GALLIARD

Charles Bigelow

A DECADE AGO THE ENTHUSIASTS OF photo-electronic composition promised a "revolution" in typography, and it is true that typesetting technology has changed significantly in recent years. Metal type has disappeared from most composing shops, and most of the great foundries have closed or switched to the making of film fonts. New manufacturers have emerged with machines aimed at the in-house typesetting and word-processing market. In their advertisements a young, elegantly groomed secretary at her electronic keyboard has replaced a middle-aged typographer in a shop apron clutching his pica rule.

Yet these are not changes in the art of typography or type design. If we critically examine the books and periodicals of today we can see that they are no better than before, and in many cases they are worse. The judges of the recent Bookbuilders West 1977 show pronounced the majority of the entries "disappointing." Moreover, there is a reactionary trend toward the truly deplorable typography of pre-World War I, an era of types and layouts so vulgar that it inspired a true design revolution, the "new typography" of Jan Tschichold, El Lissitzky, and others.

The reasons for this decline in art during an advance in technology are threefold. First, the engineers who design the new machines know nothing about letterforms: not history, not theory, not practice; and the copyists who prepare types for them have learned only to copy, not to create. Second, the lack of copyright protection for type designs in America has discouraged the creation of worthwhile new designs. American firms unfettered by laws or ethics have chosen to plagiarize existing designs rather than commission the design of new faces. These unauthorized copies (renamed "similar to . . .") lack fidelity to the originals and sensitivity to good letterforms. The results are tasteless type images that remind one of canned peas or processed cheese. Third, our art schools and universities have not been able or willing to offer coherent programs in typography and are unprepared for the technological changes. Therefore most designers who use phototypography lack a critical consciousness of the medium.

In such a climate special note should therefore be taken of the designers and introducers of new text faces which use the photocomposition medium to best advantage. Adrian Frutiger's Iridium (Stempel, 1973) is a Modern face with an ingenious modulation of the serifs, strokes, and hairlines for photographic imaging. It is less severe and more legible than the true Bodoni-Didot types. José Mendoza's Photina (Monophoto, 1972) combines a calligraphic, Old-style letterform with the serifs and a contrast of a Modern. As a serifed face, it was designed to align and mate with the sans serif Univers. Hermann Zapf's Marconi (Dr. Rudolf Hell-Digiset, 1977) is another Modern style with a softened version of the super-elliptical forms first seen in Melior. Marconi was drawn directly on the CRT (cathode ray tube) raster for digital storage and CRT output.

The above faces are Moderns, but what we really have been missing is a photocomposition Old-face for book work and extended texts. Until last year nothing had been done since Jan Tschichold's Sabon (Stempel-Monotype-Linotype, 1967) which was first cut for metal and only later released for phototype.

Recently, however, Matthew Carter has drawn Galliard (Mergenthaler, 1978), a new family of phototypes based on designs by Robert Granjon. This is a type of such artistic and scholarly merit that it would be worthwhile to examine the intricacies of its provenance.

Robert Granjon (1513-89) was born in Paris, son of a bookseller. It is believed that he was apprenticed to a goldsmith, fit training for a punchcutter, also conjectured of Griffo and Gutenberg. By 1545 he was working as a punchcutter in Paris and Lyon, and later traveled extensively.

Among sixteenth-century type designers, Granjon was the master of the dynamic line and the cursive form. His improved versions of the early Basle-Lyon italic established this Old-face style as the standard italic for the next two centuries, replacing the earlier popular Griffo Aldus and Arrighi Blado chancery italics. Of all European printers' flowers, only Granjon's arabesques have rivaled the patterns of Islam for liveliness of form and ingenuity of combination. His Civilité types were virtuoso cuttings of the French secretary bâtarde, though his attempt to popularize this cursive gothic ultimately failed. His exotic types, cut first for Plantin in Antwerp and later for the Stamperia Medicea Orientale and the Stamperia Vaticana in Rome, include Greek cursives, Syriacs, and Arabics which further demonstrate his skill in fluid forms and moving lines.

His roman types were cut in the style of Garamond, but with a more active modulation of the strokes, especially hairlines, serifs, and terminals. For Plantin he developed a "raccourci" or abridged roman with shortened ascenders and descenders, which appealed to printers economy-minded then as now. His Gros Cicero (c.1568) had an x-height comparable to a Garamond St. Augustin (14·) on a

Cicero (12·) body. In Rome (c.1583) he cut a larger, similarly proportioned face on the St. Augustine body, which is named Giubilate in the Vatican type specimen of 1628. These established the beginning of a trend which lasted through the designs of Caslon, and which is popular again today. Granjon's italics have often been revived as companions to Garamond and Jannon "Garamond" revivals of this century, but his romans have been recut only once.

In 1913 Frank Hinman Pierpont supervised the adaptation of Granjon's Gros Cicero to Monotype machines. Although Pierpont's models were photographs and reproductions from the Plantin-Moretus Museum in Antwerp, an exact revival was not achieved. Hairlines and serifs were thickened, brackets strengthened, and main strokes slightly emboldened. Other changes included an increase of x-height and the use of characters added to the font by later hands in the seventeenth and eighteenth centuries, notably a peculiar *a* by J. M. Smit.

In part these changes were due to the use of overinked proofs from worn type, the same problem which plagued Monotype's later revival of Griffo's Poliphilus cut, but it was also Pierpont's wish to adapt the type to the printing needs of the day. The resulting dark and sturdy face, Plantin 110, resembled a Clarendon as much as a Granjon, but it nevertheless has had an enduring use.

Perhaps its greatest application has been as model for the drawing of Times New Roman. Although the exact details may never be fully known, it appears likely that in 1931 Stanley Morison furnished specimens of Plantin to Victor Lardent with instructions to thin the serifs and hairlines, increase the x-height, and narrow certain of the characters. The result of this collaboration was again not a return to Granjon, but a new face destined to become a perennial bestseller.

Despite its name, George Jones's Granjon (Linotype, 1931) is actually a redrawing of a late Texte Romain by Claude Garamond. The name of this series derives from its italic which is based on a Granjon "pendante."

T HE PLAN FOR GALLIARD BEGAN WITH Mike Parker, now director of typographic development for Mergenthaler, who made an extensive study of punches and matrices at the Plantin-Moretus Museum in 1958. He later obtained fonts of several Plantinian types, intending to adapt them to photocomposition. Ultimately the drawings for the new series were done by Matthew Carter, a member of the well-known printing family, who had studied the art of hand punchcutting with P. H. Raedisch at Enschedé in Haarlem before becoming a designer of phototypes for Mergenthaler. Mr. Carter is one of the most versatile contemporary type designers, with a special skill in script forms. His previous types have included a Snell Roundhand, two variations of Shelly Script, and a series of Cochin italics with accompanying romans. He was therefore well suited to the task of redrawing the Granjon types.

With an eye to the marketplace as well as the museum, Carter and Parker sought the best of Granjon for contemporary typography. Mr. Carter has written, "Neither the Roman nor the Italic derive exclusively from particular Granjon faces, both are really aggregates of what Mike and I admire in Granjon's work as a whole . . . the object was not to make a museum replica but a vigorous and saleable typeface that would set well on Mergenthaler's machines; and no one of Granjon's Romans or Italics has a monopoly of his most personal letterforms, so Galliard is really an anthology."

For the roman design, the Gros Cicero and the Giubilate faces were the primary models, although the name for the family is an anglicization of La Gaillarde, Granjon's name for a small (9·) roman he cut in 1570. During the Renaissance a galliard was a lively dance or a spirited person. Granjon's use of the term for letters was antedated by Giovanniantonio Tagliente, who wrote in his *Lo presente libro Insegna* of 1530 that the chancery hand is improved by "qualche gagliardo tratto" (some spirited flourish) and the mercantile hand by "vivaci, & gagliardi tratti" (lively, and spirited flourishes).

When the Galliard roman is compared to careful redrawings of Garamond's romans, such as Sabon or Stempel Garamond, it becomes clear that Mr. Carter has captured that unique amalgam of Old-style forms, cursive modulations, and increased contrast which distinguished Granjon from his contemporaries, and which led to the Dutch Oldstyle forms of Van Dijck and Kis. In the lower case the thin serifs are relatively long with strongly curved brackets. Similarly, joins and bowls have strongly modulated swells from thin to thick. Terminals are treated with calligraphic variety, and the hooked terminals of *a* and *t* have rather flat angles. These, together with the generous width of the *o*, hint at a relatively shallow "pen angle" for the alphabet, well suited to the increased contrast of the letters. However, the stress axis of the *o* is not quite vertical, and those of the other rounds are tilted somewhat more, so the letters maintain an active asymmetry. The counters are open and present a pleasing set of harmonies.

The set of the letters is adapted to Mergenthaler's new 54-unit em system, and rather tight spacing is obtained even at normal setting. Tighter letterspacing is possible but should be avoided because a disturbing disfigurement occurs when narrowed letterspaces create dark blotches in contrast to the light holes of internal counters. Similarly, the text sizes look best when given some positive leading, as the large x-height places the lines too close for best readability. Negative leading is available, but this causes a confusing tangle when ascenders and descenders touch.

The capitals share many qualities with the lower case, but appear even more exuberant, perhaps because we are accustomed to the sober forms of Garamond, or the rigid forms of the Dutch and Transitional types. Long serifs with strong, curved brackets on the straight stems, and strongly modulated thickness of the curved strokes give the Galliard capitals a fluid appearance. In settings of all capitals the serif brackets tend to look too dark, therefore the letters must be spaced in an optically equal pattern; when too close they appear restless and agitated, with the serif brackets forming peculiar constellations.

The software programmers at Mergenthaler could do us a great favor by bringing out an equalized spacing program for capitals. They could use either the letter-center system advocated by David Kindersley, or the equal-area system advocated by most typographers, including Jan Tschichold. All text photo-systems now set caps poorly, and the meticulous designer must re-space them with knife and paste, an aggravating procedure.

The Galliard italic is based primarily on Granjon's Ascendonica Cursive (20·) cut for Plantin in 1570. It is a novel, even surprising style for those of us who were taught that the chancery hand of Arrighi was the best humanist cursive and the "pendante" style of Granjon the best Old-face italic. The reincarnated Ascendonica Cursive is an angular, complex chancery with several striking characteristics. The basic joins of *n, m, h, b, r* branch out close to the base-line, whereas the joins of *a, d, g, q, u* branch in close to the x-line, instead of the mid x-height branching of the Arrighi style. Serifs tend to be round or semi-round externally and pointed internally. The curves of *a, b, c, d, e, g, p,* and *q* are broken, and the tail of the *g* has an unusual leftward extension, with a peculiar counter enclosed. The italic alphabet has a narrower set than the roman but, despite its very different texture, has the same color. The late Lloyd Reynolds would, with his characteristic growl, have pronounced this italic "spiky."

This unusual alphabet was selected for several reasons.

Parker and Carter felt that the strongly sloping "pendante" style had been overused as a companion to the false (and true) Garamond revivals of this century; that the italic should be an expressive form, useful on its own, and not necessarily subordinate to the roman; that the "droite" style was too narrow for easy legibility.

The latter style, however, might have been a better choice. It has also been known as the Litera Currens Ciceroniana, the Scolastical, or, at the Oxford University Press, the Fell Pica Italic. It was chosen by Tschichold to be the model for his Sabon italic, though he had to expand the letterforms in order to duplex the italic with the roman on Linotype matrices. A narrow and rather upright italic, the "droite" nevertheless has an elegant, rounded structure which might have more appeal to the Anglo-American typographers who prefer a conservative Arrighi style.

The roman and italic fonts have Old-style figures which combine open counters with abridged ascenders and descenders to give a legible but still elegant appearance, a nice accomplishment. To give the series the versatility needed for books, reference, and tabular material, pi fonts have been made with roman small caps, superior figures, reference marks, and lining tabular figures. Given all this, we might wish that Carter would further honor Granjon and favor "fine printers" with a pi font of Granjon's unsurpassed arabesques and flowers. Fleurons for photocomp!

Series of three bolder weights of both roman and italic have been drawn. The lightest of these, the Bold, is closer to a semibold, and has enough clarity and strength to be useful for texts where a dark "color" is indicated. The bolder versions, Black and Ultra, appear best suited to display and advertising where their heavy weight and amusing forms will attract attention. Most bolds for historical serifed faces are too flabby—the bone of the strokes is obscured by the fat that was larded on by later hands—but the Galliard bolds manage to maintain a more muscular appearance. The Ultra roman is especially jolly and athletic; it reminds this reviewer of Fatty Arbuckle in his best silent comedies.

The drawing of bold weights for Old-faces is a difficult problem for even the best designers because the complex asymmetric forms descended from humanist bookhands resist simple emboldening techniques. The task is much easier with constructive types such as Moderns, Egyptians, or especially Grotesques. In fact, it is the wide range of weights available in Grotesque families such as Univers and Helvetica which has allowed the ascendance of the sans-serif Swiss style best exemplified by the work of the late Emil Ruder and his students from the Basle School of Arts & Crafts. This style has in turn fostered a demand for series of bold serifed types.

Mr. Carter was assisted in his drawing of the roman bolds by Ikarus, a remarkable computer program written by Dr. Peter Karow of Hamburg. Ikarus will interpolate or extrapolate new lettershapes from differing shapes provided by the designer. Thus, Galliard Bold Roman was interpolated and Ultra Roman extrapolated from Mr. Carter's drawings of the Roman and Black Roman. The italics were drawn by hand.

To the coming era of digital CRT and laser composition, Ikarus and programs like it will have the same significance that the Benton pantographic punchcutter and matrix engraver had to the era of hot metal composition: new technologies require new means of multiplying letter designs, but in every era good designs result from a synthesis of art and scholarship. Robert Granjon's tool-kit contained files and gravers; Matthew Carter's includes the camera and computer; but there is a shared knowledge and sensitivity to letterforms that bridges the centuries.

Many fine printers will ultimately turn to photocomposition, either because of the dwindling resources of hot metal composition, or because of the new expressive possibilities of the photographic medium. The types that are available, and the quality with which they are set, will depend upon informed and critical demand from the community of typographic designers. There must be an end to the dreary plagiarisms and deplorable spacing systems that now confront us in phototype. Matthew Carter's Galliard is a hopeful sign that the future might be as good as the past.

REFERENCES

Carter, Matthew. (Personal communication)

Dreyfus, John. "Sabon: the first 'harmonized' type," *The Penrose Annual*. London: 1968.

Dreyfus, John, ed. *Type Specimen Facsimiles I.* annotated by A. F. Johnson, Harry Carter, Matthew Carter, Netty Hoeflake, Mike Parker. London: Bowes & Bowes, 1963.

——. *Type Specimen Facsimiles II.* with annotations by H. D. L. Vervliet and Harry Carter. Toronto: University of Toronto Press, 1972.

Johnson, A. F. "The Italic Types of Robert Granjon," *The Library*, 4th series, xxi, 1941. pp. 291-97.

——. *Type Designs.* London: Andre Deutsch, 1966.

Le Be, Guillaume II. *Sixteenth Century French Typefounders: The Le Be Memorandum,* Harry Carter, ed. & trans. Paris: Andres Jammes, 1967.

Moran, James. *Stanley Morison.* New York: Hastings House, 1971.

Morison, Stanley. *A Tally of Types.* Cambridge: Cambridge University Press, 1973.

Parker, Mike, Melis, K., and Vervliet, H. D. L. "Typographica Plantiniana ii, Early Inventories of Punches, Matrices, and Moulds in the Plantin-Moretus Archives," *De Gulden Passer*, vol. 38. Antwerp: 1960. pp. 1-139.

Tagliente, Giovanniantonio. *Lo presente libro Insegna . . .* reprinted in *Three Classics of Italian Calligraphy.* Oscar Ogg, ed. Dover Publications, 1953.

Vervliet, H. D. L. *Robert Granjon in Rome.* Johnston, Alastair, tr. Berkeley: Poltroon Press, in progress.

——. *The Type Specimen of the Vatican Press, 1628.* Amsterdam, 1967.

Since the original publication of this article, the following studies of Galliard type have appeared:

Bigelow, Charles. "Galliard: Animated and Authoritative," *Publish!*, vol. 3, no. 1, January 1988. pp. 33-35.

Carter, Matthew. "Galliard: A Modern Revival of the Types of Robert Granjon," *Visible Language*, vol. XIX, no. 1, Winter 1985. pp. 77-97.

After All, What Does "Functional Typography" Mean?

G. W. OVINK

Remember the poor donkey invented by the philosopher Buridan to illustrate some scholastic problem? It found itself placed at equal distances from two wonderful stacks of hay and, unable to choose between them, starved to death.

We typographers are more or less in the same predicament, confronted on this side by the attractions of traditionalism, on that by the claims of modernism.

Traditionalism is bulwarked by solid achievement, proved by the able and learned men whose position is stated by Stanley Morison: "... According to our doctrine, a well-built book is made up from vertical oblong pages arranged in paragraphs having an average line of ten to twelve consistently spaced words, set in a font of comfortable size and familiar design; the lines sufficiently separated to prevent doubling and the composition being headed by a running title. This rectangle is so imposed upon the page as to provide center, head, foredge and tail margins of dimensions suitably related not only to the length of line but to the disposition of space at those points where the text is cut into chapters, and where the body joins the prefatory and other pages known as 'preliminaries'."[1]

On the other hand, Mr. Morison explains, "typographical eccentricity or pleasantry ... is desirable, even essential, in the typography of propaganda, whether for commerce, politics, or religion, because in such printing only the freshest survives in attention. But the typography of books, apart from the category of narrowly limited editions, requires an obedience to convention which is almost absolute – and with reason."[2]

Modernism, with all the vigor and enthusiasm of youth, is represented by Marshall Lee who writes in *Books for Our Time*:

"The very function of the book in society is being challenged by other media of information and entertainment, some of them much more accessible. Obviously our approach to book design must differ from what it was when books, and perhaps newspapers, were the only means of obtaining information – and the traveling minstrel was the book's only competitor in the field of entertainment. The publisher today is engaged in a battle for the public's attention – not against his fellow publishers but against radio, motion pictures, television, magazines, and many other distractions, ranging from war to psychoanalysis."[3]

... We take it for granted that a composition of Beethoven interpreted by Toscanini will give us a richer experience than the same work performed by a conductor of no creative ability;

yet we are expected to believe that a literary work of art is best served by an innocuous, mechanically adequate printing job.[4]

The outstanding characteristic of all modern design is the independent, creative approach to the individual problem, as opposed to the application of formulas and conventions.[5]

... The evocation of mood then becomes a primary concern of the designer. It is not enough for the designer to be 'unobtrusive'. In dealing with a literature aiming at the subconscious almost more than at the conscious mind, the mechanical neutrality of the printer's craft is a positive detriment. The book designer must now participate *actively* in the author's attempt to contact the poetic sensibilities of the reader. All the subtle and effective graphic means of the artist must be put to this service. Illustration now begins to convey the spirit and essence of the text, rather than simply representing facts. Color is used for its evocative power, not as mere gaud. Imagery and impressionism are replacing decoration. Every feature of texture, material, and format at the designer's disposal is used to convey mood and stimulate interest.[6]

It is noteworthy that neither wants the Book Beautiful, that both introduce themselves as humble servants of the public. The traditionalist backs out silently, invisibly, lest he interrupt the dialogue between author and reader. The modernist would provide an orchestration to bear the listener on the wings of songs in magic concord with the composer. Both argue as functionalists:[7] to promote communication between author and reader, to advance speed of reading, completeness of understanding, depth of emotion – measurable quantities, of no disputable artistic values.

In their common solicitude for the reader, however, each has in mind his own kind of man. For example, Updike, Rogers, C. P. Rollins, Morison, De Roos, Van Krimpen are scholarly. They study the history of printing, painting, and literature and collect fine specimens of the arts. They go at a book as a music-lover to a concert, indifferent to clothing and surroundings, intent only on the music. Or as a smoker to his favorite tobacco, the cleverly decorated tin of which is an obstacle at best – he would as soon have it in a paper bag. Their reading habits are well formed and they will not be told when to read, what to read, how to read. These adult readers demand the sovereign right to look with their own eyes, not through those of an unknown of perhaps inferior ability.

For instance, there is James Thurber's "There's an Owl in my Room" which proceeds from Gertrude Stein's "Pigeons alighting on the grass, alas" to a fascinating analysis of the nature of pigeons as opposed to that of owls, in one of the wittiest and most imaginative pieces of prose written in this century. How should this masterpiece of nonsense be printed? Consideration of this problem may clarify the pros and cons of traditionalism versus modernism.

James Thurber's work can be appreciated only by those few tens of thousands of people who know what is going on in the world, in the field of arts and literature, and who have a certain agility and playfulness of mind. A brilliant professor of philosophy may still not understand what Thurber is hitting at. A wit may not possess the literary knowledge to distinguish the styles of authors being parodied and therefore miss the subtleties of his jokes. But once a person belongs to those who understand Thurber at all, he has the interest to read this author and will do so despite all obstacles.

Conversely, no amount of cajoling into an appropriate mood will help if one has no affinity with this special brand of humor. No tricks of an "interpreting" typography could match the subtle witticisms of Thurber, let alone create a mood to help appreciate his peculiar reasonings. What kind of tricks would they have to be? Figurative or coloristic symbols of grass and pigeons in a more or less alas mood? But Thurber denies that they can convey any alas mood. Then an owl in a terrifying posture? But an owl really is not so terrifying, and Thurber can describe his own reactions much more effectively himself. No, a moody interpretation would not help at all but indeed would be a hindrance. Traditional typography would be much better.

Obviously there are certain limits. For my part, I would read Thurber anyhow, but less avidly, if he were printed in the late nineteenth-century manner with a colorless thin face and grey ink on glassy paper. Or if he were printed by one of these ease-of-reading enthusiasts among the traditionalists who have decided that nine-point Baskerville on a twenty pica em measure reads fastest, easiest. This may be true of informational texts whose meanings are developed gradually, built up consistently through many words, or of novels and detective stories and the like where a swift development of plot is essential. But the two and a half pages of the Thurber essay running smoothly through my mind in a couple of minutes – I should miss a lot.[8]

The foregoing justifies the conclusion that both the traditional and modernist styles have specific fields of use. The former will fail where the text refuses to fit into a traditional pattern or where the reader does not come up to the standard which these scholars regard as normal. The latter, on the other hand, will fail when the reader refuses to conform to the type of mass-produced, passive nitwit which the experienced modernists have learned to regard as normal, or when the text transcends usual boundaries.

Emphatically this does not mean to imply that the Updikes cater to scholars, the Marshall Lees to morons. But that all readers are in some situations scholarly, in others moronic. For example, when I read an essay on typography my attitude is that of a scholar. I do not need to be coaxed or tricked into reading, and if interest wanes the fault is the author's rather than the designer's. The same applies to detective stories, which I also approach with a scholarly attitude. If they are good I will read them printed in any degree of badness, with illumination down to half a foot-candle, in any conceivable posture. All that matters is whether Raymond Chandler's literally immortal Philip Marlowe will keep up his moral fortitude in face of the charms displayed by his female adversaries and the guns stuck in his ribs by the corrupt police of his home town.

But the same mentality confronting income tax forms, programs of new art movements, or the works of such various authors as Ezra Pound and the contributors to the *Ladies' Home Journal* dwindles pitifully to the capacity of a helpless child. The words do not penetrate the mind.

It all boils down to this: the individual pattern of conduct when reading subjects within the field of special interest, whether Updike or Raymond Chandler, is "scholarly" (absorption of content, neglect of outward form). Faced with things outside this field, whether they be fifth-rate fiction, Einstein or Ezra Pound, the same individual's response is like that of an uneducated man or even a moron, dependent on outward form to arouse interest. For everybody the set of relations will be different, one putting Pound where another places Chandler and so on. The only way to decide whether a text is to have traditional or modernist handling, therefore it seems, is by polling public opinion to determine whether the majority of readers approach the author as scholars or as morons.

Both schools of thought, then, are equally functional in the sense of serving well the purpose for which they are used – for there is a great difference of purpose. Functional typography is not a prerogative of the Bauhaus people or of the followers of Morison's *First Principles*, but of any design program making readers read as they should read.

Following this principle leads to eclecticism, an endless variety of ends matched by an endless variety of means. In such a system there would be no place for "house styles." And eclecticism – choosing among all possibilities the best for the particular case – stands low in public esteem nowadays. It suggests cowardice, a lack of participation, refusal to share in the risks while enjoying all the advantages, the passive attitude of the onlooker.

The active attitude of the creative artist might be supposed likelier to find a way out of the blind alley. Anyway some simple slogan is far more promising, more grateful than cautionary warnings to study the matter and then work out the solution with taste and insight. But in spite of the examples on the political scene, the simple typographic war-cry is out of tune with the complexities of present day life – Symmetry! Old Style Types! Renaissance Treatment! or from the other camp, Asymmetry! Sanserifs! Competition with TV! – no, this will not do.

Of course the *simple* program has a connotation of showing courage of conviction, of self-sacrifice, of advancing bravely in spite of the scorn of the not-understanding public. Everybody is for courage, against cowardice. But is the whole trend leading up to such slogans, toward an obedient following by everybody of the same style, so nice? Our best aspirations, our aims in education point another direction: toward each individual building up opinion and taste particularly suited to his own personality, his own talents and inclinations.

These ideals have been persistently followed since the Renaissance, particularly since the French Revolution. Consequently it is not astonishing that the actual products are opinions and tastes, religious and political beliefs, art movements, etc., of widely divergent character indeed.

There are many complaints today about the lack of unity among people in religious or political or artistic matters. Since John Ruskin, a romantic idealism has been accustomed to compare modern times with those in which the cathedrals were built. The popular picture is of a deeply devout population, artists all, working from daybreak till dark in perfect unity of purpose and style. So, merrily singing through life, with no thought of reward other than the satisfaction of glorifying God to their best ability, at last they hand over the task to a new generation of nameless craftsmen. But it is only fair to remember the other side which is not so rosy: toil, poverty, perpetual fear of disease or epidemic, not to mention constant feelings of guilt and doom and bodily terror of the devil. And above all the state of slavery in which these pious artists were held, completely at the mercy of some capricious and ambitious duke or bishop. Nowadays artists and craftsmen are free to pursue their own ideas and it follows that a few hundred of them of various generations put to work on a job could not be depended upon to produce a result of perfect unity in style.

Modern freedom from want and fear is, of course, relative. It is by no means complete. But in a civilized country everyone has access to all the wisdom and beauty mankind has gathered in its history. A far greater percentage of the population than ever before has reached a level of consciousness and responsibility in which the individual can start taking part in creative cultural activity. There is, then, small cause for wonder that the pocket book has a place as well as the folio edition on rag paper, that there is room for both traditionalist and so-called modernist, for people who want to read Ezra Pound and for those who do not want to read Ezra Pound.

Now to summarize the argument, with a few additional observations:

1. No theory on typographical design can claim to be the only one that practices real functionalism. One theory will serve better one function, another theory will serve better another function. Naturally, no bad typography can be functional.

2. The so-called traditionalist style can be called truly functional in those instances where the reader brings with him a sufficient amount of interest (or self-esteem) to be annoyed by any overt attempt of the book designer to help him.

3. A median position is taken by an enlightened traditionalism, which applies what one might call an interpretative method while remaining within the bounds of standard procedures of design. This school addresses itself to the same group of readers as the true traditionalists, but does not hesitate to assist the reader in a subtle way through his unconscious mind, mainly by creating an appropriate mood, e.g., by the use of "period typography," so cleverly handled by some American masters.

4. Finally, the modernists. I must confess that I cherish a kind of love-hate for them: hate, because they are so sure of themselves while making so often ugly things; love, because they are as revolutionaries the underdogs of the printing craft and because at least they try to find new ways.

Now, a little more on these new ways. It has already been pointed out that since the time of the great European cathedrals, with the beginning of the Renaissance, art became more and more an individual expression instead of a collective expression. From that turning point in the history of mankind onward, the process of individualization, of the liberation of the personality, goes forward at a rate hitherto unknown. The French Revolution is another milestone along that way, and in the nineteenth century the contemporary romantic conception of art and artist develops: the artist as a man whose *raison d'être* is to be different from anyone else, different from the craftsmen, businessmen, scientists and so on, who make up the normal membership of society. This artist is the arch-individualist, hypersensitive, unhampered by any kind of tradition or convention, who can see the invisible, put into words or music the inaudible, or express in short the things the laymen need as compensation for their daily toil but are unable to produce. He is the voluntary outcast of society who can function only by being one step ahead of all others in the march of time, who shapes the social outlook because he has already the mentality which others will not attain until the next generation at least. He is the man who can fulfill his function only when he is different from us and is useless as soon as he expresses what we actually think and feel now instead of what we will think and feel at a future stage. He is the true prophet whom we should follow because his extraordinary powers connect him with a future that we are as yet unable to grasp, though of course this future is already developing in us.

According to present day art, what is this future going to be? How much credence can be placed in the signs observable every day in and around us as to whether this future is really coming?

Present day art points characteristically to a world of dead objects, of cones, cubes and balls, of people without heads, without eyes or mouths to see or speak, of robots and machines (often fighting), of deserts and rocks, of desolation, hate and terror.

There have been two world wars with little wars in Abyssinia and Spain in between and one in Korea following. There is much desolation, hate and terror. But – this is the next question – are these the only things for the future?

That is simply not true. Anyone who looks into himself and around him will find as many if not more tendencies toward the soul and spirit, toward living, creative nature, toward human understanding, friendship, and peace.

Cold, geometrical art as the only true expression of the basic tendencies of this time, and the future, is unacceptable, though it cannot be urged that a peaceful naturalism understandable by everyone should be the true art of our time, either. A pure surface description, a sensualism without any participation in human values, is also outmoded. Modern art, expressionism and what followed after, have brought a positive gain by indeed making visible things heretofore unseen and suggesting the unspeakable. Paul Klee, for instance, or in another department such great American artists as Edward Hopper and Ben Shahn, now and then succeed in grasping things which any sensitive person will recognize as real and true, and completely new to us. And they are not morbid either. The sterile art of balance of my compatriot Mondrian is many years behind us. Accidentally it has been put into frames and hung on the wall where nobody has dared to take it off, though at best it should play a very subaltern role as a decorative element in a piece of architecture. Now once again, leading modern art is not advanced but behind the spirit of the time, as it has been sometimes before, e.g., the playful bucolic art immediately preceding the outburst of the French Revolution, or pseudo-medieval art in the midst of the ninteenth-century industrial revolution.

As for typographical design, the hygienic, antiseptic, anesthetic aspects of contemporary art – the clean-cut, clearly articulated, pure shapes – are good for certain fields of a more sensorial, physiological nature. On the other hand, the traditional, technological systems as laid down in Stanley Morison's *First Principles*, apply to the more rational parts of life.

Between those two is a field in which a truly functional typography should attempt to do what the best creative modern art has achieved, i.e., bring the reader, apart from the rational process of reading, into contact with the underlying personality, with the aims and sentiments, of the author whether he be novelist or advertiser of perfume or lubricating oil. This can be done in a most subtle and unostentatious way by choosing a suitable format, paper, color, type, and perhaps ornament. In no instance should the reader be approached with only a coldly reasoned composition of so-called maximum legibility (nine-point Baskerville set twenty ems with one-point leading), nor with the glaring contrasts of black squares on dazzling white coated paper to shake him like the blast of a horn. The human spirit and the human soul today not less – nay, more – than in former ages has approaches other than those which respond to such cold and cruel methods only.

Here in the New World – this can be said with the utmost sincerity, for which as your guest I am very grateful – I see many more manifestations of these spiritual, positive sides of man than in my own tired, disillusioned Europe; which is all the more reason to scorn the deathlike influences and cultivate the warm, vital forces of America.

1. Stanley Morison, *First Principles of Typography* (New York, 1936), p. 16.

2. *Ibid.*, p. 2.

3. Marshall Lee, "What is modern book design?" *Books for Our Time*, edited by Marshall Lee (New York, 1951), p. 20.

4. *Ibid.*, p. 16.

5. *Ibid.*, p. 19.

6. *Ibid.*, p. 15.

7. "Functionalism" has been used especially by modernists of the German Bauhaus movement who, no doubt, have been influenced by the slogan of the famous Chicago architect Louis Sullivan, exemplifier of Horatio Greenough's dictum that form follows function.

8. My experience with the humorous poems, the *Galgenlieder*, of Christian Morgenstern, is a case in point. They used to be printed in a queer kind of lapidary extrabold nineteenth-century roman, which gave the verses a peculiar, enchanting stress. Subsequently the publisher used a small size of Futura Book, and the text stood on the page very young, innocent, diffident. It was a failure: the reader takes the lines in at a glance and in doing so the sudden changes of meaning, the unexpected metaphors—in short, all the numerous jokes of the highly concentrated text—evaporate like the air of a pricked balloon.

Postscript
after Twenty-five Years

G. W. OVINK

Following our decision to reprint Mr. Ovink's 1953 article, "Functional Typography," we asked him to comment, updating his views considering typographic developments since that article was written.
L.G., *ed.*

Twenty-five years ago the salient feature in discussions on the principles of typography seemed to be the unresolved antagonism between two approaches, represented by the earlier and the later Tschichold; in short: Moholy versus Morison. There were, as usual in questions of principle, many personal loyalties and animosities involved (which pupils often inherited from their teachers), coupled with political convictions, social status, and national and personal character traits.

The post-war generation of typographic designers had fewer personal feelings about it and discovered the strong and weak points in both "systems." They saw that an analysis of the basic issues pointed to their reconciliation: learn from "the new vision" with its dynamic balance of tonal values and of successive visual stimuli, but avoid the dogmas that impose eye-hurting sans serifs, primary colors and dynamisms on a reader who needs rest to digest information or reasoning and to enjoy beauty; acknowledge the logic of industrial production without succumbing to narrow cost and efficiency arguments. Morison's "it's a free-for-all in the damned publicity jungle!" is as irresponsible as Moholy's "whip those numb readers to attention!"

I think that good contemporary design profits from the best in both systems. The means are carefully chosen for the ends, without regard for their historical origins in opposed ideologies. Eclecticism, if you like. That is usually a sign of weakness; it tends to apply outward characteristics without being imbued with the spirit that generated them; being cut off from those vital forces it cannot rejuvenate itself; it cannot point a way to the future. Are there any movements today that might lead to a new "style," i.e., a confluence of social, economical, technological and artistic impulses, manifest in a widespread consensus about form?

Scanning the contemporary typographical scene outside "fine printing" with its eclectic approach (which term I cannot and will not use today in a pejorative sense), I see first an overpowering mass of bad design and non-design, both in type and typography: an aimless drifting on a sea tossed by technological – and hence by economical and organizational – storms. Of course, a part of this mass belongs to the inevitable category of hopeless cases, but there is now an unusually large group that I believe to be the victim of the technological revolution. The problems that beset typographers today drain too much energy, time, and money away from attention to design and printing quality. I am convinced that this situation will improve once the new technologies have reached a certain level of stabilization such as we have known between 1900 and 1950.

Another phenomenon in design today is "doing what comes naturally," a clear revolt against artistic ideals and purist principles which are regarded as elitist preoccupations with useless intangibles, while communication with the ordinary man suffers. This trend stems from what in political terms is called "populism": stooping to conquer the masses with the language they understand and with the issues closest to their daily life, instead of raising them to a height of culture only easily accessible to the privileged bourgeoisie. At worst this is an excuse for people too lazy to accept the discipline demanded by mastery of techniques, by analysis of problems, by meticulous attention to detail in design. At best it may be a healthy antidote against the aestheticism that occurs in the decadent phase of any style – and that may be found, too, among adherents of both the Morison and the Moholy schools. It can lead to a return to the old country-printers' unsophisticated, but sometimes highly effective, use of good old typefaces like Cheltenham Bold Condensed (Beatrice Warde's pet aversion). The unartistic typography looks ugly according to our standards, but that is sometimes redeemed by its effectiveness. In a revolutionary technological phase, a painstaking attention to detail is bound to suffer, but in typography – which is not only an art but also a communication technique – it should return soon. That means a hefty dose of the very sophistication the populist approach wants to get rid of. So I see no real future in it, once it has corrected the excesses of aestheticism.

No one has ever been able to predict a coming design style (apart from stating generalities such as the habit of pendulums to swing back); nor can I. Having entered typography fifty years ago under the guidance of Tschichold's refreshing "New Typography," I am grateful to the editors of *Fine Print* for allowing me today to sniff the air a bit for the very first signs of another spring.

HANS EDUARD MEIER'S SYNTAX-ANTIQUA

Sumner Stone

Since the revival of edged-pen writing in modern times, a legitimate concern among typographers and letterers has been to investigate the link between written and typographic letterforms. The clear, rhythmical letters of Renaissance scribes like Poggio Bracciolini have led many to consider calligraphic forms as ideal. "Typography is properly a branch of calligraphy" is an oft-quoted phrase of Stanley Morison, and Emil Ruder writes in *Typographie*, "Handwriting can be seen to underlie any good typeface."

What are the characteristics of handwriting that can be seen to underlie a good typeface? To a calligrapher the most obvious are the shading (the difference in thick and thin parts of the letter) and the serifs. Both of these come from the properties of the edged writing tool. Old style types have thicks and thins that correspond roughly to the shading characteristic of humanistic letterforms written with the pen held at a more or less constant angle. (Variations in pen angle always occur among expert writers, particularly for branching and stroke endings, viz. serifs.) The typographic serifs of the early roman types are a combination of the serifs from Roman inscription letters and the humanist minuscule forms. According to Father Edward Catich in *The Origin of the Serif*, the symmetric serifs of the inscription letters were created by the edged brush used for laying out the letters on the stone before chiseling. These serifs are imitated in the capital alphabets of old style types, and are repeated in the serifs of many lower case letters. The other serifs found in the lower case letters are imitations of the beginning or ending of the edged-pen stroke, found, for instance, on the letter *n*, at the beginning of an ascender, or at the end of the ascender in the letter *d*.

If we construe writing to mean edged-pen writing, and hence consider serifs and variation in weight to be the essential characteristics of written letters, then we exclude from at least Emil Ruder's list of good typefaces any that do not have these two properties. This is without a doubt not what Ruder had in mind, for this would exclude any sans serif forms. However, an underlying feature of the pen-written humanistic forms that seems even more basic than shading and serifs is the essential or linear form of the letter. Imagine the forms traced out by a single point on the edge of the edged-pen (e.g., the midpoint). These

are the essential forms of the given alphabet.

It seems doubtful that Renaissance scribes thought of their letterforms as anything but organic units, but the abstractions to a skeleton form do capture the essence of the letters. Certainly, the idea is a useful one. Having determined an essential form, weight can be added to it according to different systems. There is the edged-pen pattern, but other systems of weighting are also possible. In the early 'sixties the Swiss typographer Hans Meier designed a sans serif typeface called Syntax-Antiqua using the essential forms of the humanist letters. It was originally cast as foundry type by Stempel in 1968.

The concept of an essential linear form is not unknown in the lettering pedagogy of this century. It is mentioned by Edward Johnston in *Formal Penmanship*, and was used extensively by the Austrian lettering teacher Rudolf Von Larisch and his student Friedrich Neugebauer. Father Catich also used it in his teaching of letterforms. Not surprisingly, Professor Meier uses essential linear forms in his teaching of lettering at the School of Applied Arts in Zurich.

Meier's type adds an optically equal amount of weight to the skeleton of the letter, producing no noticeable variation in thick and thin. Other schemes for adding weight using a combination of the edged-pen and pointed pen patterns produce forms with a familiar look. Recent research by this writer indicates that several common patterns of weighting that occur in typographic letters can be produced mechanically by adding weight to an essential form. The adjacent sequence of *O*'s (right) was drawn by a computer from a single ellipse, using a simple weighting principle.

It seems natural to expect that if one uses as essential forms the skeletons of written letters, e.g., humanistic ones, then the letterforms produced from them by whatever weighting system will retain some of the essential characteristics of the original letters. One of the most appealing aspects of written letters is their rhythmical quality—their dynamism. Since Syntax is based on written forms, it retains the dynamic quality of these forms. This is the thesis that was presented by Professor Meier in the lecture he gave on Syntax during his tour of the United States last fall. Indeed, it was his rationale in designing the typeface. The original drawings were begun by first writing the letters with a brush and then re-drawing. The outcome is a typeface that is distinctly different from the current sans serif typefaces in several important ways.

These distinctions have been outlined in "Syntax, a Sans Serif on a New Basis" by Erich Schulz-Anker, the Art Director at Stempel during the production of Syntax. Schulz-Anker and Meier outline the evolution of typographic forms away from dynamic forms based on the written letter toward a more static geometric basis. They point out that the essential forms of modern faces such as Bodoni or Didot do not possess the same rhythmical quality as the earlier typefaces based on handwriting. Neither do the current sans serif types for they have essential forms that are similar to the modern faces. For instance, consider the branching that occurs in the letter *n*. Meier states, "In the old face and Syntax the arches start from the stems and form angles with them. They swing lightly upwards and after making a narrow-radius curve they enter the

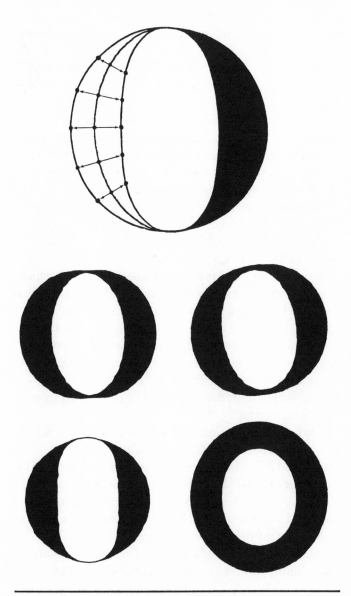

Das Erscheinungsbild der Druckschrift ist etwas komplexes, das heiß, Form, Duktus und Rhythmus sind nicht voneinander zu trennen. Bei allen formal

Das Erscheinungsbild der Druckschrift ist etwas komplexes, das heißt, Form, Duktus und Rhythmus sind nicht voneinander zu trennen. Bei allen formal

Old Style (Sabon), Syntax

Das Erscheinungsbild der Druckschrift ist etwas komplexes, das heißt, Form, Duktus und Rhythmus sind nicht voneinander zu trennen. Bei allen formal

Das Erscheinungsbild der Druck ist etwas komplexes, das heißt, F Duktus und Rhythmus sind nicht einander zu trennen. Bei allen for

Modern (Bodoni), Sans Serif (Univers)

second stem. The dynamism of a curve written with a pen is still perceptible. The arch is asymmetrical in form. In modern face and sans serif types an almost symmetrical arch is used to join the two uprights. The point where the arch leaves the stem is no longer emphasized. The motion of writing is no longer implicit." Comparisons of other forms, such as those in the word "fasten," point out other features that emphasize the dynamic nature of the old style/Syntax forms and the more static nature of the modern/sans serif forms. "The dynamic characters are based on the written script and have retained its rhythm. The open forms help to bind the characters together. The broad *g*'s and *t*'s fit into the rhythm of the face. Static characters are designed on the basis of a geometrical system. The beginnings and ends of strokes lead back into the character itself and do not join up to neighboring characters. The ends of the *a*, *t*, and *e* differ and interfere with the rhythm, while *a*, *s*, and *e* are too similar in form. The result is a monotonous and not easily legible face. Since *f* and *t* are too narrow, they give the impression of being squashed and disturb the rhythm."

One of the benefits of having a dynamic rather than a static essential form as a basis of a typeface is increased

fasten **fasten**

fasten fasten

fasten fasten

DYNAMIC   STATIC

legibility. The movement of the hand in writing the letters can promote the movement of the eye in reading them. Another feature of the old face/Syntax forms is their relatively tall ascenders. Tall ascenders tend to emphasize distinctness of letter and word shapes, hence increasing legibility.

The stroke endings of Syntax are immediately seen to be somewhat out of the ordinary. Unlike familiar serifed or unserifed types, the terminals of the strokes are at right angles to the direction of the stroke, rather than parallel to the writing line (note the *R*, *k*, *v*, etc.). Meier points out that there are early examples of alphabets with serifs in this position, "although they are rare," and that the more common parallel serifs originate in the architectural nature of Roman letters, the stems being compared to the columns of a building.

In analyzing letters in terms of their essential linear forms, one is rapidly impressed by the inevitability of making some decision about the design of stroke beginnings and endings. The common practice of ending the strokes parallel to the writing line in sans serif types does not mean that there is the absence of a stroke ending. The terminals of Syntax point this out dramatically. In comparing the usual serif system with his own, Meier says that "horizontal serifs give the letters a stabilizing, static effect. And that is precisely the effect I wanted to avoid in Syntax."

These stroke endings are used on the capitals of Syntax as well as the lowercase letters. The capitals have been constructed in varying width groups, making their proportions closer to the classical Roman inscription letters than the normalized capitals of modern and sans serif types.

Historically, there have been several typefaces with features similar to those found in Syntax. The forerunner of all of these seems to be the alphabet which Edward Johnston was commissioned to design for the London Transport System in 1916. Johnston's sans serif was followed by three others all cut in 1927—Eric Gill's Sans,

Futura designed by Paul Renner, and Rudolf Koch's Kabel.

Johnston, reviver of edged-pen writing and master lettering artist, was completely immersed in pen written forms. It is natural, therefore, that the typeface he designed should incorporate features of written letters. He chose to use the humanist "*a*" and "*g*" (as Meier did), and the lowercase "*l*" has a hook at the bottom echoing the majuscule origins of the form.

Eric Gill was a student of Johnston, and Gill Sans is obviously modelled to some extent on the letter Johnston designed for the Underground Railway. In both faces, as in Renner's and Koch's, the proportions of the capitals adhere fairly closely to those of classical inscription letters, a feature that they share with Syntax.

Koch was also a writing master, and his sensitivity to letterforms is evident in Kabel. The stroke endings and beginnings of Koch's face are interesting to compare with those of Syntax. Johnston, Gill, and Renner all constructed stroke endings that were of the horizontal variety. The stroke endings of Kabel occur at interesting slants, reminiscent of edged-pen forms. The angle of the slants, however, does not remain constant or follow any other edged-pen logic. The effect is to make the letters active in a way that is similar to the effect of the right angle stroke endings of Syntax.

Renner was an architect and associated with the Bauhaus school. His original designs for Futura contain many bizarre lowercase forms which appear to be based on geometric notions of letterforms. The final version issued by Bauer was changed considerably, and as R. Hunter Middleton has written in an article for *Sans Serif* by Taylor Poore, "one must reach the conclusion that the typefounding experience of the foundry also entered into the design of Futura as a type."

In comparing these typefaces it is necessary to note that there was some variety in their envisioned use. Syntax was designed for use as a text face as well as for display, an idea that is accepted to a greater extent today than at the time the other types were designed. Johnston's type was for use primarily in signs and, indeed, for the exclusive use of the Underground Railway. Gill and Koch also probably never intended that their types be used as text faces, but Renner certainly did.

With these distinctions in mind, some brief comparisons can be made of Syntax, Gill Sans, Kabel, and Futura. Futura and Kabel both seem quite geometric compared to Syntax or even Gill Sans. The curves are circular, and the joining of the strokes is done in a symmetric and static format. The joining in Gill Sans is closer to that of Syntax.

Another feature that bears comparing is the relative height of the capitals and ascenders. Gill Sans and Syntax have slightly shorter ascenders than Kabel and Futura, but the caps of Gill Sans are the same height as the ascenders. This has the effect of making the capitals completely dominate the lower case. Meier has followed the example of Griffo in making the caps shorter than the ascenders. This convention has also been followed by Renner and Koch, but the ascenders in their designs are already tall, so that the capitals still appear quite large in relation to the lower case.

Of the four types, Syntax is the only one that works successfully as a very legible text face. Meier's mastery of lettering will be evident to anyone who peruses his book *The Development of Writing*. He has combined his skill in lettering with a keen perception of the subtle structure of humanistic letterforms to produce a typeface of great character. The dynamism of written letters does shine through the subtle forms of Syntax. The type has the delicate proportions of the best historical examples of calligraphy.

While not well known in this country, Syntax is readily available on the photocomposition machines of Mergenthaler and Berthold. It is possible to obtain Linotype matrices and foundry type. Several weights have been drawn, including medium, bold, and extra bold. The italic is based on the cursive hand of the Renaissance.

ITC ZAPF CHANCERY

Kris Holmes

THE NEW ZAPF CHANCERY typeface, issued by ITC (International Typeface Corporation) has attracted attention and comments from many calligraphers because it is a calligraphic type, a Chancery cursive, and a design by Hermann Zapf. Depending on the school and persuasion of the calligrapher, one may hear that the bold lowercase *x* has "the vigor of Gene Kelly in his prime," that the medium-weight plain capitals are "as proud as a line of thoroughbreds," or perhaps that the stem of the swash capital *E* appears to have "turned the corner too soon," or that the bowl of the lowercase *g* resembles the "dripping faucet" warned against by a famous teacher of italic.

Vivid as such metaphors may be, we must consider not the microcosm of the individual letter but the macrocosm of the text. In type, the design problem becomes the fashioning of a true set of characters which, balancing similarity and difference, create a uniform but lively image. ITC Zapf Chancery, available in six weights (Light, Light Italic, Medium, Medium Italic, Demi, and Bold) is the boldest experiment yet in the adaptation of a calligraphic hand to photocomposition. To examine it carefully in its historic and contemporary context is to learn not only how a master designer confronts a traditionally difficult type design, but also how types are marketed and produced for contemporary equipment.

In discussing Zapf Chancery, it is well to review the origins of Chancery cursive. The writing of the Renaissance may be conveniently divided into two phases. The first is the era of Humanist scribes, whether professionals working in the Papal Chancery, like Poggio Bracciolini and Flavio Biondo, or amateurs like Niccolò Niccoli, for whom the accomplishment of writing was only part of a larger career as statesman or scholar. They wrote quick but highly legible hands, which, whether formal or cursive, were as much adapted to the production of text as to the perfection of style. This era was ended by the spread of printing, which replaced the copyists with the press. (One of the last great scribes of the fifteenth century, Antonio Sinibaldi, complained in his tax declaration of 1480 that printing had reduced him to such a state of poverty that he could not afford clothing). The Humanist cursive of these scribes was eclipsed in popularity by the later development of Chancery cursive in the sixteenth century, when typography freed writing from the demands of text production and encouraged its development as an art, thus inaugurating the era of writing masters and calligraphy. Virtuoso lettering artists such as Arrighi, Tagliente, and Palatino displayed their talents not only in their written commissions but also in their writing manuals, printed from wood blocks, of which the first was Arrighi's *Operina* of 1522.

Zapf Chancery draws its inspiration from the formal cursive of this later era of master calligraphers, though it is an original design and neither a copy nor a revival. Coming almost thirty years after Zapf's own brilliant writing manual, *Pen and Graver (Feder und Stichel)*, 1950, ITC Chancery reflects his sensitivity to the work of past designers who have accepted the challenges of this form, and his ingenuity in solving anew the vexing puzzles of translating script into print.

The first italic type was Francesco Griffo's humanistic cursive cut for Aldus's edition of Virgil's *Opera* in 1501. It was an independent form, unsubordinated to any roman, and Aldus expressed his delight in it (and its punchcutter) with a poem in the introduction of the Virgil:

> In grammatoglyptæ laudem.
> Qui graiis dedit Aldus, en latinis
> Dat nunc grammata sculpta dædaleis
> Francisci manibus Bononiensis.

(*In praise of* [*punch-*] *cut letters. Behold, Aldus, who gave carved letters to the Greeks, now gives them to the Latins, through the Daedalus-like hands of Francesco of Bologna.*) However, by the time of Granjon's zenith, c.1570, italic had been subordinated as an accompaniment to roman, on the same body and alignment, a position which it retains to the present day.

Twentieth century Chancery cursives, whether revivals or new, have been designed primarily as companions to roman text faces. The first Chancery revival, Blado, was cut by Monotype in 1923 to accompany Poliphilus roman. It was based on the later italic type designed by Arrighi, presumably cut by Lautizio Perusino, an engraver of medals, and used circa 1539 by Antonio Blado, later printer to the Camera Apostolica. Like the Poliphilus, Blado was more of a success as an imitation than as a working type, because the revival did not compensate for weight increases and distortions caused by ink spread in the handmade paper of the original sixteenth-century printing.

Frederic Warde designed Monotype Arrighi italic in 1929 to accompany the Centaur roman. Based on an earlier italic design that Arrighi used for his own press beginning in 1524, this revival is lighter and more readable than the Blado.

Condensed Bembo italic designed by Alfred Fairbank was first issued as a companion to Bembo roman in 1929. Its rather slight slant (approximately 4 degrees), narrow forms, and unusual stress-contrast resulting from a steep pen angle (55 degrees instead of 45 degrees or less) gave it too much personality for the roman. It was supplanted by a tamed version of Tagliente's Chancery type design from his *Lo presente libro* of 1525. The taming of this face broke its spirit as well and Stanley Morison was correct in saying that while "the first design had too much personality, the second has too little." In defense of the draughtspersons of the Monotype drawing office, we must remember first that they were pioneers, and second that they were working for machine-set metal type,

abcdefghijklmnopqr
stuvwxyzABCDEF
GHIJKLMNOPQR
STUVWXYZ1234
567890123456789O
&$¢£%AÇÐEŁØÃ
ÂÊßaçdełøœœ:;,.!¡?¿·
--—""''/#*()[]†‡§«»'
¶ʃfʋw ſtthoſ

START LETTERS: LIGATURES

VARIATIONS: gʋvwxyyyz
1 2 1 2 1 2 1 2 3

SWASH CAPS: ABCDEFGHI
JKLMNOPQRS
TUVWXYZ
ALTERNATES: AEILe?

FINALS: ƌdⱡkȩⱱr.ty⹁⹂·ᴗ
1 2 1 2 1 1 1 1 4 1 2 3

abcdefghijklmnopqr
stuvwxyzABCDE
FGHIJKLMNOP
QRSTUVWXYZ

abcdefghijklmnopqr
stuvwxyzABCDEF
GHIJKLMNOPQR
STUVWXYZ1234

abcdefghijklmnopqr
stuvwxyzABCDE
FGHIJKLMNOP
QRSTUVWXYZ

abcdefghijklmno
pqrstuvwxyzABC
DEFGHIJKLMN
OPQRSTUVWX

abcdefghijklmn
opqrstuvwxyzA
BCDEFGHIJKL
MNOPQRSTUV

which imposed limitations on the kerning and tightness of fit necessary to a well-composed italic.

In 1934 Jan van Krimpen, working with the brilliant punch-cutter of the house of Enschedé, P. H. Rädisch, produced a virtuoso Chancery which rivalled the historic cursives. This *tour de force*, the Cancelleresca Bastarda, contained 210 characters including alternatives and ligatures. It surpassed in variety Granjon's Civilité, rivalled Griffo's Virgil Italic, but did not quite match the 290 alternates and abbreviations of Gutenberg's original Textura. Zapf himself has said that the Cancelleresca Bastarda was one of the finest works of hand-punchcutting in this century. Although designed to accompany the Romulus roman family in hand composition, the Cancelleresca was not adapted to Monotype machine composition.

Palatino italic is Zapf's Chancery companion to Palatino roman. A narrow version with swash caps and characters was brought out for hand composition in 1951. In 1968 Zapf demonstrated his further thoughts on Chancery with Hallmark Firenze, a single alphabet with swash characters designed for photocomposition. This solo italic set the stage for ITC Zapf Chancery of 1979, an upright cursive of slight slant (approximately 3.5 degrees) with an accompanying italic of greater slant (14 degrees) but similar form. In a revolution that would have brought a cheer from the great masters of italic such as Arrighi, Griffo, and Granjon, Zapf has liquidated the roman. His transposition to an upright face of typically cursive characteristics—rhythm and movement, clubbed ascenders, swashes, and a tendency to ligature—gives a strikingly unusual and even unsettling effect. Like true revolutions, it will take some getting used to. However, let us note that the search for an upright Chancery has been like the quest of the Grail to certain visionary designers for a long time. Frederic Goudy's Deepdene italic of 1927 has a slight slant of approximately 4 degrees; as does Fairbank's Condensed Bembo italic described above, and van Krimpen's Romanée italic of 1949.

An italic is not so much a matter of inclination as of innate character.
Frederic Goudy, *A Half Century of Type Design*, 1946

There could well be a new upright italic type made in its own right that would be more readable than some existing types by virtue of its verticallity.
Alfred Fairbank, *Renaissance Handwriting*, 1960

Italic is a different style of type from roman because it is nearer to its, also different, calligraphic sources which, fundamentally, have very little or nothing to do with slope in a small or larger degree.
Jan van Krimpen, *On Designing and Devising Type*, 1957

In designing for phototype, Zapf has wisely avoided the "soft character" syndrome epidemic in type today. Compared to the sparkle and sharpness which so many historic punchcutters strove for, the rounded corners and soft, blurry quality of much modern type is deplorable. The fallacy current in the phototype industry is that this softness increases legibility and makes phototype "look like that old stuff." Every type from Janson to Bodoni has been homogenized by

this treatment. In comparison Zapf Chancery is so angular that it looks slightly like a Fraktur.

Reinforcing the Fraktur qualities of Zapf Chancery is its large x-height. Arrighi's Chancery is designed with extruders which are twice the x-height. This is a reflection of the handwritten luxury of Arrighi where every ascender or descender can be a flourish. Zapf compromised this luxuriousness by shortening the extruders to about 1-2/3 the x-height, in closer conformity to ITC's contemporary big-on-the-body style. This compromise is particularly evident in the Demi and Bold weights, and while it may alarm the purists, it does make Zapf Chancery more useful for modern commercial typography.

The weight progression shows Zapf's mature comprehension of the needs of text typography. The Light and Medium are close in weight and allow the typographic designer a subtle distinction in color for text. The Demi is distinctly bolder than the Medium and is primarily fit for display. The Bold is in turn only slightly heavier than the Demi, thus allowing for a subtle adjustment of display weight. Along with their greater weight, the Demi and Bold have greater contrast of thick and thin, which accentuates their sensuous curves and eye-catching forms.

Designing with Zapf Chancery is a challenge. The wide variety of alternate characters approaches the range of possibilities open to the calligrapher, and the proper use of these alternates requires some calligraphic sensitivity and much forethought. It is indicative of Hermann Zapf's comprehensive view of letter forms and his consummate skill with a pen, that he would use the tools of modern typesetting technology to capture the feeling of the handwritten text. The alternate characters available, including four lowercase y's and two cap A's, allow the designer to control the stress and feeling of words. Thus, one has the choice of swash or plain caps in all weights as well as small caps in the light and medium roman weights. Several connecting swashes are provided which can be joined to initial and final characters to add the touch of the flourish. Zapf designed the swash capitals to be used together in titling. Careful selection and spacing is required but the result can be elegant and refreshing.

Even the normal lowercase characters have a tendency toward ligature because of the slight lengthening of the exit hairlines and serifs, which will join to the following letter when the face is composed with a tight fitting. Thus Zapf has used photocomposition to achieve the variety and range of effects that historical masters desired, but could not practically achieve.

Given the uninspired typefaces that have come from the interregnum of metal and phototype, one might wonder why Zapf Chancery has suddenly appeared out of the fog of undistinguished designs. For this we may thank the intervention of the International Typeface Corporation (ITC) of New York, which acts as a franchiser for new photo typefaces. Type designs are submitted by a designer or produced upon specific commission from ITC, and those that are accepted are marketed to almost fifty manufacturers of typesetting systems worldwide. ITC's tremendous influence is due to its widely-read *U&lc* (*Upper and lower case*) magazine (total circulation 145,000). This free, tabloid-format quarterly has made the personalities of ITC, designers such as Ed Benquiat and Herb Lubalin, the superstars of commercial advertising typography. Because of its pronounced commercial hyperbole, ITC is considered by some to be a bastion of low taste, but whatever criticism one might have of its kinky marketing program, ITC has provided type designers a broad market for their work, and has made its typefaces widely available in their original form on a non-exclusive, ethically licensed basis. ITC has cited its ethical practices as a primary reason that Hermann Zapf has returned to type design after abstaining for nearly a decade in protest against the widespread plagiarism of his designs.

Zapf Chancery began when ITC asked Zapf to design a calligraphic typeface based on the Chancery hand. In his medieval watch-tower studio near Darmstadt, Germany, Zapf drew the letters and determined their utilization; i.e., letterspacing determined by set of characters and their side bearings on a unit-em system. They were photographed onto test fonts at Photo-Lettering, Inc. in Manhattan, and proofs were sent back to Zapf for correction and approval. The final artwork was photographed and sized at ITC and mailed to manufacturers who subscribe to the ITC program of typeface offerings.

Once a typeface leaves ITC, its fate is up to the individual manufacturer who must adapt the design to the particular typesetting machines it is selling. ITC provides a sample text with the artwork to serve as a guide to the drawing offices of these manufacturers, but an office is not obligated to follow the guidelines except through pressure to conform to other manufacturers producing the same face. The first step is for the manufacturer to select, from the potpourri of alternates and ligatures accompanying an ITC typeface, those characters which will be made available to its customers, according to the anticipated usage and point-size range of the face. It would be simplest if all the alternates provided by ITC were used by every manufacturer, since that would best reflect the intent of the designer, but this is not the case.

The second step at the manufacturer's is the unitization and actual production of the typeface for a particular machine or machines. We must note that in the later history of typography, most designers have been assisted by a punchcutter or draughtsperson—highly skilled in the craft. The contribution of craftspersons cannot be overestimated, but there is scarcely any danger of that, since we rarely, if ever, hear even their names. We all know of the great designers: Baskerville, Zapf, Mardersteig, Gill, and Morison. But who knows of John Handy (punchcutter to Baskerville), August Rosenberger (punchcutter to Zapf), Charles Malin (punchcutter to Gill and Mardersteig), or Victor Lardent (draughtsman for Morison's Times Roman)? The modern type drawing office in part fulfills the vacated role of that invisible artisan, the punchcutter, and while we cannot realistically include all the draughtspersons of the modern drawing offices in the class of those past artisans, each small decision they make—whether the adjustment of a unit value or the shaping of a light trap—contributes to the success or failure of a design.

The most crucial decision is the spacing of the typeface and of the entire family of weights and sizes of letters. Because ITC uses an 18 unit-per-em spacing system, while most manu-facturers are able to accommodate a more precise 36, 54 or greater unit system, the drawing offices can improve considerably on the unitization. In any case, the side-bearings provided by ITC are often seen to be too tight—following what Zapf has labeled the "sexy" style beloved by Madison Avenue. Since some typesetting machines can only tighten letterspace, while others can both tighten and loosen it, the best approach is to allow the machine operator the option of a relatively loose fit for text work and a tighter fit for display sizes, thus approximating the careful adjustment of spacing for each point size seen in the work of the traditional punchcutters.

In the drawing office, artistic decisions involving spacing, color, and actual design of some extra characters are only a part of the whole program of producing an ITC typeface. The draughtsperson is faced with sheets and sheets of finished artwork, a complex set of specifications, impossibly tight deadlines, personality conflicts, and enough documentary paperwork to choke a horse. Moreover, all decisions and designs must be made within the technical restrictions of the particular phototypesetting machine of the corporation. Thus, ITC type designers may sometimes be dismayed by subsequent design changes over which they have no control. Such changes reflect the various ideologies in the industry—some manufacturers prefer to painstakingly rework ITC faces, others just "lick 'em and stick 'em."

One natural extension of the new typographic technology should be the design of other new calligraphic faces. In this Chancery, Zapf has shown how a modern writing master can return to the pen for inspiration. His working method has often been to write, draw, or even paint his letters at a small reading size of 12' or so, in order to capture all the subtle optical adjustments of weight, rhythm, proportion, spacing, and detail necessary for a text type. To see him draw with a pointed brush beautiful letters at this small size is a nearly uncanny experience, especially when he apologizes that at the age of sixty, he must work larger than he could at age twenty-one. He then photographically enlarges the small drawings and refines them at a larger size for the drawing offices.

Zapf's creation of a vigorous, playful, and iconoclastic Chancery adapted to commerce rather than the museum, should be an important lesson to all calligraphers: there is more to letter design than the pen; and an equally important admonition to manufacturers: there is more to type design than a sheet of tracing paper and a camera.

FURTHER READING:

Fairbank, Alfred and Berthold Wolpe. *Renaissance Handwriting*. London: Faber and Faber, 1960.

Lubalin, Herb. "What's New from ITC; How to Use ITC Zapf Chancery," *U&lc*, vol. 6, no. 2, June 1979, pp. 33–44.

Standard, Paul. *Arrighi's Running Hand*. New York: Taplinger, 1979.

Zapf, Hermann. *Pen and Graver*. New York: Museum Books, 1952.

——. *About Alphabets*. Cambridge: MIT Press, 1970.

HIERO-RHODE ITALIC

Paul Hayden Duensing

AN ITALIC CONSIDERED on its own merits may seem an unusual topic for typographic review. In the case of Hiero-Rhode Italic, however, the surpassing merits of the type seem to me to recommend itself for whole texts, rather than only in the usual italic role, ancillary to a related roman. Overall the design is extremely well thought-out; it provides an even tone upon antique paper, without the need for corrective letterspacing. Unfortunately, this well-modulated mass effect has been achieved at the price of a brutal truncation of the lowercase *r*, but the artistic dividend is perhaps worth it. The contrast of stroke thickness between thick and thin is a bit more pronounced than in Diotima Italic, which is perhaps the closest graphic relative of this type. The serifs are largely vestigial except in *B, E, F, P,* and *R,* and give a strong feeling of the stone-cut inscriptions from which the designer must have drawn inspiration. The flow and rhythm of Hiero-Rhode Italic is eminently suited to the setting of poetry, especially in long lines (alexandrines in French, for example), or to personal narratives, such as reminiscences, or extracts from a diary. The capitals are very handsome in their own right; their proportions are balanced and classic; the drawing is quite without flaw, and the feeling of authority and elegance is devoid of pretension.

Hiero Rhode, who designed the roman bearing his name (first cast by Johannes Wagner Foundry in 1944), did not design the italic now sold as a companion font to his roman. It was Karl Hans Walter, a professor at the Academy of Graphic Arts in Nüremberg, who in 1954 began the preliminary sketches for Hiero-Rhode Kursiv. He worked steadily at the development of the concept until the final version was captured on paper in November of that year. Almost a year later, in October 1955, finished drawings were completed for the caps, lowercase, small caps, ligatures, and punctuation. From these drawings, patterns were prepared and master types were engraved as lead originals by the firm of Thebis & Bucher in Leipzig. The matrices were then deposited electrolytically, and much testing of trial casts followed before the final release of the design in 1957.

The addition of small caps to the italic is an unusual feature, but it works exceptionally well, emphasizing the strong horizontal feeling of the composed line. One suspects that the small caps were originally another artful attempt by German typographers to cope with the graphic problems created by German orthography, which demands a capital at the beginning of every noun. The small capitals are not, as one might first suspect, merely capitals of the next smaller point size, but were especially designed and cut to work as small caps. The weight was carefully adjusted to match both the capitals and lowercase, and the set width of characters was subtly changed to allow somewhat longer serifs in the small cap design.

With a pure calligraphic face of such strong individuality, one is led to wonder what to do about decoration and a companion display face. Ornament should perhaps be best forgotten in favor of letting the type work alone to its fullest potential. The problem of display first suggests perhaps the

Textprobe mit kleinen und großen Versalien der Kursiv zur Hiero=Rhode=Antiqua

Es war kein Handwerksbursch, der Arbeit suchend von Ort zu Ort ging, das sah man auf den ersten Blick, hätte ihn nicht die kleine, sauber gefertigte Ledermappe verraten, die er auf dem Tornister trug. Den Künstler konnte er überhaupt nicht verleugnen. Der keck auf einer Seite sitzende, breitrandige Hut, das lange blonde gelockte Haar, der weiche, noch

Das Läuten war lange vorüber, und noch immer stand er dort und blickte träumerisch hinaus auf die Bergeshöhe. Sein Geist war daheim bei den Seinen, in dem freundlichen Dorf am Taunus - bei seiner Mutter, bei seinen Schwestern, und es schien fast, als ob sich eine Träne in sein Auge drängen wolle. Sein leichtes fröhliches Herz aber ließ die

CORINTH-KUNST-AUSSTELLUNG

abcdefghijklmnopqrstuvwxyz z̜ äöü chck fffiflfft ß tz

ABCDEFGHIJKLMNOPQRSTUVWXYZ ÄÖÜ

ABCDEFGHIJKLMNOPQRSTUVWXYZ ÄÖÜ

1234567890 & & .,:;='()!?§+„"»«*

aabcdefghijklmnopqrstuvwxyz äöü chckfffi flftßsttz ABCDEFGHIJKLMNOPQRSTUV WXYZ ÄÖÜ 1234567890 & .,:;='()!?§*+-„"

Above, Hiero-Rhode Italic. Below, Hiero-Rhode Antiqua

capitals of Hiero-Rhode Antiqua, although graphically the relationship may be somewhat tenuous; initials from Sol Hess's Monotype Artscript 225 or the Ariadne Initials by Gudrun Zapf may provide another solution.

The roman is close to an acceptable face for fine printing, especially in its capitals (except perhaps for a bit of fussiness in the serifs of letters like *E*, *F*, and *L*, and a particularly unfortunate *M*), but the lower-case shows the eccentricities of its period of origin in the overly wide *e* and the almost cartoon-like caricature of the *g*, the upper bowl of which is far too large, and the lower of which apparently atrophied many years ago. (Some of the faces of the other talented designers of the period are subject to the same conceits, as may be seen in the Elizabeth and Marathon romans and Koch's sans serif.) If the management at the Wagner foundry could be per-

suaded to turn the talented Herr Walter loose on a half dozen revisions, plus a few flourishes, Hiero-Rhode Roman could also become a major contribution to letterpress typography.

Swash characters in the font of Hiero-Rhode Italic are unfortunately limited to two: the lower-case *z* and an alternate ampersand. One should also note that there is no $ nor are ligatures for *ffi* or *ffl* included, as is usual with European fonts. French and German accents are available and the face is cast (on Didot body and American height) in the sizes 6·, 8·, 9/10·, 12·, 14·, 16·, 20·, 24·, 28·, 36·, and 48·. Fonts are large (by American standards), 12· weighing in at 22½ pounds for a 28A 82a font. Orders may be directed to the foundry (Johannes Wagner Schriftgiesserei, D-8070 Ingolstadt am Donau, Postfach 227, West Germany).

GERARD UNGER: TYPE DESIGN AND LETTERING

Charles Bigelow

GERARD UNGER is a Dutch type designer, lettering artist, and typographer. Formerly on the staff of Enschedé en Zonen in Haarlem, he is now freelancing in Bussum, near Amsterdam, where he teaches lettering and typography at the Rietveld Academy. During the autumn of 1979, Mr. Unger was visiting professor of graphic design at the Rhode Island School of Design which honored the visit with an exhibition of his work. Most striking in this show were two families of original types he designed for digital cathode-ray-tube (CRT) composition on the Digiset typesetters manufactured by Dr. Ing. Rudolf Hell of Kiel, Germany.

Unlike most digital types which are simply imitations of traditional faces—photocopied, traced, and electronically scanned without critical reflection by the designer—Mr. Unger's types show true originality in form and painstaking attention to detail. A digital type image is comprised of thousands of minute pixels (picture elements) each of which represents one bit (binary digit) of information. The image is painted out onto photographic paper or other medium by cathode ray, laser, or other device. Mr. Unger constructed the text sizes of his faces pixel by pixel and exhaustively tested them at every stage of the design process in order to maintain complete control over the digital image and to ensure the highest quality for book work and other text composition.

His first digital face is Demos, a sturdy roman of large x-height, strong color, and low contrast. Narrow but with horizontal emphasis, it is fashioned to maximize legibility while withstanding the rigors of high-speed printing processes. It does this successfully enough that a recent gathering of newspaper designers at RISD called the face "beautiful" when used in a newspaper mock-up—unusual praise for a news face. (A more complete description of it by the designer appears in *Visible Language* XIII:2 which is, in addition, entirely set in Demos.)

His second digital family is Praxis, a sans serif designed to match Demos in form, alignment, and color. The result is a kind of "transitional sans," midway between the old-style sans like Gill and Syntax and the modern sans like Univers and Helvetica (see *Fine Print*, October 1979, "On Type," for more on this distinction). The first such mating of a serif and a sans serif was drawn by Jan van Krimpen for his Romulus family in the 1930s. Perhaps this is an aspect of the Dutch typographic collective unconscious. Praxis may be seen composed in *Typography Needs Type,* the illustrated text of a lecture given by Max Caflisch to the Association Typographique Internationale in 1977, and published for ATypI in 1979 by Hell-Digiset.

Unger has also created some experimental letterforms, including a rhythmic cursive handwriting adapted to such modern instruments as the ball-point pen and the aerosol

Basic-track recorded
at the *Music Factory*
Mastering & cutting
16-track mixdown
Over-dub **engineer**
30 input **channels**
Re-mix *engineer*
16 output busses
1000 position **patch bay**

Demos and Praxis types showing variation within the families

spray can. Italic handwriting enthusiasts take note: This is just the thing for subway grafitti and other wall-slogan writing. Coincidentally, Mr. Unger has also designed the official alphabet used for the signage system of the Amsterdam underground railway. Now, if he could only convince the Amsterdam grafitti artists and others to use his handwriting method, he would achieve an enviable domination of official formal and outlaw cursive letterforms. Counterforms for counter-culture!

Centraal Station Bijlmer

Amsterdam Subway Signage

Mr. Unger's innovative approach continues the long Dutch tradition of sensible, economical and workmanlike types, what Fournier called *le goût Hollandois*, into the modern era of electronic typography. The firm of Hell has shown good sense in commissioning original designs from this thoughtful artist who, in describing his Demos design, quotes Theodore Low de Vinne's remarks on the type of Christoffel van Dijk:

"It may not be comely, but it is legible. The letters may be stubby, but they have no useless lines; they were not made to show the punch-cutter's skill in truthful curves and slender lines, but to read easily and to wear well."

Since the original publication of this article the following essays by Max Caflisch have appeared:

"Die Hollander, eine neue Schriftfamilie," *Typographische Monatsblätter,* No. 2, 1987, pp. 1–12; and "Swift: eine neue Zeitungsschrift," *Typographische Monatsblätter,* No. 4, 1987, pp. 1–16.

DIOTIMA OF GUDRUN ZAPF-VON HESSE

Paul Hayden Duensing

WHILE TEACHING CALLIGRAPHY at the Städel Art Institute in Frankfurt, Gudrun Zapf-von Hesse produced handwritten books in the best tradition of the manuscript artists of the Middle Ages. In the spring of 1948, Städel Art Museum held a showing of Mrs. Zapf's work, much of it lettered in a wide, delicate, rounded lowercase roman, accompanied by a somewhat narrower, near-Chancery italic. These two letterforms served as the basis for the Diotima Roman and Italic.* Following the exhibition, Mrs. Zapf entered into negotiations with representatives of the D. Stempel Typefoundry in Frankfurt, and in due course an agreement was reached for the design of a roman and italic type based upon these calligraphic models.

After drawings were completed, the 36˙ pilot sizes—extraordinarily large for a trial size, which is usually in the 14˙ to 20˙ range—were cut in lead by the dean of Stempel punchcutters, August Rosenberger. (This talented *Meister* of classic engraving and punchcutting, who also hand engraved in lead plates the calligraphic alphabets for Hermann Zapf's classic book, *Pen and Graver*, died July 31, 1980 at the age of 87.)

Following careful analysis and revision of the trial cutting, brass patterns were produced at the foundry for three ranges of sizes and again carefully corrected by Mrs. Zapf to assure correct proportions, counters, serif weight, letter-fitting, etc. It is not possible to engrave all sizes of a given design from one set of patterns because of certain optical tricks played by our eyes: in order to seem the same width and weight throughout the scale of type sizes, letter designs must actually be varied every few sizes. As the size becomes smaller, the design must actually be made bolder and wider, with more open counters. As the size becomes larger, letter-fitting must be made tighter, the strokes of the letters must be made proportionately lighter, and greater subtlety must be incorporated into the drawing; hence the need for at least three sets of patterns. After approval of the patterns, the intermediate sizes were then engraved by pantograph.

Following further extensive trials and revisions, the roman was offered to the public in 1952, followed by the italic a year later. A companion set of open capitals designed by Mrs. Zapf was released as a titling letter, well-suited to accompany the original font. This design was called Smaragd, the German word for emerald. Finally the series was completed with the release in 1954 of the Ariadne initials, a free-flowing set of calligraphic forms cast in the 36˙ to 60˙ range (and of course named for the daughter of Minos, King of Crete).

The first use of Diotima in the United States was by the Zapfs' long-time close friend, Phil Metzger, at his Crabgrass Press in Prairie Village, Kansas. Showings of Diotima appeared on several of the sheets of his portfolio *Orbis Typographicus* (produced jointly with Hermann Zapf over the past ten years and finally completed and published in the spring of 1980. Professor Zapf has commented several times that Diotima remains one of his favorite types for light-sensitive texts, as may be seen in his *Manuale Typographicum I & II in extenso*).

Many type designs seem to have one size—or at best two sizes—that seem more "comfortable" than the rest; sizes in which all of the elements seem to coalesce into the ideal balance of proportion, rhythm, legibility, harmony, and visual interest. It is a rather singular feature of the Diotima Roman and Italic, that all sizes seem to work equally well. The extreme clarity of the smallest range grows into the open, legible, airy text of the middle range and finally into the visually exciting larger sizes where the details of the design's calligraphic basis become most apparent. The serifs of the roman are quite wide but, above all, the generous internal space, the openness of the counters, gives the type a light, sunny quality found in almost no other face. It is interesting to note that the lower foot of the Roman *a* ends in an abrupt stop with a foot serif. The curved, flowing foot we would have expected there is found instead in the *l*, where it echoes the *t*. The *b* has no lower left serif or spur, but rather a smooth curve into the bowl. In a lesser design this might cause visual problems, perhaps a "tumbling" effect, yet the general openness and roundness of this face assimilate these features without a ripple of disharmony.

Diotima Italic shows the charm that a calligraphic type can have; set in wide lines with generous leading and close word spacing, it can easily seem to have flowed directly from the pen of an expert calligrapher. There is a fine uniformity in this design without tediousness; no letters fail to show their right to belong to the font. Swash letters are few—only *x* and *z*, and the Ariadne initials supply the need for an occasional bit of flair. If we might wish for any alternate character, it might be the italic *y*, but that is to cavil. Two sets of figures—lining and ranging—are available, as are the usual accents and a small, charming fleuron to mark the occasional need for a

---

*Diotima was the name of a fictitious princess quoted by Socrates in Plato's *Symposia*.

break in thought. The uses of Diotima are wide-ranging and may include visiting card and letterheads in the smallest sizes, belles lettres in the intermediate sizes, and in the largest sizes, notices and posters of an elegance now seldom seen.

The roman exists as 4/6˙ and 5/6˙ caps, and as roman and italic in 6˙ through 36˙. Smaragd is also cast in 6˙ to 36˙. All members of the family are cast only on Didot bodies, but may be acquired milled to domestic height. These fonts are available from Schriftgiesserei D. Stempel AG, Hedderichstrasse 106-114, 6 Frankfurt am Main 70, West Germany.

16 didot Diotima

ABCDEFGHIJKLMNOPQRST
UVWXYZ ÆŒ Ç

abcdefghijklmnopqrstuvwxyz
ff fi fl œ æ äâà ç ï ëéè öô ü

$1234567890 &.,.:;–'!?()—¢✝*„">‹»«

16 didot Diotima Italic

A ABCDEFGHIJKLMNOPQRST
UVWXYZ ÆŒ Ç

abcdefghijklmnopqrstuvwxyz z
ff fi fl œ æ äâà ç ëêéè öô ü

$1234567890 .,.:;–'!?()—*✝✿„">‹»«

28 didot Smaragd

ABCDEFGHIJKLMNOPQRSTU
VWXYZ ŒÆ Ç $£1234567890
.,.:;!?-'·()/»« ^¨˙´

FIGURENVERZEICHNIS DER ARIADNE-INITIALEN

ABCDEFGHIJKLM
NOPQRSTUVWXY
ZLRVZ

Type specimens courtesy of Paul Hayden Duensing and Philip Metzger.

DONALD KNUTH'S *TEX* & *METAFONT*:
NEW DIRECTIONS IN TYPESETTING

Donald Day

The computerization of typesetting technology has caused many fine printers to ask whether or not the high level of typographic quality achieved during the era of letterpress printing can be maintained in the computer age. Among those who think not, a frequent complaint is that the engineers who design, and the corporate managers who market, high technology typesetting systems are alike indifferent to aesthetic values.

A significant counter-example can be seen in the work of Dr. Donald Knuth, Fletcher Jones Professor of Computer Science at Stanford University. Dr. Knuth has written two special computer languages, TEX and META-FONT, in order to improve aesthetic standards in the composition of mathematical texts. Because these languages are of general interest, Dr. Knuth has placed them in the public domain as a service to the mathematical and typographic professions.

Progress in typography has frequently resulted from the efforts of inspired amateurs, and among these we should now welcome Donald Knuth, who has set up shop not with a Columbian press and fonts of Caslon, but with a Digital Equipment Corporation PDP-10 computer, a Xerox Graphics Printer, and an Alphatype cathode-ray-tube typesetter.   C.B.

SINCE THE INVENTION of the Monotype with its punched paper tape, digital techniques have been used in typography, and during the last twenty years the computer has invaded every technical aspect of the book arts. Donald Knuth's TEX and METAFONT are the first computer aids, however, that have much to offer individual fine printers or type designers.

TEX is a computer language for typographic book design and layout, and can be used for tasks ranging from the simple (an author entering text into a pre-set design format) to the complex (specifying the complete design for a series of technical books). The METAFONT language is used for letterform design. It too has a wide range of applications, from creation of a single special symbol to design of a large family of type.

As a mathematician and computer scientist, Knuth has tried for universality in all his works. As a result TEX (pronounced, he suggests, to rhyme with blecchhh) is the most comprehensive of all the current programs for computer-aided typography, most of which have been designed for specialized uses: IBM's Printext has been used for newspaper printing and in-house manuals; Penta Systems International's Automath software has been used for setting technical and scientific texts. One would think that only unified effort by the typographic industry could have produced TEX's impressive range of features, but this was not the case, and Knuth's was largely a one-man achievement. Unfortunately, secrecy and non-cooperation (for example, encrypting fonts to protect pirated designs from further piracy) are the in-

dustry norm. Knuth has emphasized in his lectures that his programs are in the public domain, not owned by corporate giants; he plans to ensure this by publishing the algorithms—the underlying defining structures – in Pascal, a clear and explicit computer language. This should eventually make TEX and METAFONT available on small computers for use in the studio, office, or home.

The co-publisher of Knuth's book, *Tex and Metafont*,* the Digital Equipment Corporation, makes the TMS-8 and TMS-11 typesetting systems and supplies the minicomputers for many other proprietary typesetting systems: Atex, Bedford, Compugraphic, CSI, Logicon, Hendrix. Although the makers of some of these systems have criticized TEX, they will undoubtedly be among the first to order copies of the algorithms. TEX itself is not dependent on any one manufacturer's set of machines. Its input comes from a keyboard, perhaps over a telephone line, and its output can control a variety of devices, from a hot metal caster (if you really want the lead fumes) to the 5333-line-per-inch CRT phototypesetter used by Knuth for his own future books.

TEX considers that all graphic forms fall within one of two new conceptual categories: glue or boxes. Boxes are letters, words, lines, paragraphs, or whole pages; glue is the adjustable space – letter spacing, word spacing, leading. The structure of vertical and horizontal boxes within boxes was chosen to give TEX the flexibility necessary for setting mathematical text, but it could also accommodate large design features such as Jan Tschichold's page layouts based on the golden section. Detailed book design formats are also possible: the text of the forthcoming third edition of Knuth's *Art of Computer Programming* and of *Tex and Metafont* itself were executed by TEX. Knuth is a naive designer showing off his new system in *Tex and Metafont*, and it is not a beautiful book; nonetheless, the control available in TEX shows through. The second edition will have a much improved "Computer Modern" type, and setting the revised text will be a minor task with TEX.

METAFONT is part of what makes TEX a universal system. The measurements that TEX needs to space letters (equivalent to body height and set width) are already available in a METAFONT letter design. As an aid to type design META-FONT is unique; Peter Karow's program Ikarus comes to

---

*Knuth, Donald. *Tex and Metafont, New Directions in Typesetting*. Digital Press, Digital Equipment Corp., Bedford, Mass. 01730. [This is now included in Knuth's five-volume *Computers and Typesetting* (Reading, Massachusetts: Addison Wesley, 1986).]

mind, but it has been used primarily as a tool for digitizing completed type designs and interpolating between them. The style changes available on CRT (Cathode Ray Tube) typesetters to slant, expand, or embolden a font are not comparable, as they are not real design tools but gimmicks, crudely exploited outgrowths of the CRT technology. META-FONT can be used to make style changes serve the needs of the letter, not the machine; the changing angle of a slanted roman, for instance, can be linked to subtler changes in counters and serifs.

METAFONT draws letters by moving "pens" – patterns of black – along smooth curves. This method encourages the designer to follow the kinetics and topology of calligraphic models: thus the serif can be made part of the vertical stroke, rather than something tacked on to the end. Families of METAFONT letters are different flesh on a common skeleton instead of various inflations of a ballooning outline. Knuth claims not that creating a good type design using METAFONT is fast, but that in the end the designer will have created a family of alphabets and not only know which features cause the variations but be able to describe them precisely. Many of Knuth's examples are exaggerated and cartoonlike – who wants random- or backwards-slanting alphabets? But the experimental METAFONT letters designed by Matthew Carter and Hermann Zapf at Knuth's invitation are up to their usual high standards; unfortunately, Knuth's book was published before such noted professional type designers got a chance to try their hands, so these letters are not shown in the first edition.

Both TEX and METAFONT are more than mere computer programs; they are languages. In natural languages we create new words for new or expanded concepts without changing grammar. Similarly, when Zapf wanted to draw in META-FONT with a changing pen angle, Knuth was able to create sub-routines that would do this without changing the structure of METAFONT itself. The METAFONT language is not limited to the design of Latin alphabets; non-Latin alphabets such as Thai or Devanagari, or even Chinese characters, could be constructed in METAFONT as well.

If and when a transient electronic tablet is developed of sufficient graphic quality to replace dead-tree pulp, TEX may prove too awkward and METAFONT too slow to place the characters on it. If and when composing devices can intelligently recognize spoken words, TEX and METAFONT (and all other linguistic artifacts) will be drastically changed. The principal obstacle to both programs now is limited access. Since METAFONT is currently available only on a few large computer systems, the first designers to use it may work through a METAFONT expert, just as earlier type designers worked with a punchcutter; learning to design in META-FONT, however, is much easier than learning to cut punches. Knuth has given us a full set of tools to work with, but because these are languages and will grow by creative extension, it is up to us to make them into vehicles for fine printing.

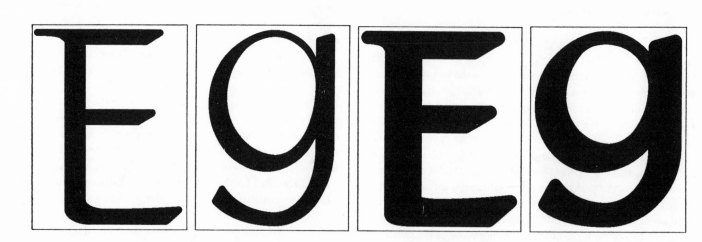

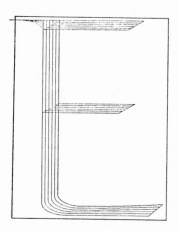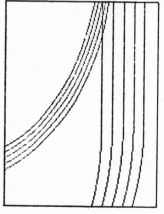

IN FEBRUARY 1980, Hermann Zapf (on a grant from the National Science Foundation) and Matthew Carter (sponsored by Mike Parker of Mergenthaler Linotype Corporation), visited Stanford University to work briefly with Donald Knuth. These experimental samples show some of Zapf's results which were too late to be published in *Tex and Metafont*.

Top row. First two examples show letters *E* and *g*. "Our main interest was in adapting standard METAFONT so that it would simulate 'pen pressure' as well as dynamic rotation of the pen angle." (From a letter from Donald Knuth.) Next two examples are the same program made bolder.

Second row, left: The internal structure of the letter *E*. Right: A portion of the *g* reproduced in original size to show edge.

THE TYPES OF JAN VAN KRIMPEN

Walter Tracy

JAN VAN KRIMPEN was one of the most distinguished figures in the world of typography. His designs for books were notable exercises in symmetry and scale, with every detail of type, spacing, and material fastidiously organized. The classic style and impeccable quality of his typographic work had considerable influence in Europe, and in America his designs were seen in several books of the Limited Editions Club. But by the time of his death in 1958 at age sixty-six, he was even better known as a designer of types. In a thorough evaulation of twentieth-century type designs (should such a thing ever be attempted), the book types designed by Jan van Krimpen would be difficult to place. All of them display a degree of refinement hardly matched by any other designs, not excluding Gill's Perpetua. They were much esteemed at their introduction, yet none of them has achieved full admittance to that select list of types known to be effective in the practicalities of everyday printing. The reason is this: each of the types, when closely examined, has some feature that amounts, in my opinion, to a defect and diminishes its chance of unqualified welcome into the typographic resources of the printer.

The circumstances of Van Krimpen's working life (except for the war years) could hardly have been better. In his youth he studied art and became particularly interested in lettering. It was a natural step to typography and the design of books. In 1923 he drew the lettering for a series of commemorative stamps published by the printing firm of Enschedé in Haarlem. Impressed with the quality of his work, the firm invited him to design a type for them to be cut and cast in their own foundry. Pleased with the result, Enschedé persuaded Van Krimpen to join their staff to supervise the design and printing of fine books, to design type specimens demonstrating the firm's remarkable collection of historic types, and, in time, to create further new types. This was wholly excellent for both parties. Enschedé acquired a person of knowledge, ability, and taste. Van Krimpen, at the age of thirty-one, gained a secure and privileged future in one of the oldest and most eminent printing houses in Europe, with the cooperation of an expert punchcutter in a working typefoundry to help him realize his type designs. Enschedé benefited from Van Krimpen's influence on the quality of their work; he had the benefit of their appreciation and encouragement during the thirty-five years he worked for them.

Lutetia

For his first type, Van Krimpen began by drawing the text of a poem in roman caps and lower case. Enschedé admired the sample, so Van Krimpen proceeded to design the full set of roman characters. His letter drawings were ready by the middle of 1924, and he went on to draw the italic. The type was first made in 16· and used in a book produced for an exhibition in Paris in 1925—hence its name, Lutetia, the early Roman name of Paris.

In August 1861 I wrote another novel for the *Cornhill Magazine.* It was a short story, about one volume in length, and was called *The Struggles of Brown, Jones, and Robinson.* In this I attempted a style for which I certain

A B C D E F G H I J K L M N
O P Q R S T U V W X Y Z
abcdefghijklmnopqrstuvwxyz
12345 ﬀﬁﬂﬃﬄ 67890

A B C D E F G H I J K L M N
O P Q R S T U V W X Y Z
abcdefghijklmnopqrstuvwxyz
12345 ﬀﬁﬂﬃﬄ 67890

Lutetia with italic, the original version, 16·

In 1926 the roman was reviewed by Stanley Morison in *The Fleuron* V. He observed that the type was not derived from any historic predecessor or school, that the designer had "kept himself free from current English, German, or American fashions" (*were* there any?), and that the design was "an exceedingly handsome one, its proportions . . . most agreeable." He did not care for the e with the sloping crossbar and would have been pleased if the E could be reduced a little in width, but he clearly regarded Lutetia as a remarkably fine design.

During the next two years the Enschedé foundry completed the production of seven sizes of roman caps and lower case, three of titling caps, and five sizes of italic (some of the punches were cut in Germany). These were shown in a specimen inset in *The Fleuron* VI in 1928, and this time the italic was reviewed. The reviewer noted that it was a true "chancery" letter and the most legible of its kind so far, but that it was "so good in itself that it cannot combine, with the proper self-effacement, with its roman." (Perhaps by "good" he meant "distinctive" or "expressive.") *The Fleuron* inset shows some of the alternative swash letters made for the italic, and it must be said that they prettify the text only at the expense of comfortable reading. Swash letters were made for the roman too; they can be seen in the Enschedé specimen books of 1930 and 1932. Many years later, when Van Krimpen wrote a survey of his type designs for the Typophiles, he expressed disapproval of such extraneous aids to elegance as swash characters.

Mention should be made here that under Van Krimpen's direction, P. H. Raedisch, Enschedé's punchcutter (one of the last practitioners of that ancient craft), created an attractive decorative type by engraving a white line into the 36· and 48· sizes of Lutetia capitals. In the Lutetia Open, the white line was cut through the edges of the letters. In the Romulus Open, the profiles are intact.

ABCDEFGHIJK LMNOPQURS TVWXYZ

Lutetia Open, 36·

There was general admiration for the Lutetia design. Oliver Simon, who visited Holland in 1928 and met Van Krimpen, ordered Lutetia for the Curwen Press. In America the Grabhorn Press installed the type in 1927 and used it frequently. (They tried the 18· size for an edition of *Leaves of Grass*, but not surprisingly found it unsuitable for Whitman's reverberant verse.) The Merrymount Press had Lutetia but used it sparingly; Updike preferred a limited typographic palette. As it happened, the next chapter in the story of Lutetia emanated from the United States, producing a development that, though not unique, is certainly unusual.

Porter Garnett, an expert printer, had since 1923 been in charge of the School of Printing at the Carnegie Institute of Technology in Pittsburgh and of the Laboratory Press connected with the school. The Press had been awarded the task of printing the catalogue of the Frick art collection, a monumental work of great prestige. In 1928 Garnett visited Van Krimpen to say that he wanted to use Lutetia for the work, but would Van Krimpen agree to the re-design of certain characters? His published reason was "to amend such characters as seem to fall short of perfection," but he may have had another reason: to be able to tell the governing body of the

Frick collection that the type to be used in the printing of the catalogue would be, in a sense, original. Van Krimpen willingly agreed to the changes—because, as he wrote nearly thirty years later, they accorded with the changes he would have made himself if it had been possible to do so.

REVISED LUTETIA

Irascimini, et nolite peccare: quæ dicitis in cordibus vestris, in cubilibus vestris compungimini. Sacrificate sacrificium iustitiæ, et sperate in Domino. Multi dicunt: Quis

HERE THE ORIGINAL FORM IS FOLLOWED
BY THE REVISED:

CC EE FF GG LL QQ
ee hh ii jj mm nn ss 88
?? !! .. ,, ;; :: () () -- " " [] []

The revised characters in the Lutetia roman

A study of the Porter Garnett revisions is instructive. The e, having a level rather than slanted crossbar, is more appropriate for this type that owes nothing to Jenson. (It was the only one of the changes to be adopted by Enschedé for their own use of the type.) The wider h, m, and n are in better balance with o and the other round letters. The new s, though, is too narrow. The dot of the i and j, too small and isolated in the original (even more so than in Bruce Rogers's Centaur), is in better relationship with the stroke of the letters. The stronger punctuation marks are more effective. Rather than altering the figure 8, Garnett should have increased the width of the 2, 3, 4, and 5, which are oddly cramped. The short-tailed Q is less likely to suffer breakage than the elegant original. The new version of C seems hardly necessary. The shorter vertical in G was evidently to Van Krimpen's taste; it appears in all his later designs. The changes in E and F are particularly interesting. The excessive width that Morison noted in the original version of the type and the high crossbar had not previously been favored in Van Krimpen's drawn lettering; but they *are* characteristic of De Roos's types, which Van Krimpen knew well (for that matter, they appear in several

ABCDEFGHIJK LMNOPQRS TUVWXYZ

Romulus Open, 36·

of Goudy's early types). The Garnett versions, narrowed and with the crossbar lowered, are certainly better.

Most of these revisions are distinct improvements, elevating a good roman into a positively distinguished one. It is a pity that it was not found possible to incorporate them into the standard Lutetia fonts, especially when Monotype, by arrangement with Enschedé, began to produce the face in 1928. When the completion of the Frick catalogue was taken on by the Thistle Press of New York around 1945, the proprietors offered to release the revised sorts for general use. Van Krimpen declined the offer, believing that the introduction of alternative characters at that time would cause confusion.

In any case, the italic remains a problem. It is not a good working companion for the roman: too narrow, dazzling, and too dark. Van Krimpen said he took a long time to decide whether to design the face as a conventional italic or as a chancery letter, which suggests that he was thinking of it as a separate entity. He had not grasped the fact that an italic intended for use as a *secondary* letter can be successfully designed only by first trying out groups of tentative letters within a sample passage of the roman, seeking to achieve harmony of style, proportion, and weight. But the empirical attitude and the practical method were not, it seems, Van Krimpen's way—neither then, when he was a novice in type designing, nor later, when the lesson should have been learned.

To the growing number of people who were taking an interest in typography at that time, Lutetia was clearly unlike the recently revived Garamonds, the ubiquitous Caslon, or the familiar old styles and moderns. It was original, yet refined and unassertive. It made Van Krimpen's reputation as a type designer, and the types he created during the following twenty years were received with the greatest respect.

ANTIGONE

In 1927 Van Krimpen designed a Greek type, Antigone, as the first part of a scheme to create a complete set of characters and symbols for mathematical textbooks (only the alphabets were actually produced.) The Antigone type is one of the best of Van Krimpen's designs; the Δ and the Ξ look too large and the Φ looks too small, but these are minor faults. The lower case is distinctly calligraphic, so the type is nearer to Wiegand's type for the Bremer Press of 1923 than to Scholderer's New Hellenic face of 1926, and it is better suited to

ABCDEFGHIJ
KLMNOPQRSTU
VWXYZ
ΓΔΘΛΞΠΣΦΥΩ

Open Capitals, Roman and Greek, 24·

literary than to mathematical texts. To work with the Antigone, Van Krimpen added eleven Greek letters to the handsome set of open roman capitals he had already designed for use in title lines.

οὐ βραδύνει κύριος τῆς ἐπαγ-
γελίας, ὥς τινες βραδυτῆτα ἡγο-
ῦνται, ἀλλὰ μακροθυμεῖ εἰς ὑμᾶς,
μὴ βουλόμενός τινας ἀπολέσθαι
ἀλλὰ πάντας εἰς μετάνοιαν χω-
ρῆσαι. Ἥξει δὲ ἡμέρα κυρίου ὡς
κλέπτης, ἐν ᾗ οἱ οὐρανοὶ ῥοιζηδὸν

Α Β Γ Δ Ε Ζ Η Θ Ι Κ Λ Μ Ν
Ξ Ο Π Ρ Σ Τ Υ Φ Χ Ψ Ω
αβγδεζηθικλμνξοπρσςτυφχψω

Antigone Greek, 16·

ROMANÉE

The firm of Enschedé possesses a remarkable collection of punches and matrices, many of them acquired by purchase during the eighteenth century, others created by their own punchcutters, including Fleischman and Rosart. Among the collection there had been a roman and an italic attributed to Christoffel van Dijck, "greatest of Dutch letter cutters," as Harry Carter described him. The faces were included in a type specimen book issued by Enschedé in 1768, but only the punches and matrices of the italic had survived, and only in the 16· size. It was decided to create a roman to work with the italic. It is not clear who made the decision. Van Krimpen himself, writing in 1957, said that he had never been in favor of copying or adapting historic typefaces. This may have been his view also in 1928, but he was probably in no position to oppose the plan in any case.

There is only one way to accomplish the task of adapting type copying easily and successfully: make bleached-out photographic enlargements of samples of the type to be imitated; carefully paint over the characters, modifying them as necessary, and then give the resulting collection of enlarged characters to the punchcutter. This was the method suggested by Emery Walker and adopted by William Morris for his Golden type and by Bruce Rogers for his Centaur. Van Krimpen did indeed study photographic enlargements of the Van Dijck roman, but he did not work them over. Instead he *drew* a roman, retaining little more than the proportions and some of the features of the original. As could surely have been predicted, the resulting roman, called Romanée, was, as Van Krimpen frankly admitted, a "distinct failure" as a companion for Van Dijck's italic.

Considered by itself, the Romanée roman has great merit. Except for the w and y, which are rather cramped, the letters in the lower case are in better proportion to each other than in the original version of Lutetia. This second major type is

In August 1861 I wrote another novel for the *Cornhill Magazine*. It was a short story, about one volume in length, and was called *The Struggles of Brown, Jones, and Robinson*. In this I attempted a style for which I certainly was

A B C D E F G H I J K L M N
O P Q R S T U V W X Y Z
abcdefghijklmnopqrstuvwxyz
12345 ff fi fl ffi ffl 67890

abcdefghijklmnopqrstuvwxyz
12345 ffifflfflffi 67890

Romanée with italic, 16·

therefore an advance on the first. This may be due to the influence of the Porter Garnett revisions of Lutetia, but that cannot be said of the punctuation marks or the dots on i and j, which are too light to be properly effective. The r and g look good enough to me, though they have been criticized by others. The ligatures are excellent (they are not always so in Van Krimpen's types). The numerals are the best he ever designed. The capitals, always his strong point, are very fine, except for W, which is a little obtrusive. In all the characters the thin strokes are firm, no doubt because the designer was attending to a model, the print of the lost seventeenth-century roman. Said the reviewer in *The Fleuron* VII: "The general form, proportion, and relation of upper to lowercase remind us of the Bembo. . . ." This is going a little high—Romanée is rather bland in comparison with Bembo—but the type is certainly a distinguished design. It is ironic that when, about ten years later, the Monotype Corporation decided to make their own version of the missing roman (Van Dijck, Series 203), it was Van Krimpen who, doubting now that the roman and italic in the old Enschedé specimen book were by the same hand, discovered an edition of Ovid printed in 1671 in which the Enschedé italic could be seen with a different roman, which Van Krimpen judged to be a true relation to the italic.

In spite of the lack of harmony between the Romanée roman and the original Van Dijck italic, four sizes of the roman were cut, and it was the existence of these types in the Enschedé foundry's stock, while the Van Dijck italic remained in only one size, that persuaded Van Krimpen twenty years later to design a new Romanée italic to work with the roman. (To keep matters in chronological sequence, this italic will be discussed later.)

ROMULUS

After the Romanée roman there was an interval until 1932, when Van Krimpen conceived the idea of a family of types for book printing, comprising a roman (which came to be called Romulus), an italic, a script, bold and condensed romans, at least four weights of sans serif, a Greek, and possibly more—

In August 1861 I wrote another novel for the *Cornhill Magazine*. It was a short story about one volume in length, and it was called *The Struggles of Brown, Jones, and Robinson*. In this I attempted a style for

A B C D E F G H I J K L M N
O P Q R S T U V W X Y Z
abcdefghijklmnopqrstuvwxyz
12345 fffiflffiffl 67890

A B C D E F G H I J K L M N
O P Q R S T U V W X Y Z
abcdefghijklmnopqrstuvwxyz
12345 fffiflffiffl 67890

Romulus with italic, 16·

all to be related in style and consistent in alignment. He was therefore intending to create a larger family of types than had Lucian Bernhard, about whose roman, "italic" (in the form of a sloped roman), and script Morison wrote, in *The Fleuron* VII of 1930: "Professor Lucian Bernhard is the first type designer to put into practice the principles laid down in successive articles in *The Fleuron* as to the relation of roman, sloped roman, and script—the trinity in which, it was forecast, contemporary type faces must henceforth appear."

In his account of the Romulus roman, Van Krimpen remarked that Romulus was related to Lutetia. "The lower case of Lutetia being, on the whole, on the narrow side, it was to be expected that Romulus should be wider. . . . A number of the capitals of Lutetia were, against the classical Roman tradition, too wide . . . ; their width has been reduced. . . ." In my opinion, the alphabets of Romulus are exemplary as letter shapes, being the most satisfying in the display sizes, but less so in the text sizes, where the limited contrast between the thick and thin strokes makes the face look rather lifeless.

The "italic" in the form of a sloped roman was a departure from historical practice. It was in 1926 that Stanley Morison had propounded in *The Fleuron* V that the logical and ideal form for an auxiliary face to a roman was a *sloped roman* rather than a true italic.[1] It seemed at the time a revelation of truth and was taken seriously. (W. A. Dwiggins, for example, adopted the principle for the "italic" of his Electra type in 1935.) Van Krimpen accepted the theory, though he was aware that

1. The sloped romans current at the time of Morison's writing were mostly jobbing faces, such as the italic of the De Vinne face introduced by the Central Type Foundry of St. Louis in 1894—a popular type in Europe for many years. Lucian Bernhard's "italic" of 1926, designed to accompany his roman of the year before (called Bernhard Antiqua Zarte by the Bauer foundry), was one of the first sloped romans designed for the secondary role in *text* setting. Morison observed approvingly that in Bernhard's "italic" (sloped roman) only the comma showed any calligraphic influence.

Morison himself not only had been obliged to allow the introduction of a few informal letterforms into the "italic" for Perpetua, but had evidently thought that a traditional italic was the only kind that would be tolerated in the Times Roman newspaper type made under his supervision in 1931-32.

Van Krimpen began to draw the Romulus sloped roman in the autumn of 1932, though the face was not completed until late in 1936. The width of the letters is very similar to that of the roman, and all of them without exception follow the roman shape—though the t has lost most of its crossbar.

After it was introduced, reviewed, and tested in the field, Morison and Van Krimpen decided that the doctrine of the sloped roman was not valid.[2] There is no evidence of any attempt to modify the monotony of the Romulus sloped roman by substituting an informal form of *a*, *e*, and *g*, as had been done in the Perpetua italic—though there is an alternative italic-style *f* in the Monotype version. Van Krimpen would not have agreed to such a compromise with principle. In any case, he was much occupied with, and no doubt investing great hope in, the script type that, according to plan, was to be the third member of the Romulus family.

Van Krimpen had evidently discussed the script in correspondence with Morison who, in August 1932, offered the suggestion that the scriptorial quality ought to manifest itself in the first and last letters of the words (that is, in swash letters) and in the capitals. He felt the script should possess both cursive and formal qualities, that it should, in fact, be a *cancelleresca bastarda*—and that was the name adopted for the

Farai che la distantia da linea a linea
de cose che scriverai
in tal littera Cancelleresca
non sia troppo larga, né troppo stretta,
ma mediocre.
E la distantia da parola á parola
sia quanto e uno n:
Da littera ad littera poi nel ligarle,
sia quanto e il biancho
tra le due gambe de lo n.

Cancelleresca Bastarda

type. In the full font there are indeed swash and other alternative items—more than a hundred of them—and several of the regular capitals do have an informal, though not particularly calligraphic, treatment of the serifs. It is the lower case that holds the most interest. The curves are much rounder than those in the Lutetia italic, so they bring the characters nearer to the kind of italic letterforms that experience shows work best with roman. The ascenders and

Cancelleresca Bastarda, 16·

descenders, though, are another thing—noticeably long and, in the case of the *f*, whose stem is both ascender and descender, obtrusive and distracting. The type has been described as "beautiful" and "entrancingly graceful," and it has been favored by several eminent printers for select books intended as objects of beauty for collectors. Thus used (as Vicentino used a similar type in the early part of the sixteenth century), the type makes a stylish effect. But I find it mannered and pretty rather than beautiful, lacking the vigor of the Blado chancery italic revived by the Monotype Corporation in 1923—or, for that matter, the vigor of Van Krimpen's own handwriting.[3]

Twenty years after the introduction of the type, Van Krimpen expressed disapproval of the exercise—not of the principle of a *cancelleresca* as the third companion to a roman, but of the technical basis he had devised for its design and manufacture. To furnish the script with the extra-long ascender and descender strokes he thought appropriate, he decided to place the face on a body one-quarter larger than that of the corresponding face size of the Romulus roman. Thus for 16· roman the appropriate size of Cancelleresca would be 20·, and for 8· roman it would be 10·. A one-quarter increase of 12· would result in 15·, an "unnatural" size, so the Cancelleresca would be cast on a 16· body. These three sizes were produced in the Enschedé foundry according to that plan. But the plan would not work for 10·, the one-quarter increase of which results in 12½·. Since 13· was out of the question and 14· was not a popular size in Holland at that time, the 10· Romulus could not be given a Cancelleresca companion. Van Krimpen came to regard this as a serious flaw in the plan, for which he and Morison (who had presumably approved it) were culpable. And he also expressed doubts about the rectitude of such a wealth of swash and ligatured items, feeling they gave the type too "playful" and personal a character. Perhaps he had realized, too, that in order to use Romulus roman and Cancelleresca in the same line, the compositor would have to add compensating spacing material above and

---

2. At the present time, when the use of the anamorphic lens and the adjustable CRT raster have made us familiar with sloped romans, it is the aesthetic effect, rather than the doctrine, that needs discussion.

3. A facsimile of his handwriting may be seen in Van Krimpen's *A Letter to Philip Hofer on Certain Problems Connected with the Mechanical Cutting of Punches*, with introduction and commentary by John Dreyfus. Cambridge, Massachusetts, 1972.

below the roman words—a tiresome business for more than a few lines—or a font of roman specially cast on the Cancelleresca body size would have to be obtained from the foundry, at due expense. In practical terms the Cancelleresca cannot function as a fully versatile member of the Romulus family; it is valid only as a separate type.

Van Krimpen thought highly of the principles that governed the design of Romulus Greek, even if he was not finally satisfied with some of the character shapes. His ruling principle was that between the roman and the Greek there should be as little differentiation as possible. Not only should the Greek be upright and the lower case equipped with serifs, but also letters such as lower case ζ, κ, and ν, should be similar or identical to letter shapes in the roman. And there is the fallacy: in the very book in which Van Krimpen is explaining this (it is in English), the occasional French and Latin phrases are in italic, providing the reader with the traditional visual sign of a sudden change of language. And the same should apply to Greek. To make the Greek letters look like roman (and to give the lower case ζ and ξ unfamiliar forms on the ground that calligraphic characteristics must be eliminated) is to assume that letters can be reformed by "logic" and, in short, to allow theory to override practical sense. (Eric Gill had followed the same cul-de-sac in designing his own Greek type). Much more in accord with Van Krimpen's original plan would have been an upright Greek, in familiar style, with an italic Greek as a companion. The printer would have thus been well served. For a Greek phrase interpolated into a text in, say, English, he would use the italic Greek. For a Greek text book the upright version would be used, with the italic in a secondary role. As it is, Romulus Greek mixed with

Α Β Γ Δ Ε Ζ Η Θ Ι Κ Λ Μ Ν Ξ Ο Π Ρ Σ
Τ Υ Φ Χ Ψ Ω
A B C D E F G H I J K L M N O P Q R
S T U V W X Y Z

ου βραδυνει κυριος της επαγγελιας, ως τινες βρα-
Non tardat Dominus promissionem suam, sicut
δυτητα ηγουνται, αλλα μακροθυμει εις υμας, μη
quidam existimant: sed patienter agit propter vos,
βουλομενος τινας απολεσθαι αλλα παντας εις μετα-
nolens aliquos perire, sed omnes ad pœnitentiam
νοιαν χωρησαι. Ηξει δε ημερα κυριου ως κλεπτης,
reverti. Adveniet autem dies Domini ut fur: in quo
εν η οι ουρανοι ροιζηδον παρελευσονται, στοιχεια
cæli magno impetu transient, elementa vero calore
δε καυσουμενα λυθησεται, και γη και τα εν αυτη
solventur, terra autem et quæ in ipsa sunt opera,
εργα ευρεθησεται.
exurentur.

αβγδεζηθικλμνξοπροςτυφχψω
abcdefghijklmnopqrstuvwxyz
fbfffffifflflfhfifkfl
1234567890

Romulus Greek and Roman

Irascimini, et nolite peccare: quæ dicitis in cordibus vestris, in cubilibus vestris compungimini. Sacrificate sacrificium iustitiæ, et sperate in Domino. Multi dicunt: Quis ostendit nobis bona? Signatum est super nos lumen vultus tui Domine:

A B C D E F G H I J K L M N O P
Q R S T U V W X Y Z

abcdefghijklmnopqrstuvwxyz
12345 ffffifflflfifl 67890

Romulus Semi-bold, 12·

In finem in carminibus; Psalmus David: Cum invocarem exaudivit me Deus iustitiæ meæ: in tribulatione dilatasti mihi: Miserere mei, et exaudi orationem meam: Filii hominum usquequo gravi corde? ut quid diligitis vanitatem, et quæritis mendacium? Et scitote quoniam mirificavit Dominus sanctum suum: Dominus exaudiet me cum

A B C D E F G H I J K L M N O P Q R
S T U V W X Y Z

abcdefghijklmnopqrstuvwxyz
12345 ffffifflfifl 67890

Romulus Semi-bold Condensed, 12·

Romulus roman does not harmonize but rather becomes confused with it.

As for the other members of the family, there is little to be said for Romulus Semi-Bold, which sprawls in a most ungainly way. The Semi-Bold Condensed is a better design, but it can hardly be used as a mate for any other member of the family—and that, after all was the object of the scheme, as was emphasized in the rationale for Romulus Greek. For the sans

A B C D E F G H I J K L M N O P Q R S T U V W X Y Z
abcdefghijklmnopqrstuvwxyz
12345 fbffffifflfifhfkfl 67890

A B C D E F G H I J K L M N O P Q R S T U V W X Y Z
abcdefghijklmnopqrstuvwxyz
12345 fbffffifflfhfifkfl 67890

A B C D E F G H I J K L M N O P Q R S T U V W X Y Z
abcdefghijklmnopqrstuvwxyz
12345 fbffffifflfhfk 67890

A B C D E F G H I J K L M N O P Q R S T U V W X Y Z
abcdefghijklmnopqrstuvwxyz
12345 fbffffifflfhfk 67890

Romulus Sans Serif

serif, punches were cut in the 12· size and matrices struck in the Enschedé foundry, but specimen settings of the four weights make it clear that the work stopped at an early stage of development.

SPECTRUM

The tranquil concentration needed to design a type was not easy to achieve in Europe in 1938. Van Krimpen created a private type, Haarlemmer, to be used for an association of bibliophiles, but it was not successful, and the project was terminated. Available specimens of Haarlemmer (Monotype Series 531) show some characteristics—distinct contrast between the thick and thin strokes and markedly oblique stress in the curves—that were to be fully realized in his next major type, Spectrum. The war and the occupation of Holland by an enemy did not stop all creative endeavor. Spectrum was designed in the period 1941–43, and trial alphabets were cut and cast in 14· in the Enschedé foundry. Like Haarlemmer, Spectrum was intended to be a private type for the publishing house of that name, to be used first for the composition of a bible and later for other publications, as soon as the Monotype Company was able to produce a series of sizes. In the event, the Spectrum Company relinquished its rights to the design to Enschedé who, in 1950, arranged with Monotype that a range of sizes should be developed jointly for general distribution.

The differences between the roman of Spectrum and Van Krimpen's earlier romans are plain to see: increased height in the lower case and ample contrast between the main and thin strokes. The tops of the arches in m and n are sharply defined, and the upper serifs in those and other letters are wedge-shaped. The effect is crisp and positive, like that of seventeenth-century book types; indeed, the face seems to have some of the characteristics of the old face type cut by Hendrik Claesz which is in the Enschedé collection. The italic is a distinguished design in itself, but it does not quite harmonize with the roman, being too narrow and a little too heavy in comparison with the broad-countered roman; a foreign phrase or a longish book title in a page of Spectrum becomes overemphatic and the total effect is patchy.

Spectrum roman is the most practical of Van Krimpen's book types, being suitable for a broad range of work in general publishing. But it is not without faults. The f ligatures are too narrow (the fact that the letters are tied at the top is no reason for reducing the space between the uprights). That can be tolerated. So can the narrow crossover W—though it is not so easy to accept in the italic. It is the non-ranging numerals, cramped and diminished, looking as though they belong to a type two sizes smaller, that are hard to take. Van Krimpen gave no explanation for this curious departure from tradition. It was certainly not an accident: the numerals were included on his original drawing of the lower case alphabet. The makers of the type would be applauded by many grateful typographers if they could bring themselves to produce an alternative set of non-ranging numerals in natural scale with the lower case.*

---

* No specimen of Spectrum is included in this article; *Fine Print* is composed entirely in this face.

SHELDON

The Sheldon design was Van Krimpen's response to a commission from the Oxford University Press in 1947 for a type to be made in 7· and used for the composition of an octavo bible, the text to be in two columns. He decided to make the lower case unusually large and to center it on the body, shortening the descenders and ascenders considerably. This, he thought, was better than reducing the descenders only. Having some personal experience in designing types much smaller than 7·, I can assert with some confidence that Van Krimpen was wrong in his premise. The channel of white between lines of type is an indispensable aid to the reader's eye in its traverse across the page or column. The channel is composed of the space below the letter m in line one and above the m in line two. If the lower case letters are enlarged too much, the reduced width of the channel will be detrimental to the reading process, and in a fairly narrow column the space between the lines may even be less than the average space between the words, still further disturbing the texture of the setting. Paradoxically, Sheldon would be easier to read if the lower case letters were a little smaller.

IN FINEM IN CARMINIBUS, PSALMUS DAVID. Cum invocarum exaudivit me Deus iustitiæ meæ: in tribulatione dilatasti mihi. Miserere mei, et exaudi orationem meam. Filii hominum usquequo gravi corde? ut quid diligitis vanitatem, et quæritis mendacium? Et scitote quoniam mirificavit Dominus sanctum suum: Dominus

IN FINEM IN CARMINIBUS, PSALMUS DAVID. Cum invocarum exaudivit me Deus iustitiæ meæ: in tribulatione dilatasti mihi. Miserere mei, et exaudi orationem meam. Filii hominum usquequo gravi corde? ut quid diligitis vanitatem, et quæritis mendacium? Et scitote quoniam mirificavit Dominus sanctum suum: Dominus exaudiet me cum clamavero ad eum. Irascimini, et nolite peccare:

A B C D E F G H I J K L M N O P Q R S T U V W X Y Z

A B C D E F G H I J K L M N O P Q R S T U V W X Y Z

abcdefghijklmnopqrstuvwxyz

abcdefghijklmnopqrstuvwxyz

1234567890　　1234567890　　*1234567890*　　**1234567890**

Sheldon Roman and Italic

The unnatural shortness of the ascenders is another reason the Sheldon type is less effective than Van Krimpen intended. Ascenders are more important than descenders to the reader's comprehension of the text. The letters g, p, and q may have their descenders shortened and yet not be confused with other letters; j and y with shortened descenders can be prevented from looking like i and v by careful designing; but the ascender parts of h and l are essential to their identity and cannot be reduced without seriously affecting their natural appearance and that of the words in which they occur.

ROMANÉE ITALIC

The italic that Van Krimpen designed in 1949 as a companion for the Romanée roman is not entirely satisfactory in that role. As he wrote himself: "I am afraid that, despite the fact that the roman and the italic are undeniably by the same hand, the distance of twenty years between the coming into existence of the one and the other in a way tells." (His

English is awkward, but the meaning is clear enough.) Once again the contrast in color and texture between the generous roman and the narrow italic is too great. But in itself this italic is a notable design. It is so nearly upright (the angle is only four degrees) that it was thought possible to dispense with italic capitals, the roman being used instead. In fact, if the lower case were not so narrow, the roman capitals would work better than they do. As it is, the generous width of the roman capitals makes them too prominent in an italic text. And because the lower case letters are so narrow, the descender strokes seem excessively long; the *f* sometimes has the momentary effect of an opening bracket.

The Romanée italic was the last of Van Krimpen's types to be completed, though it was not his last essay in the designing

A B C D E F G H I J K L M N
O P Q R S T U V W X Y Z

Irascimini, et nolite peccare: quæ dicitis in cordibus vestris, in cubilibus vestris compungimini. Sacrificate sacrificium iustitiæ, et sperate in Domino. Multi dicunt: Quis ostendit nobis bona? Signatum est super nos lumen

abcdefghijklmnopqrstuvwxyz
fb ffffffl fhfifkfl
1234567890

Romanée Italic

of type. Shortly before his sudden death in 1958, he had started a design for use in a photo-typesetting machine. Since the design, when completed, would have been photographically transferred to the font disc, one wonders how Van Krimpen would have judged the outcome, in view of his stated belief that the punchcutter Raedisch had always made an essential contribution to the appearance of his type designs. In a review of Raedisch's autobiography, published last year, William Ovink referred to the value to Morison, Mardersteig, and Van Krimpen of the skills of the punchcutters Plumet, Malin, and Raedisch.

Working with an interpreting reproductive craftsman suited Van Krimpen and his friends: it was easy, relaxing and stimulating. Easy because they did not have to keep making new sets of drawings; it was relaxing to be able to escape from the desk and drawing-board to the restful company of the solitary craftsman and sit there for hours at a time, talking as creative artist to executant; it was stimulating because the typecutter's technical questions forced the designer to become aware of and to formulate his motives, intentions and perceptions, so that perhaps ideas also came to him more easily than when he judged the results on his own.

Precisely what, and how much, Raedisch contributed to the work is not clear. Van Krimpen's drawings were immaculate and unambiguous. It is most unlikely that there were any deficiencies that Raedisch had to make good. It is more likely that Raedisch was so skillful in making a perfect copy on steel of the character in the drawing, without any deviation, that his contribution was to Van Krimpen's peace of mind rather than to the designs themselves. That is speculation, merely; Van Krimpen gives us no detail. Indeed, his writings in the last four years of his life are not very informative regarding his ideas about type design in relation to what is actually printed and how it is read. He provides little evidence that he thought of himself as one among many engaged in the everyday realities of printing. Speculation seems necessary.

CONCLUSIONS

It was almost certainly Stanley Morison[4] who wrote the review of the Lutetia italic in *The Fleuron* VI in 1928. He began by referring to the roman, observing that it was "in no recognizable way purloined from ancient times but instead rose freshly from the reasoned canons of type design." The first part of that statement is acceptable; indeed, it can be applied to all of Van Krimpen's roman types. They certainly stand apart from the ranks of historical types from Aldus to Fournier (to say nothing of Firmin Didot), and they are visibly different from the types designed by such contemporaries of Van Krimpen as Mardersteig, Dwiggins, and Ruzicka, whose designs are all in the mainstreams of typographic letterforms. Only Gill's Perpetua, perhaps, prevents Van Krimpen's types from being *sui generis*.

The second part of Morison's statement is harder to accept. "The reasoned canons of type design" suggests that Van Krimpen had thought thoroughly about the requirements of particular kinds of printing and about the nature and purpose of type, had identified certain principles of design, and had then proceeded to the act of creation. It is no disrespect to Morison (after all, in 1928 he was still forming his own ideas about typographic matters) to suggest that things were otherwise: that Van Krimpen's view of printing was a narrow one, and that he worked, not from a set of considered principles, but from a single ideal. Most type designers, drawing upon their knowledge of printing types past and present, approach the task of creating a new typeface with an array of typographic referents in mind and a consciousness of the circumstances in which the type will have to function. It is hard to believe that Van Krimpen worked like that. On the evidence of the types themselves it seems reasonable to conjecture that, in spite of his presence in a great printing house, his considerable knowledge of typefaces of the past, and his experience as a book designer, Van Krimpen was not ruled by the designer's sense of "fitness for purpose." Instead, his habit of thought was that of the classicist, the man with a vision of the perfect; his ideal letters were the Roman inscriptional

---

4. It does not actually say so in *A Handlist of the Writings of Stanley Morison*, compiled by John Carter (Cambridge, 1950), or in his *Additions* and *Corrections* in *Motif* 3 (London, 1959).

capital with a lower case designed to match, and his criteria were restraint, dignity, and beauty of form. (It cannot be an accident that, referring to the capitals of Lutetia, he spoke of the "classical Roman tradition.") From this idealistic standpoint it would not have occurred to him that there is a difference between drawing the lettering for a monumental inscription and drawing an alphabet for a printing type; that is to say, he would not have perceived that one is an end in itself, the other the means to an end.

An examination of the character of Van Krimpen's designs seems to support this hypothesis. To begin with, compared with that of other type designers, his range was unusually limited: his four roman book types—Lutetia, Romanée, Romulus, and Spectrum—are remarkably similar in style. It is as though he carried in his mind an image of a single perfect alphabet, the quintessence of letters, and could do no other than produce a representation of it on each occasion—even when, as in Romanée, a particular model was clearly in view and the task was specified. Only in the Spectrum roman, a late work, is there any sign that Van Krimpen had added to his vision an awareness of *typographic* characteristics; but the awareness is not very obvious.

The hypothesis holds good for his italic types too. His ideal was evidently the written chancery hand of Arrighi and other masters of calligraphy of the early sixteenth century, to the exclusion of later typographic models. If this were not so, if he had shown equal willingness to take the italic types of, say, Granjon or Fournier as exemplars, he would have worked as they did, from a *practical* standpoint, aware of the need to make his italics true secondary types, subservient to and thoroughly harmonious with his romans. But the italics for Lutetia, Romanée, and Spectrum, and the Cancelleresca Bastarda intended to work with Romulus, show that—whatever he thought he was doing—he was actually concentrating single-mindedly on the design of a perfect alphabet in the chancery mode, and was probably oblivious to external considerations.

Van Krimpen thought like an artist, not like a designer; he worked from an inner vision, not from a broad view of practical realities and requirements. This is not the best frame of mind (and it is not even the right one) for creating something to function in different sorts of texts to the full satisfaction of publisher and reader. In Van Krimpen's case such an attitude produced, in my opinion, types that, though not wholly adequate in the functional sense, are unequalled as representations of *classic* letterforms in print (especially the capitals). That is the significance of the types of Jan van Krimpen

in the history of type design. And it is also the reason that a close study of his types is essential for anyone who aspires to a clear understanding of something that Van Krimpen seems not to have appreciated: the crucial difference between art and *design*.

ACKNOWLEDGMENTS

I am deeply grateful to my friend Sem Hartz for reading this essay in manuscript and offering valuable comments. And like countless others, I am glad to thank the staff of the St. Bride Printing Library for their unfailing assistance.

I am particularly grateful to Joh. Enschedé en Zonen for specially composing a number of type specimens and supplying reproduction proofs of them, together with proofs of some (those in Latin) where type is not available and which were made from the settings done for Van Krimpen's Typophiles book, fortunately still standing.

For information about supplies of the types mentioned in this article write to Joh. Enschedé en Zonen, P.O. Box 114, 2000 AC Haarlem, Holland. The types are on Didot body sizes, for which spaces can be supplied. Type can be planed at the base to American height-to-paper. On occasion there may be a delay in supply until there is a sufficient accumulation of orders for a type to justify the casting of additional stocks.

WORKS CONSULTED

For this essay, two sources have been invaluable: John Dreyfus, *The Work of Jan van Krimpen: A Record in Honour of his Sixtieth Birthday*. London, 1952. J. van Krimpen, *On Designing and Devising Type*. The Typophiles Chap Book, no. 32. New York, 1957.

Also consulted were articles by Van Krimpen in various journals including *The Fleuron*, *The Penrose Annual*, and *Printing and Graphic Arts*. Reviews of Van Krimpen's types by Stanley Morison appear in *The Fleuron* V, VI, and VII. A. F. Johnson, review of Romulus roman and italic in *Signature*, no. 13, 1940. John Dreyfus, "Romulus" in an appendix to Stanley Morison's *A Tally of Types*, with additions, Cambridge, 1973. John Dreyfus, "Spectrum," *The Penrose Annual*, vol. 48, 1954. Harry Carter, "Johannes Enschedé & Zonen," and "Postscript" in *Signature*, nos. 4 and 5, 1947 and 1948. Nicholas Barker, *Stanley Morison*. 1972.

G. W. Ovink, "Grandeurs and miseries of the punchcutter's craft," a review of *A tot Z. Een Autobiografie van P. H. Raedisch, staalstempelsnijder*. In *Quaerendo*, vol. X, no. 2 (Amsterdam, 1980).

Published by Enschedé & Zonen, Haarlem: *A Selection of Types from Six Centuries in Use at the Office of Joh. Enschedé en Zonen*. 1930. *Letterproef*. 1932. *The House of Enschedé, 1703–1953*. 1953.

For further reading on the analysis of type by Walter Tracy, see *Letters of Credit* (Boston: David R. Godine, 1986).

THE CENTURY FAMILY

Paul Shaw

The rugged simplicity of the Century family of types has made it an enduring favorite of American typographers for almost one hundred years. Beginning as foundry type, Century has withstood a series of technical transformations into Linotype, Monotype, Ludlow, phototype, transfer type, digital type, and Xerox-like "toner type." The American Type Founders' original drawings for the Century family, along with thousands of their other drawings, are now in the archives of the Smithsonian Institution. In transferring a type design to a new technology, the selection of the best model is of critical importance, and original drawings by the designer are obviously the best possible choice. Curiously, American type manufacturers, usually so eager to "emulate" existing designs, have not taken the trouble to seek out the true and original forms stored in the priceless collections at the Smithsonian Institution. This account of the Century family, based on recent research at the Smithsonian, indicates the richness of the Institution's collection for the scholar, designer, and manufacturer. C.B.

DECRYING THE "growing effeminacy" of late nineteenth-century types, Theodore Low DeVinne (1829–1914), eminent printer of *The Century* magazine, convinced the publishers to support the design of a new face. DeVinne designed a stronger, bolder, and more readable face than others then in use and commissioned Linn Boyd Benton (1844–1932) of the nascent American Type Founders Company to cut it. The punches were subsequently cut on the newly invented Benton punch-cutting machine and, in November 1895, the face, christened Century Roman after the magazine, made its first appearance. It proved well-suited for use in *The Century* and other magazines and books having double column pages with narrow margins. DeVinne had achieved strength and boldness through thicker hairlines and increased readability through a larger x-height. However, the latter change gave the face a compressed look that hindered its readability when used in books set in a broad measure. Consequently, a companion to Century Roman was created for ATF by L. B. Benton: Century no. 2, later called Century Broad-face. This face became the basis for Century Expanded, designed by L. B. Benton's son, Morris Fuller Benton.

The younger Benton (1872–1948), upon graduation from Cornell in 1896, had joined ATF with the express chore of selecting the usable typefaces from among the thousands ATF had inherited from its twenty-three constituent foundries. Four years later, upon successfully completing the job, he was chosen to head ATF's Department of Typographic Development, a position he held until his retirement in 1937. Despite his relative obscurity (the result of his great modesty), Benton was arguably America's most influential type designer. With over 200 faces to his credit, he was certainly the most prolific. Among his numerous designs are many of today's stalwarts: Cheltenham, Clearface, Cloister, Hobo, Souvenir, Stymie, Garamond, Bulmer, and their families. Between 1900, when he designed Century Expanded, and 1928, when he completed Schoolbook Italic, Benton created eighteen different versions of the basic Century face. Along with Henry Lewis Bullen, the company's librarian, he was responsible for ATF's revival program, which antedated Stanley Morison's at the Monotype Corporation by nearly a decade and a half.

The Smithsonian Institution has about 14,000 drawings of characters for typefaces designed by ATF. The standard ATF sheet is 13 x 26 inches with identification of the characters and typeface for which drawn in the lower left-hand corner. The characters are pattern drawings, not rough sketches, representing the final stage before the design is transferred, via the Benton matrix-engraving machine, to metal. Although virtually finished, they still bear measurements, notations, doodles, and other comments regarding the design of each character, and offer insights into the creation of the ATF typefaces. The Smithsonian's ATF drawings constitute an invaluable, yet practically unknown and untouched, resource for the study of type design.

None of the drawings at the Smithsonian are labeled Century Roman or Century Broad-face, while those marked Century Expanded show only the 42' through 72' characters. However, there are three incomplete and undated sets of drawings, watermarked 1890 or 1893, that relate to the transition from Century Roman to Century Broad-face to Century Expanded. One set is unlabeled, one is marked "Century Caps," and the other simply "Century." The unlabeled set contains four pairs of capitals marked "Copy group #16" and an H marked "Copy Bruce #16." The same cryptic notation also appears on the H–Q–O sheet in the Century Cap set, and the counter of the H is marked "Bruce H= 64.0" (a reference to the set width of the letter). Apparently, Bruce #16 refers to the number 16 roman produced by George Bruce's Sons, a New York typefoundry that ATF acquired in 1900. Although the sheet is dated September 29, 1897, ATF was surely long familiar with the face, since DeVinne had edited the 1877 Bruce specimen book in which it first appeared. Examination of Bruce #16 reveals a face that could easily pass as the model for Century Expanded. Not surprisingly, the basic differences between the two are thicker hairlines and an increased x-height for Century Expanded.

The Century sheets are most likely designs for Century Broad-face, except for one that bears the comment "l.c. g for

Century Roman 10 pt Ordered Sept. 24 1902 by I Baas Drawn Sept. 25 by L.B.B." Five of the other sheets are labeled "Revised l.c. for 'Century'" and contain characters with wider set widths than those found on similar characters elsewhere in the set, leading one to the conclusion that they represent the transition from Century Roman to Century Broad-face.

With the design of Century Expanded in 1900, ATF, under the direction of M. F. Benton, set about creating an entire family of Century typefaces. The concept of type families is often considered to be Benton's most important achievement. His families, Century included, were conceived as such from the beginning. What sets today's type families (including the Century family currently issued by the International Typeface Corporation [ITC] apart from their ATF forerunners is a differing conception of what constitutes a family. For example, the standard ITC family contains four weights, each with an accompanying italic and a corresponding condensed roman and italic—sixteen variations in all. ATF families were not so tidy. Instead, they began with only four variations—book and bold weights with matching italics—and added others as the market developed.

Century Expanded Italic was designed in 1900, Century Bold (originally called Bold Century Expanded) in 1904, and Century Bold Italic in 1905. Between the issue of different weights Benton made a number of changes in the design of certain characters. The most obvious difference between the romans is to be found in the h, m, and n, where the inner serifs of the bold weight have been lopped off. This was done for practical rather than aesthetic reasons. Retention of the serifs would have closed the counters and decreased the readability of the face. In addition, in the bold weight the arm of the r is no longer curled up and the loop of the g is less compressed. In the italics the distinctive copperplate-like entrance strokes of many of the x-height letters have been replaced by horizontal serifs in the bold version.

Once a face had been italicized and made bolder, the next step for ATF or Benton was to vary its width. Because of the squeezing and stretching that went into the creation of the original Century Roman and Century Expanded, this was not done for the original weight. However, the Smithsonian has a set of drawings labeled Century Extended, a name that fails to show up either in ATF specimen books or in matrix records. Two of the sheets contain 1899 dates that suggest Century Extended was an earlier name for Century Expanded. Extended and condensed versions of Century were first offered with the bold weight in 1908 and 1909 respectively, though the extended was begun as early as 1906. The degree of condensation and expansion was forty percent. This expansion of Century Bold made it possible for Benton to reintroduce the inner serifs of h, m, and n.

At the same time that ATF was developing new weights and widths for Century, the family was being expanded in yet another, more fundamental, way. With the introduction in 1906 of Century Oldstyle, Benton began an entirely new series of Century faces. While the essential appearance of Century Roman and Century Expanded derived from Bodoni and Didot, that of Century Oldstyle seems to have been based on Caslon. The top serifs of the new face are angled, the stress of curved strokes is diagonal, and many vestigial parts of letters (the beard on the G and the tail of the a) have been dropped. The result is a vastly different face, heavier and sturdier, though not quite as readable.

Just as the Oldstyle roman diverges greatly from the original Century, so too does the Oldstyle italic, begun sometime in 1907 and completed the following year. The entrance and exit strokes are much sharper, resembling Chancery italic more than copperplate; the stress of the curves has been shifted; some letters have pointed serifs; ball terminals have been replaced by lobe endings; and several letters (g, p, r, R, and y) are radically changed. The g is of the looped variety, the p resembles that of Caslon Italic, the r branches low, the cap R has a straight leg, and the y is v-shaped. That the face was inspired by Caslon can be seen in rejected versions of several characters, such as the w (originally with a looped middle). There were also ct and st ligatures in the initial drawings.

Three variants of Century Oldstyle were produced by ATF: Century Oldstyle Bold (1909), Century Oldstyle Bold Italic (1910), and Century Oldstyle Bold Condensed (1913). The only changes of any significance occasioned by the heavying-up process occurred in the Century Oldstyle Bold Italic where the f no longer has a descender, the p no longer has an ascender, and the neck of the g has become softer and more rounded.

At the same time that Benton was developing Century Oldstyle, he was working on a very similar face titled Norwood, designed at the suggestion of J. S. Cushing of the Norwood Press. Several years earlier Cushing had caused ATF to produce Cushing Old Style (Cushing Roman), Cushing Monotone, and Cushing Antique. The Norwood sheets indicate a relationship between Cushing Old Style, Norwood, and Century Oldstyle, since several sheets bear all three names. It is very likely that Norwood was a second attempt by Benton to provide an oldstyle face for Cushing and that its essential ruggedness and high degree of readability suggested the development of an oldstyle equivalent of Century. The intent behind both Cushing Old Style and the Century family was similar, as comments from J. W. Phinney, the head of ATF's "Foundry A" in Boston, indicate:

The Cushing Old Style was the result of Mr. Cushing's needs in mathematical composition and other educational book work where emphasis in words and sentences required heavier type than the body type used. In cutting the face it was intended to be as condensed as legibleness would permit and conform as far as may be to Old Style Roman characteristics.

Furthermore, Norwood and Century Oldstyle appear virtually identical at first glance. Only the italics differ greatly, Norwood Italic resembling Century Italic rather than Century Oldstyle Italic.

The Norwood sheets contain many unfinished characters that reveal the ATF drawing procedure. Apparently, there were three basic steps: first, the rough letter was drawn in reverse, probably using a graphite transfer process, on the back of the sheet; second, the letter was traced through to the front of the sheet; and third, the image was cleaned up and carefully redrawn with the aid of French curves and specially made templates. Unit markings and other notations were not

Century Schoolbook

ABCDEFGHIJKLMN
OPQRSTUVWXYZ&
$ 1 2 3 4 5 6 7 8 9 0
abcdefghijklmnopq
rstuvwxyz.,-:;!?'`
fi ff fl ffi ffl

ABCDEFGHIJKLMN
OPQRSTUVWXYZ&
$ 1 2 3 4 5 6 7 8 9 0
abcdefghijklmnopq
rstuvwxyz.,-:;!?'`
fi ff fl ffi ffl

Century Schoolbook Bold

ABCDEFGHIJKLMN
OPQRSTUVWXYZ&
$ 1 2 3 4 5 6 7 8 9 0
abcdefghijklmnopq
rstuvwxyz.,-:;!?'`
fi ff fl ffi ffl

Century Bold

ABCDEFGHIJKLMN
OPQRSTUVWXYZ&
$ 1 2 3 4 5 6 7 8 9 0
abcdefghijklmnopq
rstuvwxyz.,-:;!?'
fi ff fl ffi ffl

Century Bold Condensed

ABCDEFGHIJKLMN
OPQRSTUVWXYZ&
$ 1 2 3 4 5 6 7 8 9 0
abcdefghijklmnopq
rstuvwxyz.,-:;!?'
fi ff fl ffi ffl

THE CENTURY FAMILY
Reproduced courtesy of ATF.

Century Oldstyle

ABCDEFGHIJKLMNOPQRSTUVWXYZ&.,-:;!?'`""[]()
abcdefghijklmnopqrstuvwxyz$1234567890fiffflffiffl st ct
Small Caps, 6 to 18 pt.   ABCDEFGHIJKLMNOPQRSTUVWXYZ&

ABCDEFGHIJKLMNOPQRSTUVWXYZ&.,-:;!?'
abcdefghijklmnopqrstuvwxyz$1234567890fiffflffiffl st ct

Century Catalogue

Characters in complete font: ABCDEFGHIJKLMNOPQRSTUVWXYZ&
abcdefghijklmnopqrstuvwxyz.,-:;!?'`""fiffflffiffl$1234567890

Characters in complete font: ABCDEFGHIJKLMNOPQRSTUVWXYZ&
abcdefghijklmnopqrstuvwxyz.,-:;!?'fiffflffiffl ct$1234567890

Century Nova

ABCDEFGHIJKLMNOP
QRSTUVWXYZ
$1234567890
abcdefghijklmnopqrs
tuvwxyzfiffflffiffl
&$¢£%.:.,;----·.()?![]'`""*

ABCDEFGHIJKLMNOP
QRSTUVWXYZ
$1234567890
abcdefghijklmnopqrs
tuvwxyzfiffflffiffl
*&$¢£%.:.,;----·.()?![]'`""**

Century Expanded

ABCDEFGHIJKLMN
OPQRSTUVWXYZ&
$1234567890
abcdefghijklmnopqrst
uvwxyz.,-:;!?')[fiffflffiffl

ABCDEFGHIJKLM
NOPQRSTUVW
XYZ&
$1234567890
abcdefghijklmnopq
rstuvwxyz.,-:;!?'
fiffflffiffl

Original drawings

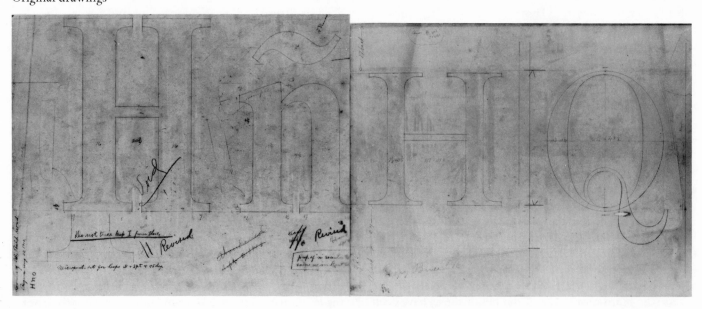

added until after the character had gone through this stage.

Following the completion of Century Oldstyle Bold Condensed, Benton set out to design Century Oldstyle #3. It was begun September 20, 1912, but three years later all the characters had been either revised or cancelled. Redevelopment of the face began on November 1, 1915, and it was renamed Century Book. It was still oldstyle in appearance but was slightly wider than Century Oldstyle. Completed in 1916, it was renamed Century Catalogue. Its development repeated the same stretching process that attended the birth of Century Expanded.

At the same time that Century Catalogue was being finished, ATF was approached by Ginn & Co., the textbook publishers, with a request to design a typeface for use in schoolbooks. Benton began the project by reviewing research done by Clark University on the relationship between legibility of type and the eyesight of children. In addition, he consulted the "Report of the Influence of School Books upon Eyesight" written for the British Association for the Advancement of Science, and other academic studies on the subject. All of these tests and experiments indicated that children required larger and more distinct typefaces than did adults. Consequently, Benton increased the space between letters, the x-height of each letter, and the weight of each stroke, and balanced the color of the type by opening up the counters. The result was Century Schoolbook, completed in 1919, a face that is sturdier and more open than Century.

The italic counterpart of Schoolbook, begun in 1919 in a bold weight, is basically a sturdier version of Century Expanded Italic, but the top serifs on the lowercase letters are flat as in Century Bold Italic. Thus, there is a strong x-height line for the eye to follow. Oldstyle counterparts for Century Schoolbook, under the name Schoolbook Oldstyle and Schoolbook Oldstyle Italic, were begun in 1920 and completed in 1926 and 1928 respectively. They completed Benton's extensive family of Century faces and represented the last major reworking of the basic Century theme for the next three and a half decades.

In 1964 ATF commissioned Charles E. Hughes to design a new proportion of Century Expanded. The result, Century Nova, is more condensed than its predecessor, thus returning the face to its original DeVinne-conceived look. Yet in the recent version, designed by Tony Stan for International Typeface Corporation under license from ATF, the face has been re-expanded. Developed between 1975 and 1980, the ITC Century family contains sixteen members consisting of four weights—light, book, bold, and ultra—each with accompanying italics and condensed romans and italics. Thus, it is more methodical than the ATF family, while the latter is more varied, primarily because of the oldstyle versions. The ITC version differs from its ATF model both in overall appearance and in detail. Following ITC policy, Stan has increased the x-height, thus further opening the counters and increasing the airiness of the face. This is especially noticeable in the e and g. Furthermore, as a personal touch, Stan has selectively eliminated the inside serifs of h, m, and n throughout the family. Benton dispensed with several of these serifs only where counter space was at a premium. All of these changes give ITC Century a more contemporary appearance, but the ruggedness that once typified Century has been lost.

The story of Century is yet another chapter in the quixotic search for the ideal readable typeface. Despite all the redesigning that Century has undergone over the course of eighty-five years, DeVinne's original conception has survived virtually intact. Like an accordion, Century has had the vitality and strength to undergo repeated stretchings and squeezings without loss of identity.

CITATIONS

American Type Founders Company. *Specimens of Type, Borders & Ornaments, Brass Rules & Electrotypes*, New York, 1898, p. 100. The excerpt by DeVinne from the March 1896 issue of *The Century* is also included in several other ATF specimen books.

American Type Founders, Inc. *The Book of American Types*. Elizabeth, New Jersey, 1965, p. 15, Century Family.

Lakeside Press. *American Type Designers and Their Work*. Chicago: R. R. Donnelly & Sons, 1948.

Murphy, John Allen, "Morris Benton—Type Designer—Executive." In *The Inland Printer*, March–May 1936.

Letter from J. W. Phinney to H. L. Bullen, 1913, in ATF Collection, Columbia University.

See the ATF specimen book for 1965 and *U&lc*, Fall, 1980. Comments about Tony Stan are from a telephone conversation on March 20, 1981.

American Type Founders
200 Elmora Ave.
Elizabeth, NJ 07202

International Typeface Corporation
2 Hammarskjold Plaza
New York, New York 10017

THE NEW TYPE SPECIMEN BOOKS: A CRITICAL VIEW

Charles Bigelow

H. Berthold, AG. *Berthold Fototypes E 2. Body Types, vol. 1.* Götz Gorissen, editor and designer. Berlin: Berthold; Munich: Callwey, 1980. 30 x 21 cm., lxxi + 776pp. Cloth, $40. Order from: H. Berthold AG, Teltowkanalstrasse 1-4, D-1000 Berlin 46, West Germany, or Berthold of North America, P.O. Box 624, Paramus, New Jersey 07652.

Mergenthaler Linotype Company. *Mergenthaler, Linotype, Stempel, Haas Specimen Books.* Leonard Battipaglia, editor and designer. 8 (of 9) vols. 1977–1981, and continuing. 21 x 15 cm., 540pp. Wire spiral bindings, $50 the set. Mergenthaler, 201 Old Country Road, Melville, New York 11747.

The Monotype Corporation Ltd. *The Specimen Book of 'Monophoto' Filmsetter Faces.* 2 vols. 27 x 22 cm., 150pp. (approx.). Looseleaf, ring binder, £9. Monotype, Salfords, Redhill RHI 5JP, England.

The Alden Press. *Photocomposition at the Alden Press, Oxford: A Printer's Type Specimen Book.* Designed & edited by Hugh Williamson. 1981. 18.5 x 24 cm., xiii + 156pp. Cloth, £8.50. The Bodley Head, 9 Bow Street, London, WC2E 7AL.

Volk & Huxley. *Mergenthaler VIP Typeface Catalog.* Designed by Tony Esposito. 2 vols. New York: Van Nostrand Reinhold, 1980. 30 x 22.5 cm., 1000pp. (approx.). Paper, $24.95 per volume.

King, Jean Callan and Tony Esposito. *The Designer's Guide to Text Type.* New York: Van Nostrand Reinhold, 1980. 30 x 22.5 cm., 320pp. Paper, $24.95.

Rice, Stanley. *CRT Typesetting Handbook.* New York: Van Nostrand Reinhold, 1981. 28.5 x 22 cm., 409pp. Boards, $35.

Compugraphic Corporation. *Typeface Analogue: A cross-reference guide to typeface names.* 1979. 21.5 x 28 cm., 16pp. Paper, gratis. Compugraphic Corporation, 66 Concord Street, Wilmington, Massachusetts 01887.

Association Typographique Internationale. *A.Typ.I. Index of Typefaces.* 1975. 30 x 21 cm., 60pp. Paper, gratis to members. A.Typ.I., Kattowitzer Strasse 57, D-6230 Frankfurt am Main 80, West Germany.

WE TYPOGRAPHERS collect type specimen books, in part because we need them and in part because we desire them. They are needed to design intelligently; they are desired because typographers like type, and the more type the better.

The commercial success of phototype and digital type has made traditional letterpress specimen books obsolete for an accurate representation of the way type will be reproduced under most contemporary conditions. Unfortunately, many of today's manufacturers of typesetting equipment have devoted their resources to the development of new machines rather than new types and type specimens.

The specimen books of those manufacturers who have chosen to plagiarize type designs rather than innovate them are generally a dismal lot, containing for the most part an unappetizing collection of wretched clones, re-drawn and re-named imitations of deservedly famous designs. Further, such specimens seldom show us what we need to see—text settings and alphabets in a variety of sizes, measures, and leadings. Instead we are fortunate if they display more than a single alphabet or line—sufficient for us to identify, if we care to do so, the original design upon which the plagiarism has been perpetrated.

The reasons for this distressing situation should by now be familiar to readers of *Fine Print.* Type designs are unprotected by copyright law in the United States. Therefore, manufacturers take the attitude that hardware development requires real investment, whereas type designs are free for the stealing. Why go to the expense and risk of commissioning and promoting a new design which may take several years to become popular, when, for example, Hermann Zapf's Palatino is just a sitting duck, waiting for the plucking, roasting, and re-issuing under the pseudonym of "Palindrome"?

Nevertheless, the firms that are serious about type have generally made an effort to provide typographers with useful phototype specimen books. Following is a sampling of some of them.

Berthold Fototypes E 2, Body Types, vol. 1
This is a thoroughly impressive effort. Successor to Berthold's earlier *E 1* volume, now out of print, it is in the same league as the compendious *ATF Specimen Book and Catalog* of 1923 or the *Specimen Book of Linotype Faces* of 1939. The Berthold *E 2* displays 577 typefaces. Each is shown as a complete upper- and lower-case specimen, with all figures, punctuation, signs, and accents, in 9·. Text types are additionally shown in sample text settings, in German, from 5· through 16·, with English and French texts in 10·, and Spanish and Italian texts in 8·. A single word (Berthold) is given in display sizes from 14· through 36·. Display types are given in text from 6· through 12·, and in a display line (Berthold's quick brown fox jumps over the lazy dog . . .) from 14· through 36·.

There is also a comprehensive introduction (in German, English, and French), which explains the organization of the book's information, and also discusses the manner in which Berthold's fonts are drawn, showing examples of extensive correction by Günter Lange, Berthold's type director, and giving the distribution of typefaces according to average character width, stroke height, and x-height. The introductory text, set in ITC Zapf International, is the most sensitive use of that face that this reviewer has yet seen. Designed and compiled by Götz Gorissen, the book is beautifully printed and handsomely bound; for the serious typographer, a book worth having.

The Mergenthaler, Linotype, Stempel, Haas Specimen Books
Some 1000 faces from the collective type libraries of the Mergenthaler-associated firms are shown in this projected nine-volume set, which includes original designs, as well as designs licensed from other firms. Originally announced in 1977, only eight volumes have been produced to date: *General Typefaces, Text Typefaces, Display Typefaces, 54 Unit General Typefaces, 54 Unit Display Typefaces, ITC Typefaces, Script and Specialty Typefaces,* and *News and Classified Typefaces.* Each type is shown in an upper- and lower-case alphabet and figures in 18·, with text specimen in 10·. The 10· text specimens suffice for many common text design applications, if what one needs is more a feel for the type rather than an exact size for a mock-up.

Although less detailed than the Berthold *E 2* volume, this is a handsome series, designed and produced with delicacy and taste by Leonard Battipaglia. The lightweight and handy size of these books makes them more accessible for quick reference than a single large volume. One wishes, however, that something better than a wire spiral binding had been used. Best would have been a ring binder, so that the loose-leaf pages could be removed for comparison and "comping." Also, it is a source of annoyance to those of us who ordered and paid for these volumes four years ago, that the final volume showing non-Latin typefaces is not yet released, nor even in production.

'Monophoto' Filmsetter Faces
The Monotype Corporation has for many years offered an excellent series of ring-binder loose-leaf specimen books for their Monotype faces and carries through the same format for Monophoto, displaying some 150 faces. Each type is shown in text settings from 6· or 8· through 14·, and in upper- and lower-case alphabet with figures and punctuation from 14· through 24·. Many of the familiar Monotype faces are here displayed in their photo forms, and newer designs like Apollo and Photina produced especially for photocomposition are also displayed. The typographic format is workmanlike and quite usable.

Photocomposition at the Alden Press, Oxford
This is essentially a specimen book of Monophoto faces, specifically those available at the Alden Press as set by the digital Lasercomp typesetting system. Much more than a "bread and butter" specimen, it is quite possibly the most lovely typographic book so far produced in the Digital Era.

From the overall conception down to the smallest detail, it is a superb demonstration of the consummate artistry of designer Hugh Williamson.

The book begins with an intelligent introduction to the equipment, fonts, and composition methods of the Lasercomp system, and then provides a set of character-count tables for casting off, with a discussion of how the tables were prepared, how to use them, and what precautions to take. Each typeface specimen is introduced by three or four paragraphs (set in that face) discussing the origin and designer of the type, its revival or adaptation to Monotype, and its further adaptation to Monophoto, with comments on particular aspects of the Alden Press version. There follows a series of complete fonts of upper- and lower-case letters, figures, punctuation, signs, accents, alternate sorts, ligatures, and small capitals (if available) in 6· through 24·. Following the font synopses are fourteen columns of text settings in sizes 9· through 12·, in a variety of leadings and measures. The essay in the text samples, written especially for the book, is a discussion of type specimens, historical and modern, that shows the range of the types by involving the use of small capitals, italic, superior figures, and footnotes. The text sections end with a column in which Greek and bold face alphabets and mathematical formulas appear. These superb showings are provided for Baskerville, Bembo, Century, Ehrhardt, Garamond, Photina, Plantin, Times, and Univers. Additional abridged sections are devoted to Times Semi-Bold, Times Phonetic, and Porson Greek. Text outside the specimens is impeccably set in José Mendoza's lovely Photina.

The binding is handsome, in maroon cloth with gold stamping, and even the dust jacket is a model of tasteful composition with type, rules, and ornaments. This book is a masterpiece; don't miss it!

Mergenthaler VIP Typeface Catalog
These two large volumes display the 562 typefaces available for VIP photocomposition by Volk & Huxley, a New York typographic house. After a brief introduction to the methods of VIP composition and copyfitting, the books launch into the real stuff, over 1000 pages of alphabets and text samples. Each type is shown as an upper- and lower-case alphabet with figures, from 6· through 36·, and as a short text, set solid, from 6· through 18·. These are followed by a complete synopsis of the 96-character font in 12·, and a 12· lower-case alphabet set with normal, tight, and very tight letterspacing. The overall design by Tony Esposito is workmanlike and usable.

As specimens, these books are obviously not intended for specialized book designers, but for the general range of graphic designers, commercial artists, and type buyers. The most obvious indication of this intention is the generally too tight letterspacing. For sizes 6· through 9·, the spacing is normal, whereas a book designer would have it slightly loose. For 10· through 36·, the spacing is tight, whereas a book designer would prefer "normal" spacing at least through 14·, but tightened thereafter. Admittedly, many modern typefaces designed especially for photocomposition and for promotional text and display look their best with tight spacing, but most of the traditional typefaces do not. Therefore, the careful designer needs to study the specimens here with some imagination regarding how the types might look with more breathing room.

The Designer's Guide to Text Type
This is a needed companion to the two-volume VIP catalog described above, showing VIP text settings of fifty-one typefaces in 6· through 14·, leaded solid, one, two, and three points each. The choice of faces is generally appropriate to the broad spectrum of commercial text composition, but several excellent text faces readily available for VIP have been omitted. These include Zapf's Aldus; Dwiggins's Electra; Frutiger's Frutiger, Iridium, and Méridien; Carter's Galliard; Gill's Sans; and Meier's Syntax. For the book designer, these text settings are also too tightly letterspaced. The 6· through 9· samples are set "normal," but the smaller sizes could be a bit looser and thus more readable. The 10· through 14· samples are set tight, and these could have been set normal with some improvement in readability. Despite these problems, it is an enjoyable experience to browse through the more than 1,600 subtle variations in tone and texture assembled here.

CRT Typesetting Handbook
This is an interesting but somewhat puzzling book. It is the first type specimen book to come to grips with the awesome problems and potentials posed by digital typesetting. In this first match, technology rather than aesthetics appears to have been the victor. In an earlier book (*Book Design: Systematic Aspects*) author/designer Stanley Rice notes, "The aim of this study is to help the book designer with the nonartistic or 'systematic' aspects of the design function."

In this present volume he also shows greater attention to the systematic programming of computerized cathode-ray-tube typesetting machines than to the design of the book beautiful. The book begins with a thirteen-page introductory outline of typesetting in the digital computer era. For designers who have not yet grappled with the new technology, this is an adequate introduction to the subject. It covers the complexities of sizing, distorting, spacing, kerning, formatting, paging, and copyfitting for CRT devices. Occasionally the welter of detail obscures the sense of the exposition. Greater attention to actually *explaining* the subject through illustrative principles and diagrams might have helped.

The sample settings demonstrate our helplessness in the face of the powers of computer technology. Seven types— Century Expanded, Geneva (an imitation Helvetica), Malibu (an imitation Palatino), Souvenir, Tiffany, Times, and Univers —are displayed in a small fraction of the possibilities available on the CRT typesetter. Yet these seven faces occupy nearly 400 pages! The author points out that a more complete demonstration of the possibilities for just twenty faces would require over 16,000 pages! Each face is shown first as a single line in 133 sizes, from 6· through 72· in 0.5· increments. This is followed by roman text specimens from 6· through 13.5· type, set in electronic condensations from 70% of normal through electronic extensions to 120% of normal, in 10% increments. An electronically obliqued roman and a bold roman text are shown at each size increment, in normal width only. Then

come the display specimens of the same faces, from 14· through 24· in 0.5· increments, and from 24· through 36· in 2· increments. Each of these is set from 80% condensation to 110% extension, in 10% increments. Next is a series of text specimens of normal width, from 6· through 13· in 1· increments, each with leading of 0.5, 1, 1.5, and 2 points. Wrapping it up comes a series of text specimens, in 10· and 12· with normal width and 1 point leading, but with four reductions of letterspacing: normal, 2/100 of an em tight, 3/100 tight and 4/100 tight. Altogether, this is an impressive display of programming, which Mr. Rice credits to John Pierson of Autologic, Inc.

Now we must ask a fundamental question: Why is this book, despite all its marvelous variations, so much less satisfying and so much less beautiful than the Alden Press specimen reviewed above? The difference is design. Both are set by a digital typesetter and printed by offset lithography, but the *CRT Handbook* is a pedestrian display of programmatic possibilities without real consideration of their perceptual consequences, whereas the Alden Press specimen is a virtuoso design performance in the best Anglo-American book tradition; it demonstrates in itself how a typographic book should look and feel. Also, the Monotype Lasercomp digital fonts in the Alden Press specimen are more accurately and sensitively crafted than the Autologic CRT digital fonts (two of which are plagiarisms) used in this book.

Mere proliferation of programmatic variation is senseless without true aesthetic comprehension of the visual effects of the typographic images. Machines can spew out oceans of this stuff, but we *humans* have to read it! As designers, we don't really need to see all the astronomical possibilities available. We need instead to understand both artistic and technical principles in order to choose the relatively few types and formats needed for any given design problem. Technological revolutions have antiquated many traditional typographic practices, and we need to re-assess our concepts of text to navigate successfully in the expanding alphabetic universe.

Typeface Analogue
This is a sordid little pamphlet for the delectation of the typographically depraved. In its disingenuous, self-serving introduction it commends type manufacturers for devoting "much time and expense" to what in fact amounts to the piracy of type designs. Purporting to be an aid to the typographer, it cross-indexes the re-named pirated versions with the original designs, though it never so much as hints at the true provenience of the faces. Neither designer, nor originating firm, nor date of first release is mentioned. For example, here we may learn, if we can stomach it, that Melior (another sitting duck) has been ripped off and reissued as "Mallard," "Medallion," "ME," "Ballardvale," "Hanover," "Uranus," "Ventura," and so on *ad nauseam*.

Far from being a service to the profession, this is a not-too-subtle attempt to legitimate the wholesale theft of artistic and intellectual property and the debasement of our typographic heritage. The text is unillustrated, no doubt a gesture of mercy on the authors' part, for to have to view this entire parade of type perversions would surely send one to the neuro-psychiatric ward with extensive perceptual damage.

Regrettably, the authors of this dissimulating tract have cloaked themselves in the anonymity of the Compugraphic Corporation. Otherwise, we could credit this *copyrighted* catalogue of distortions to their rightful names, or, of course, to any pseudonyms they might have preferred.

A.Typ.I. Index of Typefaces

A.Typ.I. (Association Typographique Internationale) is the major international organization of typographers, type designers, typographic equipment manufacturers, scholars, and educators. Among its purposes are the improvement of education and research in letterforms, the promotion of the creation of new typefaces, and the protection of typeface designs against unauthorized copying. A.Typ.I. published this index of typefaces in 1975 as a reference service for its membership. It lists the names of 3600 typefaces, the name of the manufacturer of each type, the name of the type designer, and the year the typeface was first offered for sale. Although it is not a complete listing, it is at least a first step in organizing this basic information about types and their designers and producers.

As A.Typ.I.'s publication of this information is in the public domain, there is little reason that the authors of *Typeface Analogue* reviewed above could not have included the true origins of the type designs in their pamphlet. It would have added immeasurably to the *Analogue*'s informational and ethical value, and, of course allowed easier identification of the pirating firms.

We will not see a general improvement in the quality of "high-tech" typefaces until typeface designs are given protection equal to that offered other intellectual and artistic property. Active participation in A.Typ.I. and organizations like it is one step in that direction.

ERIC GILL'S PERPETUA TYPE

JAMES MOSLEY

ONCE ERIC GILL had been persuaded that making designs for printing types was a proper use of his talents, he became, in England at least, one of the most prolific type designers of the century.[1] Yet the progress of his first book type, Perpetua, the development of which is outlined here, was an oddly halting one.

The record of Gill's type designing would have been impressive, even for a designer without his other distractions. If we take into account his unceasing work in sculpture, wood engraving, and lettercutting, his flow of published polemical literature and private correspondence, and his involvement in the printing office of his son-in-law Rene Hague, it is an astounding performance. For someone with Gill's reservations—deeply felt and publicly expressed—about the relationship of the atist to industry (see page 96), it is also a rather puzzling one. The explanation lies partly, perhaps, in Gill's need for a regular income, however modest. Supporting an extended family of children, sons-in-law, and apprentices in the harsh economic climate of the 1930s, Gill must have welcomed his designer's retaining fee. But he would hardly have continued to work with such application in this field without his growing respect for the company that made most of his types, the Monotype Corporation, and his affection for their typographical adviser, Stanley Morison.[2]

The English Monotype Corporation of the interwar years looks in retrospect rather like one of the great public bodies of the period, for example the British Broadcasting Corporation or London Transport (Gill made sculptures for the palatial headquarters of both bodies), benevolent monopolies ruled by autocrats who reveled in the role of patron of the arts on a scale exceeding that of Italian Renaissance princes.

Monotype enjoyed, in Britain at least, something approaching a monopoly in book and better-quality magazine typesetting. Initially this may have been favored by the innate conservatism of the British printing trade which, faced with the

need for machine composition, opted for the only system capable of delivering separate single characters that were identical in all essentials with those that the hand compositor was used to. Later, in the 1920s and 1930s, Monotype exploited the glamor of its new typefaces and the technical advantages of single-type composition with brilliant publicity, for which Morison and his devoted young American recruit Beatrice Warde were partly responsible. As a live artist, Gill was to be one of their most valuable assets.

The Lanston Monotype Corporation, as it was first known, had been established in London in 1897 in order to secure the British and British Colonial market for Tolbert Lanston's American Invention. The dominant personalities of the English company were both American: Harold M. Duncan, who had been Lanston's friend and early technical adviser, was the Managing Director; Frank Hinman Pierpont, the works Manager, was a former Pratt & Whitney apprentice who had worked in Berlin with the German manufacturer of the Typograph, a slug composition machine of American origin. He equipped the new Monotype works at Salfords, twenty-three miles south of London, to the highest standards, redesigning the Benton-Waldo punchcutting machines on which the accuracy and quality of the product ultimately depended. He had brought with him from Typograph a draughtsman, Fritz Max Steltzer, who became head of his Type Drawing Office. Their partnership, which lasted until Pierpont's retirement in 1936, was one of the most formidable and, until recently, least appreciated in the history of type-making in the twentieth century.[3] Pierpont was an autocrat and an engineering genius with an obsessive passion for accuracy and efficiency. But he was also, as William Ovink remarks, "the counterpart at Monotype in England of Morris Fuller Benton at American Type Founders, namely the engineer who had a far greater share in type design than our mainly artist-oriented histories of type production suggest."

Monotype's early faces were, quite simply, facsimiles of existing types. "Series 1," for example, a modern face, was adapted from a type of the Edinburgh foundry Miller & Richard. When kerning was introduced in 1908, the works acquired the capability of making facsimiles in Monotype that were virtually indistinguishable from the original foundry type. These were sometimes historic faces: Caslon Old Face (originally ca. 1734) and Miller's Old Roman (ca. 1814), later known as Scotch Roman, were both made at the request of the Scottish printers R. & R. Clark in 1916 and 1920 respectively. Each size was individually drawn, following with scrupulous care the differences apparent in the hand-cut original foundry type.

---

1. Gill was more or less directly involved in the making of thirty-seven Monotype series, twenty-four of which are accounted for by Gill Sans and its variants. His five other types are the Golden Cockerel Press type (1929), Joanna (1930), Aries (1932), and Bunyan (1934), all of which were made privately by H. W. Caslon, and Jubilee (1934), which was sold commercially by Stephenson Blake.

2. I am grateful to the Monotype Corporation (and especially to John Latham and Graham Shepherd) for granting access to some of the records on which this account is based, and also to other holders of Gill's drawings and letters. Particular thanks are due to John Dreyfus and David McKitterick. The most comprehensive account of the making of the classic Monotype faces is that given by Nicholas Barker, *Stanley Morison* (1972). Other information has been drawn from Gill's own collection of drawings, proofs, and specimens which was acquired by the Monotype Corporation in 1955 and is extensively reproduced in the *Monotype Recorder*, vol. 41, no. 3 (1958). In 1976 this collection was presented to the St. Bride Printing Library, London.

3. The first adequate account is in Barker, *Stanley Morison*. See also Willem Ovink's long review-article "Two books on Stanley Morison," *Quaerendo*, vol. 3 (1973), pp. 229-43, and John Dreyfus, "Matrix making and type design 1900-13," *Typos* 1 (1981), pp. 14-16.

ABCDEFGHI
JKLMNOPQR
STUVWXYZ

abcdefghijklmn
opqrstuvwxyz &
1234567890

ABCDEFGHI
JKLMNOPQR
STUVW&XYZ

abcdefghijklmn   o
opqrstuvwxyz

Alphabets drawn by Gill for Gerard Meynell of the Westminster Press (capital height 1½ inches, x-height of lower case 1 inch).   (*St Bride Printing Library.*)

Eric Gill by London photographer Howard Coster. (*Albert Sperisen Eric Gill Collection, Gleeson Library, University of San Francisco.*)

Early state of Felicity italic with (below) Gill's sketches for alternative characters. The sloped roman "a" was experimentally cut, but abandoned in the final design.   (*St Bride Printing Library.*)

An alternative approach to historical models was to re-draw them in a manner that suited modern machine printing while keeping as much as possible of the spirit of the original. Imprint (1912), a kind of Caslon, and Plantin (1913), based on a roman of Robert Granjon, are classic examples of this method, which would be used for such later faces as Baskerville, Bembo, and Ehrhardt. They are deeply satisfying faces, beautifully fitted and (in Updike's phrase, quoting Didbin) "comfortable" to the eye. While Imprint was a commission (for Gerard Meynell's new magazine), Plantin, interestingly enough, may well have been Pierpont's own idea. This reworking of the face that appears in the introductory pages of the 1905 specimen of types surviving at the Museum Plantin-Moretus in Antwerp is now known to be the Gros Cicero type by Robert Granjon. It is to Pierpont that credit is thus due for making the first twentieth-century revival of the classic French interpretation of the letter cut by Griffo for Aldus, which dominated European book production for over three hundred years. Did Pierpont have an intimation of this historic lineage? It seems unlikely. He had a far better eye for type than he has been given credit for, but he possessed neither the breadth of culture that enabled D. B. Updike to write his authoritative *Printing Types,* first published in 1922, nor the historical curiosity of the younger men who were to find the answers to so many of the questions that Updike had left unresolved. One of the outstanding personalities in this younger generation was Stanley Morison, who would become Monotype's "typographical adviser."

Writing over thirty years later, Morison was to claim in his *Tally of Types* that in 1922 he had laid before Monotype "a programme of typographic design, rational, systematic and corresponding with the foreseeable needs of printing."[4] This program would consist of the cutting of a repertory of classic typefaces drawn from good historical models. "The original twentieth-century book type might come in due course," said Morison. "But certain lessons had first to be learnt and much necessary knowledge discovered or recovered. The way to learn to go forward was to make a step backward."

Morison's account of this process fails to convince entirely. The evidence assembled by his biographers suggests that he was responsible for rather less of the early part of Monotype's program than he implied. Even in the case of Bembo (1928-9), a type with which he was deeply involved, he found it impossible to get it provided with the italic he wanted. When making Fournier, a model that was undoubtedly Morison's choice, the works took advantage of his absence to put in hand a version of which he disapproved. Frustrations of this kind were to continue to plague Morison's relations with Monotype from time to time.[5] Harold Duncan had died in October 1924 and his successor as Managing Director was William Burch, who was decisive but diplomatic—and respectful of Frank Pierpont's authority within his own empire at Salfords.

And yet the voice in which Monotype addressed the public in its publications and specimens was increasingly that of Morison. His historical essays, by means of which he worked his way (with some retractions) towards a coherent view of the development of printing types, were to form the typographical education of his readers, who learned with him as he seized on topic after topic with restless energy, arguing his case in clear, vigorous prose. There were obvious dangers in the technical expertise that made it possible to create literal facsimiles. "It is hoped, in the course of time, to make available to the present day other distinguished faces of the past and in addition at least one original design," said the writer (presumably Morison) in introducing Monotype Poliphilus to the world in the *Monotype Recorder* for January-February 1924. By the following year he had not only discovered a potential designer (Gill) for an original twentieth-century book type, but evolved a strategy for getting it past the twin rocks of Burch's caution and Pierpont's hostility.

"Eric Gill is at present engaged upon designing an alphabet for a new type which Morison wishes to have cut for use here in London," wrote Frederic Warde to Giovanni Mardersteig on November 5, 1925. Gill was an obvious choice, but it can have been by no means certain that he would agree to cooperate. His creative life was often reined in by self-imposed disciplines. Having been fired with enthusiasm by his gifted teacher George Catt for the exhilarating "new art," lettering, on which he looked back wistfully in his *Autobiography* ("I could almost wish I had that freedom now"), he had submitted to the severity of broad pen calligraphy. Gill's pen and brush-drawn lettering, including some of the most exquisite work he ever did, began to appear on title pages and in headings, but this work, which had been reproduced by means of relief etchings, became so repugnant to him that he turned to a more direct medium. "Drawing for photographic reproduction is so beastly in itself and so unsatisfactory in result that even inexpert wood-engraving seemed preferable," he wrote in the 1929 edition of his engravings published by Douglas Cleverdon.

Gill might well have rejected the suggestion that he should make a design that would be subjected to the mechanical processes used by Monotype. Clearly Morison must have made the approach with some subtlety. Moreover, he had chosen his time well. Gill had just begun his association with the Golden Cockerel Press, newly under the direction of Robert Gibbings, and he would become increasingly involved in the practicalities of bookmaking. Morison was in any case in no hurry to approach Monotype.[6] Having secured drawings from Gill, Morison, rather than send them to the Monotype works, sent them to a Parisian hand punchcutter, Charles Malin, to have cut at his own expense a set of 12· (Didot) capitals and lower case and a companion set of titling capitals. Monotype would be faced with a fait accompli.

"You will remember that when I made you those drawings of alphabets I expressly disclaimed the suggestion that I was type designing," wrote Gill to Morison in June 1928. "I did not & do not even now profess to know enough about it (i.e. typographical exigencies)." Malin, on the other hand, though very well aware of the exigencies of making a type, needed guidance from Morison on points of detail, particularly since the design style with which he was working was strange to him. Part of Malin's side of their correspondence survives,[7] ten letters written between May and December 1926, but unfortunately there is no trace of the drawings that he used as models. Morison

4. Stanley Morison, *A Tally of Types, cut for machine composition and introduced at the University Press, Cambridge* (Cambridge, 1953), p. 9

5. Barker, *Stanley Morison,* pp. 177-8.

6. During 1925 he and Frederic Warde had already acquired some experience in commissioning a veteran hand punchcutter, Charles Plumet, who lived in Paris, to make the punches for their Arrighi italic.

7. Now in the University Library, Cambridge.

certainly retrieved them from Malin, for they were to be referred to during the course of Monotype's recutting of the new type, but there is a hint in the Monotype records that they may possibly have deteriorated, perhaps in transit.[8] On the other hand, if Morison kept them, they may well have been destroyed during the air raid of May 10, 1941.

Morison submitted his new type to Burch, who passed it on to Pierpont in March 1927. At the same time he planned to show it in *The Fleuron*, of which he was now the editor, together with reproductions of the original drawings and a note on the face by Gill. (Neither project materialized.) Now that he saw the type in print, cast from the matrices made for Morison in Paris (before he had only seen smoke proofs from the punches), Gill was struck by the number of changes needed.

> I think a very nice fount can be made from these letters, but agree with you in thinking that several details must be altered before it can be passed, and certainly before I should like to see my name attached to it. Not that I think it is unworthy of me, but simply that it makes me shy at present.
> (i) The y must be altered—the blob removed . . .
> (ii) The tail of the "g" is rather heavy. You see it all over the page . . .
> (iii) I think the bow of the lower case "r" is too heavy.
> (iv) I agree the space between the letters is too great.
> (v) I agree that the capitals are too short . . .
> Apart from these details which, if corrected, would I think make the page effect very much better, I agree in thinking that a nice useful type can be made. Will it be for sale to all and sundry?

Faced with these detailed criticisms of a fount that was now out of the original punchcutter's hands, Burch asked Morison to get his drawings from Malin so that the works could see them. Some months later (nothing was to happen with any urgency in the making of this type) an unexpected figure briefly enters the story: Gerard Meynell. It emerged that Gill had made a second set of drawings during July 1926, when Malin was already engaged on cutting Morison's type, for Meynell, one of the begetters of Imprint and also, in a sense, of Edward Johnston's Underground sans serif. Morison was asked to report on these drawings to Burch. "Mr. Meynell is of the opinion," noted Morison, "that the drawings which Mr. Gill made for him are so nearly identical with those previously made for me, at present in Mr. Pierpont's hands, that he feels that a type made therefrom will be satisfactory. The main difference in the drawings lies in the italic capitals, and I think later when we come to that question certain details in the other (Meynell's) series might be substituted for those in my own. Mr. Meynell has no doubt that when the type is ready he will require considerable use of it."[9]

What purpose did Meynell have in mind when he commissioned these drawings? In the event, he seems to have used them simply as a source of large display letters. Reproduced by relief line block, the capitals, but not the lower case, appear in the type specimen book issued by the Westminster Press in about

1928. In 1927, however, they very nearly supplanted Morison's drawings and his type as the model for Perpetua. After considering the rather desperate expedient of trying to make "one face represent both types"—that is, presumably, to conflate the two designs, picking details from each—a set of roman and italic trial characters were cut from Meynell's drawings and on October 15 a specimen of this type, 14· "Gill face," was proofed.[10] Shortly afterwards a similar exercise was performed using the Malin type as the basis and casting it on 13· to accommodate the original 12· Didot characters. A proof was forwarded to Burch by Pierpont in January 1928.[11] He could not resist a sardonic comment: "The g is as ugly as the original. The Gill drawings show a very satisfactory g and if we produce the fount it should be substituted for the one which we have cut."

In the end, it was the Malin-Morison face that was to be cut by Monotype, and Gill himself, still disclaiming expertise as a type designer, was drawn into the slow process of refining its detail. It was Gill, writing to Morison on September 1, 1928, who suggested that the lower case "a" with its serifed foot—a shape derived from his own stonecut letter—had a "clumsy heaviness" as it stood. It would be better, he thought (illustrating his idea with a sketch) if a curved stroke were substituted. It was one of several occasions on which he was to learn the limitations placed on the designer by reduction in scale.

The next problem was that of the italic. Grasping the nettle, Burch sent Gill's original drawings for the italic to the works in January 1929. A couple of months later both the roman and italic were formally baptized Perpetua and Felicity after the second-century saints mentioned in the text that Morison had planned to use for the specimen of his new type to be shown in *The Fleuron*. Gill had been persuaded to fall in with the idea that Morison had set out in his essay "Towards an Ideal Italic" (*The Fleuron 5*) that a type intended for use as a subordinate companion to a roman should be, in effect, a "sloped roman" while a fully cursive type was to be kept for independent use. This is the Perpetua Italic that is shown, rather tentatively, in the seventh number of *The Fleuron*, where it is hinted that the fount would be completed with a third element, the "avowedly calligraphical" Felicity Script. This never came to pass, however, and even this first "italic" or sloped roman was hardly ever seen again, except when the experimental matrices that were supplied to the Cambridge University Press (printers of *The Fleuron*) were pressed into service.

Was Pierpont the obstruction? He had given Burch his characteristically candid opinion in September 1927: "The Meynall [sic] italics are good," he wrote, "but should be given a somewhat greater inclination, as it is a little difficult to distinguish them from the Roman. The Morison italics are worth-

8. The record cards of the Type Drawing Office summarize a note sent on May 13, 1927: "Enc. original drawings—are these in a satisfactory condition?"

9. Quoted by Burch in memorandum to Pierpont, August 15, 1927.

10. A 14· size of Perpetua was also cut by Stephenson Blake in the early 1930s and is far more closely related to the Meynell drawings than to Morison's. Stephenson Blake, who cast Perpetua in hard metal by arrangement with Monotype, followed their patterns in the other eight sizes. It seems more than a coincidence that this type, which reproduces the rich color, the relatively narrow proportions and large x-height, and also the characteristic lower case a of the Meynell drawings, should also have been cut in 14·. Did Monotype perhaps complete the roman fount and pass it to Stephenson Blake?

11. The surviving specimen, from Gill's own files, is dated 1-14-27, which is obviously wrong. It seems to fit the remarks made by Pierpont in his memorandum of January 14, 1928. (Type Drawing Office file).

less in my opinion." Once again, it must have seemed doubtful whether Morison's Gill type would ever appear. The solution was to jettison the old models. In January 1931 Gill was asked to draw a new italic. This face, still roman in its serif structure, but far more steeply inclined, more fluid in its drawing, and with some decorative elements in its capitals, was put in hand. Monotype Perpetua, with its new Felicity Italic, was issued to the printing trade in 1932.

"The sloped roman idea does not go down so well in this office as it does outside," was Morison's comment to Jan Van Krimpen. "The reason of this is that when the doctrine was applied to Perpetua, we did not give enough slope to it. When we added more slope, it seemed that the fount required a little more cursive in it. The result was rather a compromise."[12]

So indeed it was, and so are all enterprises in which such forceful personalities are engaged. Imprint had been made in scarcely more than two months. Why had Perpetua dragged on for seven years? One can hardly avoid the conclusion that, Pierpont's bloody-mindedness apart, it had been an ill-judged exercise, begun by Morison for political reasons at Monotype and for doctrinal ones. He was now caught up in the creation of Times New Roman, the project that was to secure him a lasting reputation in the field of typography, and he was losing his faith in the theory of the sloped roman. "The italic of '*The Times New Roman*' owes more to Didot than to dogma," he later remarked. In Times Roman, Monotype had produced a twentieth-century book type that eclipsed Perpetua. It owes some of its elements to Gill's type, but far more (as Pierpont no doubt noticed) to Plantin.[13]

In the end, Monotype was on safer ground adapting established classics than trying to create new ones. Gill developed Perpetua from the idiosyncratic letter that he used in his letter-cutting and which he had evolved from a number of sources, principally broad pen calligraphy and inscriptional lettering of the second, the fifteenth, and the seventeenth centuries. "While the relations of the thicks and the thins and the serifs are perfectly judged, and all the essentials are present in correct balance, certain departures from the norm, set up by centuries, distract and therefore estrange the reader, though only to a slight extent." This was Morison's verdict on Perpetua in his *Tally of Types*, making it more appropriate, he wrote, for "the semi-private printing with which Gill was for a long time associated."

It should be remembered, in considering the protracted gestation of Perpetua, that Gill Sans might well have had a similar history. "I can see nothing in this design to recommend it and much that is objectionable," wrote Pierpont to Burch in July 1927 when he first saw Gill's designs for the capitals. It is impossible not to feel sympathy for him and (especially) for Steltzer. If the design for Gill Sans were to fail, the disgrace would be theirs. If they succeeded in correcting its considerable naivetes, Gill and Morison would get much of the credit, as in the event they did. As it happened, the very qualities in the protagonists that had frustrated the making of Perpetua now conspired to produce an outstanding type. Gill made a graceful reworking of the sans serif letter drawn by Edward Johnston for the London Underground in 1916, keeping its fifteenth-century Florentine M and adding his own spring-tailed R from the same source. He avoided the trap into which Johnston drove himself: namely, the necessity of constructing the lower case from strokes of unvarying thickness. (In Gill Sans they vary by as much as a factor of three.) The Monotype works resolved the problems set by the drawings and they fitted the type with exemplary skill. Morison must receive the credit for initiating the production of a design that was perfectly timed: Erbar, Futura, and Kabel were all sans serif faces of 1926-7. But Gill Sans had the advantage (for the British market) of appearing so much closer to a conventional old face roman that the most conservative of readers put up only token resistance. Burch, for his part, had the wisdom to support Morison on this occasion.

Unlike Gill Sans, Perpetua is a design that has never suffered from heavy over-exposure. Its openness and small x-height make it far from economical in use, and the delicacy—even spindliness—of its cutting are a severe handicap. It reveals its qualities best in the richly-inked and crisply-machined first specimen text entitled "The Passion of Perpetua and Felicity," in *The Fleuron* (1930). The likelihood that such care will again be devoted to printing from metal type is, paradoxically, greater now than it would have been at almost any time in the fifty years since Perpetua appeared. Despite the arguments that raged during its making (far more, no doubt, than we shall ever know), Perpetua, as an example of a type that simultaneously engaged the talents of such great typographic figures as Gill and Morison, Pierpont, Steltzer, and Malin has a special claim to the attention of typographers.

12. Barker, *Stanley Morison*, p. 343.
13. John Dreyfus, "The Evolution of *Times* New Roman," *Penrose Annual*, vol. 66 (1973), pp. 165-74.

This article is set in Eric Gill's Monotype Perpetua, 10· and 12·. Monotype composition by Los Angeles Type Founders, Los Angeles, California.

Robert Bridges, Poet-Typographer

DONALD E. STANFORD

IT WAS ONCE WELL KNOWN that two scholarly amateurs, William Morris and Robert Bridges, did much to revive the art of fine printing during its decline in the late Victorian period. Today we are all familiar with the work of Morris. The achievements of Bridges seem to be almost forgotten. I think they are worth reexamining.

Robert Bridges, poet laureate of England (1913–1930), revealed an interest in typography and book design beginning with the publication of his first book, *Poems* (1873). From then until the end of his career he was involved in the designing of almost all of his many books.

Beginning in the early 1880s, Bridges started his collaboration with Henry Daniel, provost of Worcester College, Oxford, and owner of the Daniel Press. The story of how this collaboration revived interest in good printing and good design in England is interwoven with the recovery of the Fell types and their eventual reestablishment and use by Horace Hart of the Oxford University Press.[1] John Fell, Dean of Christ Church and Bishop of Oxford, in the latter half of the seventeenth century set up presses for the university in the Sheldonian theater at Oxford and sent his agents to Paris, Frankfurt, Antwerp, and elsewhere to secure the best punches, matrices, and type available. They brought back to Oxford splendid types, many cut in the sixteenth century. Then for almost a hundred and fifty years the types were forgotten. In the early 1870s they were discovered by Daniel and Bridges. In 1876 Daniel printed in a Fell type a volume entitled *New Sermon*, a satirical piece by a seventeenth-century Royalist. It was issued in 1877 in an edition of fifty copies, the first book in Fell for a century and a half. Bridges must have known of the Fell collection several years earlier than Daniel's book for in *his* first book, *Poems*, 1873, published by the reputable firm of Pickering, he uses an ornamental border from the Fell collection. Bridges is generally credited with encouraging Daniel to continue his use of Fell types on his private press, and it was the typographical success of these privately printed volumes, authored and designed by Bridges, that led to the eventual reestablishment of the types at Oxford.

Bridges's first poem set in Fell appeared in 1881. It is in a very rare book, *The Garland of Rachel*, an anthology of poems printed by Daniel to celebrate the first birthday of his daughter. Among the other seventeen contributors were Andrew Lang, Austin Dobson, and Edmund Gosse. The volume is considered to be the first adequate specimen of a Fell type.

Beginning with *Prometheus the Firegiver* in 1883, Daniel issued fifteen volumes by Bridges, most of them well received by authorities on typography. But Bridges's excursion into Fell's black letter, which included his sonnet sequence, *The Growth of Love* (1890), had a mixed reception. Most twentieth-century readers consider black letter an archaic affectation. But Bridges occasionally liked being archaic. For example, he insisted (again counter to the tastes of our century) on retaining archaic poetic diction in his verse. Bridges had another reason for using black letter. He is reported to have said: "The tempo at which verse should be read should be controlled typographically e.g., by the use of unfamiliar black letter which gives just the check to hasty reading which thoughtful and elaborate poems need." Black letter is good then because it forces the reader to read poems slowly. The statement irritated almost everybody, including Holbrook Jackson who snorted, "Trial by black-letter will never do. It is the business of the reader, not the printer, to administer that 'check to hasty reading which thoughtful and elaborate poems need.'"

There has been little or no disagreement about the typographical excellence of the *Yattendon Hymnal*, Bridges's collection of the words and music of one hundred ancient hymns, which he compiled with his good friend Harry Wooldridge and published 1895–1899. It was printed not by Daniel but by Horace Hart at the Oxford University Press. The title page has the same border as Bridges's first book, the 1873 *Poems*. The musical notation is set in the fine music types cut in the seventeenth century by Bishop Fell's punchcutter Peter Walpergen; these blend well with the Fell Small Pica used for the words of the hymns. The typographical success of this book led to Hart's decision to reestablish the Fell types for use by the university press. Stanley Morison said, "But for the Yattendon enterprise it is almost certain that the use of the Fell types in our time would have been restricted to private use." A poet's personal enterprise, then, had a significant effect on the history of printing in the twentieth century. Morison again: "The rehabilitation and canonization of Fell's types was not to be expected from *practical* men." But practical men now began to use them. In 1896 the London firm Kegan & Paul issued E. Gordon Duff's *Early English Printing* in Fell's Great Primer type. Over fifty books were printed in Fell types by Oxford University Press from 1902 to 1927, including Bridges's masque *Demeter*.

In 1899 Bridges returned to his old love, black letter, when Daniel published a selection of hymns (words only) from the *Yattendon Hymnal*. The title page has Fell's famous leaf ornament. Morison spends one and a half folio pages discussing it. He says, "The decorative leaf is a decoration of immemorial antiquity, stemming from the Romans of Vespasian's time." He traces its typographical history from 1512 in Venice and he

---

1. The history of Fell types and their reestablishment at Oxford is told in detail and illustrated with specimens of the entire collection in Stanley Morison's great book *John Fell: The University Press and the 'Fell' Types.* Oxford, 1967. Reprinted by Garland Publishing, 1981. Quotes of Morison included in this essay are from that volume.

says that Fell's version comes from the Venetian Aldus. By the time Bridges put out his *Collected Works, 1898–1905* (published by Smith & Elder but printed at the University Press, Oxford), he was revelling in Fell ornaments. The pages of these six volumes are crowded with flowers, tailpieces, ornaments, and borders.

In 1915 Charles Longman of the firm Longmans Green commissioned Bridges to compile an anthology suitable for wartime reading. Bridges not only edited the anthology, *The Spirit of Man*, but also helped design it and see it through the press. He chose Sir Emery Walker, friend of William Morris, to do the calligraphic title page which has been widely admired. The volume, reprinted (including the title page) in 1973 with an introduction by W. H. Auden, had a popular literary success. Bridges included several poems in it by his then unknown friend Gerard Manley Hopkins. Their publication marked the beginning of Hopkins's reputation.

In 1918 Bridges went back to the Oxford Press and the Fell types and ornaments for the first edition of Hopkins's poems, now considered to be one of the most important books of verse published in the twentieth century. The volume was successful typographically also and, as Bridges's letters to Hopkins's family show, Bridges took great pains with it, not only as editor but as designer. In a letter[2] to Kate Hopkins on March 15, 1918, he writes:

Dear Miss Hopkins

Thank you for your letter. You can assure your Mother that things are moving as fast as can be expected. It is just the stage where patience is much needed. About 32 pages are in print, but I am now busy in getting the first sheet of 16 pages satisfactorily arranged. There is a great deal of trouble in getting the proper types for headlines, and half titles and titles of poems. I have just spent two hours in pasting a sample initial page together. When once the first sheet is set up properly the printers can go on copying it—and then no further delay arises. I would send you one of the proofs of first sheet, but it is so utterly unlike what it will be that I should mislead and disappoint you. I should think now that we should get the 1st sheet done next week, that is a Se'nnight hence. I will send it as soon as it looks at all right . . .

Bridges was fortunate in his choice of associates. The firm of William Pickering, which printed Bridges's first book, is now considered to be one of the best, typographically speaking, of the mid-Victorian period. The press of his friend Henry Daniel was one of the best private presses of its day. In 1923 Bridges became acquainted with the man who was to become known as the greatest typographer of his time, Stanley Morison. In the fall of 1923 Morison wrote Bridges a letter complimenting him on the design of his books published by Oxford, and asking if he designed his own books. Bridges invited Morison to his home, Chilswell, on Boar's Hill, shortly thereafter. The story of their friendship, which lasted until Bridges's death in 1930, is told by Nicolas Barker in his privately printed

volume *The Printer and the Poet* (1970). Their association led to what I consider to be Bridges's most successful typographical venture, *The Tapestry*, privately printed in 1925, in the first use of Arrighi type. A calligraphic type like Arrighi is not suitable for all occasions. I would not like to see a long, heavy, philosophical poem such as Bridges's last poem, *The Testament of Beauty*, set in it. (*Testament* was, in fact, impressively designed by Morison in Bembo type.) But I think Arrighi's light and graceful texture is exactly right for some of Bridges's short lyrics such as "Noel." Below are lines five to eight set in Arrighi:

And from many a village
in the water'd valley
Distant music reach'd me
peals of bells aringing:

We owe *The Tapestry* to a happy collaboration of several persons including Bridges, Stanley Morison, Frederic and Beatrice Warde, a French punchcutter, French typefounders, and Mrs. Bridges, an expert on penmanship with a favorable attitude toward calligraphic type. Morison, about the time he was becoming acquainted with Bridges, became deeply interested in the calligraphic printing type designed by the Italian Ludovico degli Arrighi and used by him in books first printed in 1524. Morison wanted to reestablish this type. He got in touch with the typographer Frederic Warde who designed the new type based on that of Arrighi and pushed its manufacture in Paris to completion. Morison wanted now to put out a book with his new type. He approached Bridges who agreed to give him a number of poems from his volume *New Verse* forthcoming from the Oxford University Press. These poems formed the content of *The Tapestry*, which then, in order to be a first edition, had to be published *before* the Oxford volume. As shall be seen, delays caused it to precede the Oxford publication with only a few weeks to spare, in November 1925.

Bridges had a lifelong obsession. He wanted to reform English spelling and make it logically consistent and *phonetic*. He invented a phonetic script and produced some manuscripts of his poems written entirely in this script. He also wanted to produce a type that was completely phonetic. This was not practical, so he decided to sneak his reformed spelling into his printed works gradually. In *The Testament of Beauty* he frequently spells *have* without the final *e*. In *The Tapestry* he decided at the last moment to introduce two separate types for the letter *g*, one to represent the soft *g*, the other the hard *g*. This decision delayed and in fact almost stopped the printing of *The Tapestry* while everyone waited for the new *g* to be manufactured. It almost broke up the Bridges-Morison friendship. Fortunately, Morison got *The Tapestry* out before the Oxford edition of *New Verse* and all was well.

In the last three years of his life, Bridges began publishing his collected essays and papers, and for this purpose he began, with the aid of Morison, manufacturing special phonetic types. In all, twenty-eight phonetic sorts were included in this Monotype Blado which became known as the Chilswell Font. The font was used in the ten volumes of Bridges's *Collected Essays* which began publication in 1927. Nicolas Barker considers it one of Morison's most successful designs.

2. From my forthcoming book, *The Selected Letters of Robert Bridges* (University of Delaware Press).

did not run more than one night, because it did not please the million; and that the million did not relish it, because it was unseason'd with their common spice. Without pressing Shakespeare's apology beyond its necessary meaning, it is a confession that he had himself deliberately play'd false to his own artistic ideals for the sake of gratifying his audience. Now this is just the piece of knowledge which we require, and it conveys the inference that

Monotype Blado with phonetic symbols, designed by Bridges and Stanley Morison. From Bridges's *Collected Essays*, 1927.

Robert Bridges's contributions to the art of the printed book lack the intricate showiness of Morris's work, but they have merits which should not be forgotten or disregarded. Bridges designed his books to be read rather than to be looked at. I think he would have agreed with Holbrook Jackson's doctrine as stated in *The Printing of Books*: "Self-effacement is the etiquette of the good printer," and with Paul Valéry's remark, "The mind of the writer is seen as a mirror which the printing press provides."

Dr. Stanford's article on Bridges was originally given as a lecture to The Art of the Printed Book Conference at The University of Nebraska at Omaha in April 1980. Our thanks to conference director Mel Bohn and to the university for facilitating its publication in *Fine Print*.

THE ROMANCE OF WOOD TYPE

STEPHEN O. SAXE

WOOD TYPE is a unique expression of the great commercial and geographical expansion of America in the nineteenth century. It is an American invention, originating in the early years of that century and dying with its last years, flourishing during the nation's industrialization and movement westward. Indeed, it was an important aid to both. Wood type in broadsides and billboards advertised everything: public land sales, steamship and railway transportation, political candidates, army recruitment, and government proclamations.

Wood type is display type—for advertising, pure and simple, with no function as text or body type. It is commercial, brash, inventive, expansive—and thus close in spirit to nineteenth-century America. It was seldom made smaller than six lines pica (72 points, or one inch); the largest examples were seven feet high. The advantages of making large type of wood rather than foundry metal were noted by Darius Wells in 1828 in the first wood-type specimen books

> These types are prepared with a machine, which gives them a perfectly even surface, and renders their height exact and uniform, while large metal types are more or less concave on the face, arising from the unequal cooling of the metal when cast.... The perplexity and loss arising from the breaking of metal types through the centre, as well as of the descending and kerned letters, is completely obviated by my wood letter. This advantage, all printers, especially those at a distance from foundries, will know how to appreciate.... The use of wood types when carefully prepared in the manner of those in this specimen, are in no respect objectionable; ... they are more convenient in many respects, are more durable, and cost only from one quarter to one half those of metal.

Wood type was much more highly developed in this country than in England or Europe. Yankee ingenuity, combined with an enterprising spirit, expanding markets, and easily available supplies of raw material and power, gave this country the decided edge over foreign competition. There were more suppliers of wood type in America than in Europe and their product was more varied, more complex in design, and more innovative. In America the production of wood type was the specialty of a small number of manufacturers. The major figures in the business were Darius Wells, William Leavenworth, Edwin Allen, William and Samuel Day, John Cooley, Ebenezer Webb, William H. Page, Charles Tubbs, and James Hamilton. In the last part of the century Hamilton managed to take over and consolidate most of the business of his predecessors, but the victory was short-lived: wood type was on the way out.

Darius Wells, a New York printer, was the first to produce wood type commercially, in 1827. As far back as the fifteenth century, carved lettering appeared in German block books, and many printers since then had carved letters on blocks of wood. But it was Wells who first used the end, rather than side, grain of wood, which made possible much greater detail and increased durability. The preferred woods were maple, pear, and cherry, and to a lesser extent boxwood, mahogany, and holly. By midcentury maple was the wood most often used.

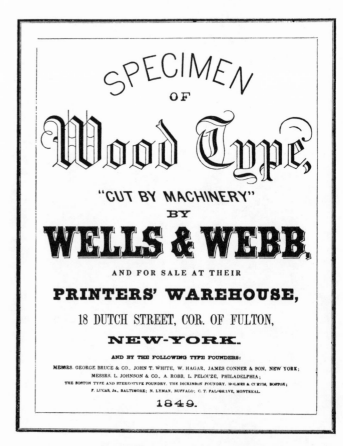

Title page of the wood type specimen book of Wells & Webb, 1849. (Author's collection reduced to 45% of original size.)

The fine detail that could be cut into the end grain of these hardwoods made possible the great proliferation of wood-type designs.

Wells's most important contribution was the application of mass production methods to wood type. In 1827 he invented the machine-router which enabled him to reproduce wood types in great quantity and to sell them to printers at low prices. The router consisted of a flat-faced, half-round cutting tip powered by steam and rotating at a high speed of 14,000 revolutions per minute. (The machine-router was never patented by Wells, and it soon became an essential tool in woodworking and other industries.) At first, Wells's router tip remained stationary; the material had to be moved around it. But before long it was improved and made to move around the material. Wells, who had a good eye for letterforms, produced the first wood-type specimen book in 1828. A copy is at Columbia University's collection of historic type materials from the American Typefounders Company.

In 1834 William Leavenworth, of New York, added a pantograph[1] mechanism to the router for the first time, and soon a profusion of wood-type designs became available. With the pantograph it was an easy matter to copy a competitor's wood type by using his font as a pattern for the pantograph's tracing finger. The high-speed router tip, moved by the arm of the pantograph, duplicated the original font faster and more accurately than it could be traced with a pencil. Often two

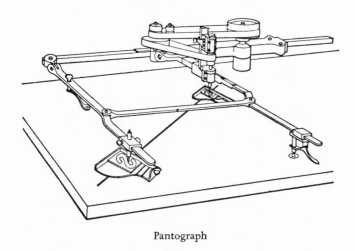

Pantograph

fonts of old wood type are found to be identical, except that one is an eighth of an inch larger; clearly, one is a pantographic copy of the other. As other manufacturers went into business with the router-pantograph, there was widespread pirating of wood-type designs. (Similarly, widespread pirating of foundry type occurred after the development of the electrotype matrix in the early 1840s.)

But the pantograph also inspired the creative imagination of the wood-type manufacturers. Using a standard pattern

letter, it was relatively simple to cut inlines, outlines, shaded letters, reversed letters, italics, backslopes, condensed, expanded, and ornamented faces. A glance at a page of any nineteenth-century wood-type specimen book will demonstrate the enormous variety and inventiveness of the designers and makers. The pantograph could produce a new type style in wood at a fraction of the time and cost involved in producing new designs for foundry type.

The most inventive, fanciful, and beautiful of the wood types were the multi-colored or "chromatic" types. Ringwalt in his *American Encyclopedia of Printing and Bookbinding* (1871) defines chromatic type as "type made of metal or wood for color printing and so arranged that there are duplicate or triplicate copies of each letter, which, after being printed, respectively, in different colors, on a given space, blend together in a harmonious whole." Chromatic wood type is seldom encountered today; it was always a very small proportion of total type production and is now a rarity and a treasure.

The peak of chromatic type production came in 1874 when the William H. Page Wood Type Company, of Connecticut, issued its extraordinary folio-sized specimen book of chromatic types. Henry Lewis Bullen described it thus: "This is the most notable of wood type specimens. Page outshone all competitors in imparting a degree of artistry in designing wood type and borders, most of which could be printed in several colors. . . . [It is] a work of unusual excellence, well worth preserving."[2] (See illustrations, page 65.)

Lithography was rapidly making wood type obsolete by the end of the last century, but it was not until 1969, when Rob Roy Kelly published his important book, *American Wood Type: 1828–1900*, that anything substantial was written on the subject.[3] Kelly described in detail for the first time the manufacturing process, the makers, and the entire historical development of the industry. In addition, he devoted an immense amount of effort to describing and annotating the profusion of type designs he had encountered.

Rob Roy Kelly's pioneering effort is impressive; wood type is not easy to study and to document. Take the simple matter of identifying the origin of a font of type. With metal type, a foundry's identifying pinmark was almost always cast on the side of all characters in a font. But wood-type manufacturers only occasionally stamped their imprint on the side of the capital A's in a font; quite often there is no mark whatsoever to indicate the maker. And one cannot always identify wood type by referral to old manufacturers' specimen books—the catalogues of type styles and sizes issued by the manufacturers for their customers—because these books are extremely scarce. Kelly lists only fifty-eight different specimen books

1. The pantograph is an open steel frame in the shape of a rhomboid, with the joints pivoting freely. A projection at one end holds a tracing stylus; projection at the opposite end holds a pencil (or, in this case, the rotating router bit). By adjusting the pivot-points of the frame, a design traced by the stylus can be accurately reduced or enlarged by the pencil or router at the other end.

2. Henry Lewis Bullen, *Duplicates of Type Specimen Books, etc. . . . for sale by the Typographic Library and Museum of the American Type Founders Co.* (Jersey City: American Type Founders Co., 1934), p. 36.

3. Brief descriptions of wood type and its manufacture can be found in J. Luther Ringwalt, *American Encyclopaedia of Printing* (Philadelphia: Menamin & Ringwalt, J. B. Lippincott & Co., 1871), p. 502, and Theodore Low DeVinne, *The Practice of Typography: Plain Printing Types* (New York: The Century Co., 1900), p. 345. Rob Roy Kelly's book is currently available as a large-format paperback from Da Capo Press, 233 Spring Street, New York, New York 10013, $8.95.

between 1828 and 1919, less than a tenth of the number of type-founders' specimens issued during the same period. Some wood-type specimen books survive in only a single copy. To make identification even more difficult, much wood type is of such large size that some specimens of a font consist of no more than a single letter from the font, perhaps filling the entire page. Moreover, wood types, unlike foundry types, were rarely given names. The customer ordered by a catalogue number. Any given number might be used by several type makers to describe different types. And unlike type-founders of the period, few wood-type manufacturers registered their new typeface designs with the United States Patent Office. (William H. Page is an exception, but his patents cover only about a dozen faces in 1870.) Thus we have no documentation of the designers and dates-of-origin of wood-type designs as we do for many metal types.

Finally, a true disaster for the modern wood-type researcher occurred soon after 1906 when the Hamilton Manufacturing Company of Two Rivers, Wisconsin, having completed a specimen book of all the wood-type designs in their possession, destroyed all the original paper designs and patterns for the individual letters. Since the Hamilton company was the successor firm to the William H. Page Wood Type Company, Morgans and Wilcox, and Vanderburgh, Wells & Company, Hamilton thus destroyed at one blow the complete alphabet designs for all the faces of its predecessors, some designs dating back to Darius Wells. As Rob Roy Kelly points out, now the only way it is possible to reconstruct complete alphabets of wood type is to find, preserve, and make proofs of the actual fonts of type.

That, fortunately, was done by Rob Roy Kelly himself (his collection is now at the University of Texas) and by Douglas and Lloyd Morgan of Dobbs Ferry, New York. The Morgan brothers began to collect wood type in the 1940s, at a time

NEW YORKERS

Boats

Samples from an early Morgan Press wood type specimen book. The original is printed in red. (Reduced to 50% of original size.)

when commercial printers and printing equipment dealers considered the type to be worthless, much as foundry type today is thought to have no value except as scrap metal. It was their father, Willard, an artist and photographer, who first became interested in antique type. His interest quickened when he found in Connecticut a small press for sale for $100, along with a paper cutter and a few cases of old type. He purchased these, and soon his sons were printing for amusement. Fond of the antique, and not having much money to buy new type, the brothers often bought used wood and foundry type for a dollar a case from Damon and Peets in New York. (Damon and Peets, a printers' supply house since about 1868, had sold second-hand type as far back as 1883 at least.) The type was considered "junk type"; most printers would not buy it because no replacement sorts were available.

The brothers' growing awareness of the beauty of nineteenth-century type led them around the country in search of it. Paul Hayden Duensing, the well-known private press printer and typefounder, and former schoolmate of Doug Morgan at Carnegie Institute of Technology, recalls that the Morgan house in Scarsdale was "like a storeroom for the British Museum; there was literally type stashed under the bathtub and in the closets, and the basement was jammed full of specially made boxes [of foundry type]...." Doug and Lloyd found wood type in New England, New York, Pennsylvania, Virginia—along the seacoast and rivers of nineteenth-century industrial America.

Some of the Morgans' collection came to them by a convoluted route. Elrie Robinson was a printer of St. Francisville, Louisiana, who called himself "The Horse and Buggy Printer" because the types he used were popular "when the horse and buggy was the favorite means of locomotion." Much of his collection of hundreds of fonts of nineteenth-century type came to the New York Public Library in 1957, soon after his death, through the gift of Carl Pforzheimer, a wealthy book collector who had been a long-time friend of Elrie Robinson. Known as the Robinson-Pforzheimer Collection, the metal type was available at the library for many years to provide commercial repro proofs of type designs. (The collection has since been "deaccessioned" and is now located at the State University of New York at Purchase.) What is not generally known is that when N.Y.P.L. accepted Robinson's foundry type collection, they politely declined his wood type collection. It was given instead to the Upton Printing Company in New Orleans. Upton in turn gave it, for the cost of trucking,

Samples from the specimen book of the Hamilton Mfg. Co., ca. 1900. (Author's collection, reduced to 75% of original size.)

to Standard Printing of Parkersburg, West Virginia. Neither of these companies wanted the collection, but neither could quite countenance throwing it out. Enter the Morgan brothers who located the collection in about 1961. They bought a full truckload of wood type—about fifty cartons—from Standard Printing for $200.

When the brothers incorporated their printing company, Morgan Press, in 1958, they offered reproduction proofs of their antique types to advertising designers and agencies. For advertising and display, wood type has certain characteristic virtues not found in metal. The letterforms are bold and direct because they were originated for advertising use and were

Zietbedürfnisse

SHARP POINTED BRAMBLES

LEIDE

COAST SURVEY

Samples from *Wm. H. Page & Co.'s Specimens of Wood Type, 1867.* (Courtesy of The Kemble Collections, California Historical Society, San Francisco. Reduced to 80% of original size.)

not derived by enlarging and thickening the strokes of text types. (Ultra Bodoni and similar fat faces of early nineteenth-century origin are exceptions.) Wood type lends itself to manipulation and distortion in an amazing variety of ways. Because it seldom has more than the shortest of ascenders and descenders, wood type can be placed quite closely together horizontally. Often in a playbill style of setting, a simple change of type styles provides an optical break between lines, eliminating the need for leading.

The Morgans built up a steady business in advertising during the 1960s and early 1970s. Leading advertising typographers were soon using their types: Pushpin Studio, Herb Lubalin, Milton Glaser, Lou Dorfsman of CBS, Henry Wolf and then Sam Antupit of *Harpers Bazaar*. At first, wood type was used only for advertisements with Victorian or Old West themes. But as these leading designers became aware of the great potential of wood type, they began using it for other themes. Wood type began to appear in newspaper ads for television, in high fashion magazines, on record albums. Primed by this knowledgeable, pioneering use of wood-type letterforms by Glaser, Dorfsman, and the others, a second wave of designers began using the Morgan brothers' wood type. By the late 1960s the Morgan Press was pulling about a dozen repros a day. About fifteen faces accounted for eighty percent of the orders, an indication that certain typefaces become fashionable in advertising typography and are used repeatedly until their novelty wears off.[4]

After several years of supplying repros directly from the wood type, the Morgans saw that photocomposition of display types was becoming important in advertising. They made a deal with Headliners, Inc., to put on film many of their wood type fonts. Once made into film negatives, the letters could be supplied to customers as positive proofs in any size and with the letterspacing adjusted to the customers' specifications.

Other companies also developed sources of display photocomposition. In 1967 Visual Graphics started making available antique typefaces from the great collection of T. J. Lyons, a Boston printer and collector. The Lyons collection of metal type, similar in scope to the Morgan collection of wood type, was sold some time ago to the Compugraphic Corporation.

As sources for photocomposition of antique typefaces began to proliferate, demand for repro proofs made directly from the type slackened. As Lloyd Morgan describes the situation, "Here we had a collection of over 40,000 pounds of type, taking up a great deal of space, bringing in only a few hundred dollars each month in business, and rapidly becoming completely obsolete in an industry that was almost entirely photocomposition. We knew we had to sell the collection, and there were only two choices: to keep it as a collection or to break it up and sell it piecemeal."

---

4. Some display types of the twentieth century show the influence of wood type, and some are direct adaptations. Some of the more important faces influenced by wood type are: Chisel (Stephenson Blake, 1939), Fontanesi (Nebiolo, 1954), Playbill (Stephenson Blake, 1938), Profil (Haas, 1946). A more general influence of wood type on today's display types is seen in the widespread use of drop shadows, inlines, and shaded type. In fact, type is being manipulated and elaborated by the camera today in very much the same way it was by the pantograph in the last century.

Although it seemed likely that the collection would bring in more money if it were sold piecemeal, the Morgans preferred to keep it together. Lloyd and Doug Morgan had a strong sentimental attachment to the collection, "the hobby that had turned into a business."

Dr. Elizabeth Harris, Curator of the Graphic Arts Division at the Smithsonian Institution, was keenly interested in the collection from the outset: "Though the nineteenth century was the heyday of the type trade in America," she said, "and America was leading the world, very little remains to show for it today. This collection simply couldn't be duplicated." The Smithsonian's purchase of the Morgan collection was not, however, to be entirely smooth sailing. The collection was also sought by other institutions, including the University of Texas and the Rochester Institute of Technology. Could the money be raised in time? Or would the other institutions take the initiative? A year and a half after the collection was first offered, the Smithsonian had raised the $250,000 purchase price. The money came from the Regents' Fund, a special Smithsonian fund established for large extraordinary purchases. The Smithsonian took title to the Morgan collection in May 1981. The Morgans were delighted. "It went to where it should be," Lloyd said. "The Smithsonian has the right people and the right facilities. I couldn't be more pleased."

The Smithsonian had previously acquired from American Type Founders matrices representing type designs from the many individual typefoundries of the nineteenth century that had consolidated in 1892 to form ATF, but the Institution had had little to show of the metal type itself and less of wood type. The Morgan collection brought approximately 1000 printed items ranging from pamphlets and monographs to histories, manuals, and type specimens; approximately 700 fonts of wood type; approximately 2000 fonts of foundry type; about 5000 wood and metal cuts; and over 500 sets of borders and ornaments. Dr. Harris proposes to combine the American Type Founders Collection, the Morgan Collection, and a library of specimen books and reference books "into a scholarly center where type can be traced from design through manufacture to the market."

Much depends on raising more money for the center. As Dr. Harris envisions it, the study center would include a study area and laboratory/workshop adjacent to the collections themselves. There would be typecasting equipment, a proof press, photocopiers, microscopes, equipment for comparing printed images, microfilm readers, and a library of microfilms of material from other collections. The study center would be used by practicing printers and printing historians, social historians, and students of popular culture, technology, and business.

The first step, now under way, is the proofing and cataloguing of the collection. "A small army of volunteers" is proceeding to do this under the direction of Harris and Stan Nelson, Museum Specialist. Apparently undaunted by the arrival of four large truckloads of wood and metal type, the Graphic Arts Division has begun the work of removing the metal type from its cases, proofing it, and then fonting it on galleys or in small boxes. The wood type is proofed and then stored as compactly as possible. The cataloguing will be aided considerably by the foundry and wood-type specimen books that are part of the Morgan collection. The Morgan brothers also printed their own specimen books during the period when their type was used to supply repros to the trade. Their foundry-type specimen book is still in print, and it is the first resource of the puzzled antique type collector trying to identify an unknown nineteenth-century typeface. So far, the wood type has been used to produce four newspaper-sized posters announcing events at the Smithsonian. In the late spring of 1983 the Graphic Arts Division will mount its own exhibition of wood type from the Morgan collection, and the public will have a chance to sample the delights of this national treasure.

An Investigation of the Interdependency of Paper Surface, Printing Process, and Printing Types

This paper is based on a lecture given at a symposium of book publishers sponsored by the Albert Ziegler Paper Company in Grellingen, Switzerland in 1973. The lecture derived from a study in which sixteen typefaces in three sizes were reproduced on nineteen different kinds of paper by the three most commonly used printing processes: letterpress, offset, and gravure. A collection of proofs was produced which allowed one to determine which method of printing reproduces best on a particular paper, the subtle refinements of a particular typeface, and what influence paper tints have on legibility. Copyright ©1974 by Max Caflisch; this English translation by Inga Wennik published with permission of the author.

The Choice of Type and Paper—Yesterday and Today

Just as the most "beautiful," or rather, the most suitable piece of paper can be deprived of its effect by the choice of an unsuitable typeface, so can reading turn into torture when a typeface is reproduced on the wrong paper.

When designing a book, the first step, other than deciding on the format of the book, is always to select a readable typeface that also harmonizes with the contents of the book. The early printers had a considerable advantage: they generally had at their disposal just one typeface which was printed on a handpress with heavy ink on moistened paper, a process which certainly differs greatly from printing on our fast modern printing presses. The proof was pulled by hand and a strong impression was created on the backside of the paper. This relief impression is still the characteristic sign of letterpress printing, but it is often so slight that one can hardly discern it; nowadays, letterpress is really just a "light touch." The paper is much smoother and more even; it is no longer moistened, and we print with considerably less ink. Papers with low ink absorption qualities can tolerate a much smaller amount of ink used in high-speed printing.

In contrast to his colleague of yesteryear, the modern printer has a large number of typefaces at his disposal. If, however, one disregards the poor or unsuitable types, one is left with just a dozen or two well-designed, easily readable typefaces, so the present assortment is hardly excessive, especially in view of the fact that many typefaces are designed only for certain manufacturing systems and thus are not readily available to every printer or publisher. Today's printer *does* have at his disposal a rich assortment of papers with different surfaces especially made to accommodate the various printing techniques. If the early printer was familiar with a variety of

more or less rough handmade papers, he could not have imagined today's coated and glossy paper finishes, nor the bright white papers we know today. Yet this very abundance of choices poses the threat that the publisher or printer will use the wrong combination of type, paper, printing process, and ink.

Glossy Paper—A Legitimate Need of the Printer

Rough paper has always been a thankless surface both for writing and printing, and this is especially true for printing letterpress. Thus, it is understandable that calligraphers and printers were forever hoping to write and print on smoother surfaces in order to produce more even and crisp letters, and to reduce the amount of ink required. Originally papers were smoothed manually by means of an agate stone, but by the mid-sixteenth century smoother paper surfaces were achieved in Germany through the process of *schlagstampfen* (strike-stamping). Though still somewhat more porous than today's glossy papers, these surfaces were much better suited for reproduction since they no longer showed gross structural irregularities as did the unfinished papers.

In the eighteenth century several famous printers tried to produce printing paper with smoother surfaces. In Holland, a method was developed by which sheets of paper were pressed between wooden rollers made from logs, the forerunners of modern satinizing calenders. The English typefounder and printer John Baskerville, creator of the charming baroque types named after him, possessed a secret method for smoothing and evening paper. His books distinguish themselves by both the silky sheen of their paper surface and the excellent reproduction quality of his types. The German philosopher and physicist Georg Christoph Lichtenberg visited his house and shop shortly before Baskerville's death. He was shown punches and matrices but was unable to discover the secret behind the smoothing of the papers. Certain experts believe that the paper was pressed between hot plates made of copper. Albert Kapr writes that Baskerville's sheets (whether printed or unprinted he does not mention) were smoothed between polished steel rollers. The Italian master printer Giambattista Bodoni also used smoothed, handmade paper on which the subtleties of his neoclassical types were shown to their best advantage. The end of the eighteenth century brought the introduction of vellum paper, and most important for us, glossy or coated papers came in the nineteenth century, a development that has its culmination in the mirror-finish papers so highly regarded currently. Today's printer can choose from a large complement of more or less satin-finished natural papers as well as from matte, glossy, or high-gloss paper.

Paper Surface and Printing Results

In due course the demands for improved paper surfaces also affected the design of typefaces. The much-desired glossiness of paper required different conditions for the reproduction, and, therefore, the cut of printing types. The early printing technique, hand letterpress on handmade moistened paper, demanded that the typefounder take the inking conditions (the inking of the form and the spreading of the ink over the edges of the letters) into consideration when cutting punches for type. The type image had to be reduced to allow for the ink that would be squeezed around the letters during the printing process, making inked letters on the printed sheet appear heavier and stronger than the metal type in direct proportion to the amount of ink squeezed out by the impression. If, today, we were to cast letters from existing matrices of the incunabular period, such as the roman of Jenson, and print them on glossy paper, the types would be too fine and too thin, but also too crisp, and their legibility would be correspondingly poor. The early types needed a lot of ink and much pressure, even on moistened papers. It is important to take this into account if one wants to re-cut historical types: the modern versions of Bembo or Garamond are designed to produce a more or less heavy effect when printed on today's glossy paper in order to replicate the impression the original types made when printed on early handmade papers.

An especially beautiful example of this adaption can be found in the Garamond roman. The Linotype as well as the Monotype Garamond roman recuts were based on old specimens of printing. Therefore, the hairlines and serifs of these true-to-the-original cuttings are relatively heavy. In reality, however, the cut of the historical Garamond was much finer as we can see on the first printer's proofs of this face, which Jeanne Veyrin-Forrer found in the Bibliothèque Nationale. Further evidence that early types were cut more finely than they appear in print are the types cut by the excellent typefounder Robert Granjon, who was a younger follower of Claude Garamond. Both the Musée Plantin in Antwerp and the Oxford University Press own punches and matrices of types cut by both typefounders. This makes it possible to compare punches and proofs. (Incidentally, this is the very manner in which typefaces for the IBM Composer were designed. In order to prevent the types from producing too heavy an imprint on the paper after striking the keys, the letters were reduced by a carefully measured percentage.)

The Influence of Copperplate Engraving on Type Design

While the printing techniques of the sixteenth and seventeenth centuries differed but little from those of the incunabular printers, a major change occurred in the techniques for the reproduction of pictures, and consequently, of letterforms, toward the end of the eighteenth century: the development of copperplate engraving. Fine-line titles and texts, engraved by hand in copper, increasingly defined the type styles of that period; sharpness and fineness in letterforms were elevated to an ideal to be imitated by calligraphers and

Type design was influenced by letterforms created by pointed pen and copperplate engraving, as for example, these elaborate engraved letters from the lettering book of Ioseph de Casanova, 1650.

the punchcutters. And as they turned away from the natural, form-giving effects of the broad pen, they gradually turned toward the unnatural pressure demanded by the pointed pen which corresponded to the techniques of copperplate engraving. In order to give printing types the delicate appearance that the engraver's burin makes possible in copperplate, the punches had to be cut even finer, impairing the durability of steel punches and cast letters. When printed on very glossy papers, these neoclassical types appear still finer and sharper, and their hairlines are barely visible; their legibility diminishes correspondingly. Therefore, it stands to reason that when using most types designed between 1780 and 1810, for instance Didot or Walbaum Antiqua, it is best to select a rather smooth book paper in order to show them to their best advantage, but under no circumstances can coated paper be recommended.

Width or Letterspacing of Types

Letterspacing is important to legibility because the rhythm of a word image depends on the size of the counters[1] and on the width of the body or the spaces between the individual letters (the side-bearing measurement). Even the smallest width variation can have an irritating effect on the reader. Faulty letter width or letterspacing produces uneven and spotty word images, especially if the type has been set too tightly—a practice far too often embraced today by phototypographers. Tight letterspacing that may be quite acceptable for larger sizes is only rarely, or not at all, suitable for

1. The counter is empty space inside the letterform; e.g., the bowl of the *b*.

RQEN
baegn *ba*

A photographic enlargement (approximately 4½ ×) of type printed letterpress on handmade, moistened paper in the sixteenth century (from the *Hypnerotomachia Poliphili*, Paris, Jacques Kerver, 1546), clearly showing how ink-spread distorts a typeface.

text setting in 8· to 12·, especially if the small type sizes are printed on paper with a rough surface. Under these circumstances strong sans serif typefaces, for instance the regular or medium weights of Helvetica, often produce unsatisfactory results, whereas they hold up considerably better if printed on glossy paper with a stronger impression, with increased effectiveness produced by the white color of the paper.

Sharpness as a Standard for Judging Printing Methods

If one judges the quality of a printing method by the sharpness with which it reproduces type, one finds that letterpress does not work as well as offset printing, since the edges of the typeface appear heavier than they really are due to the ink-squeeze, and the contours of the metal types tend to lose some of their sharpness depending in degree on the structure of the paper surface. In offset printing, however, the sharpness of typographic reproduction is unsurpassed. The ink-spread disappears from the letter's edges and only its surface appears in print; the impression becomes crisper, sometimes even absolutely razor sharp. Technically speaking, offset printing provides a maximum of sharpness and is, therefore, superior to letterpress. Since, however, most of the types used in offset were originally designed for reproduction by letterpress, they appear unnaturally "pointy" and bloodless in offset.

In gravure printing many of the subtleties of a type are lost in the screen; the finer the typeface, the greater and more apparent the loss of resolution, a real disadvantage when using finely cut types in gravure printing. Regular weights of sans serif typefaces will not show as large a loss of resolution as would romans. Typefaces with counters too tightly cut or with too little letter space or width of the body are not desirable for gravure printing as they will tend to produce "fly specks."

Printing Methods and Paper as Criteria for the Design of Type

Generally speaking, historical type designs do not lend themselves easily to offset or gravure printing unless their image is particularly heavy. As a rule, they appear too fine, too thin.

Each method of printing demands its own designs. It is desirable that typefaces are now being designed especially for offset and gravure (or photogravure) printing processes with stronger hairlines and serifs. In other words, typefaces in which the edge definition of a letter, as it appeared in letterpress, is taken into consideration.

These ideas have been scientifically examined in the United States and in England, where they have been incorporated into the typeface development program of the Monotype Corporation. Monotype developed special typefaces designed for the specific requirements of different printing methods and paper, for example their Plantin, Erhardt, Emerson, and Times. Times Roman (1931) was an especially promising beginning because it was created for newsprint and newspaper printing. Times Roman is, however, not too well suited for printing on rough antique wove papers, especially the version that contains the stronger capitals. Typefaces designed especially for optimum reproduction quality include, among others, Monophoto Photina, Linotype Rotation (for rotary letterpress) as well as Hermann Zapf's Optima (letterpress and offset), Matthew Carter's Olympian (newspapers), and Adrian Frutiger's Iridium (offset) and Gerard Unger's Demos

---

Times New Roman *and Italic*, Serie 327

Die Times New Roman ist wohl eine der weitestverbreiteten Antiqua-Schriften. Ursprünglich für *The Times* unter der Aufsicht von Stanley Morison in den Ateliers der Zeitung 1931 geschaffen—die erste Nummer der Zeitung im neuen Kleid erschien am 3. Oktober 1932—, wurde sie bereits 1933 der Fachwelt zur Verfügung gestellt. Nach dem Schnitt der Schrift durch die englische Monotype Corporation folgten Linotype und Intertype mit analogen Schnitten. Damit begann der eigentliche Siegeszug der Times New Roman: die Zeitungsschrift fand bald Eingang im Bereich von Zeitschriften und sogar Büchern. Die kräftige

Bembo Roman *and Italic*, Serie 270

Die von Aldus Manutius im Druck *De Aetna* von Pietro Bembo 1495 in Venedig verwendete Antiqua wurde von der englischen Monotype Corporation 1929 nachgeschnitten und der Fachwelt vorgestellt. Die zugehörige *Kursiv* geht auf eine von Giovantonio Tagliente 1524 gezeichnete Type zurück, ausserdem existiert noch die von Alfred Fairbank gezeichnete *Bembo Condensed Italic 294*, von der Stanley Morison sagt, 'it looked happier alone than in association with the Bembo roman'. Obwohl die Bembo *als Buchdrucktype geschaffen* ist, hat sie dank ihrer ausgeglichen kräftigen Zeichnung auch für die Wiedergabe in Offset gerade noch genügend Substanz. Vorteil-

bn bn

(left) The sober letters of classical type design: Bodoni Antiqua.   (right) Linofilm Iridium, designed for photo typesetting by Adrian Frutiger, based on a classical design but with stronger hairlines, and larger x-height and counters.

i i i

In order to obtain the image desired for photo typesetting, the drawing has to be corrected, as shown in the third letter "i." The second "i" shows how the first "i" would reproduce if uncorrected.

Times New Roman *and Italic*, Serie 327

Die Times New Roman ist wohl eine der weitestverbreiteten Antiqua-Schriften. Ursprünglich für *The Times* unter der Aufsicht von Stanley Morison in den Ateliers der Zeitung 1931 geschaffen—die erste Nummer der Zeitung im neuen Kleid erschien am 3. Oktober 1932—, wurde sie bereits 1933 der Fachwelt zur Verfügung gestellt. Nach dem Schnitt der Schrift durch die englische Monotype Corporation folgten Linotype und Intertype mit analogen Schnitten. Damit begann der eigentliche Siegeszug der Times New Roman: die Zeitungsschrift fand bald Eingang im Bereich von Zeitschriften und sogar

Bembo Roman *and Italic*, Serie 270

Die von Aldus Manutius im Druck *De Aetna* von Pietro Bembo 1495 in Venedig verwendete Antiqua wurde von der englischen Monotype Corporation 1929 nachgeschnitten und der Fachwelt vorgestellt. Die zugehörige *Kursiv* geht auf eine von Giovantonio Tagliente 1524 gezeichnete Type zurück, ausserdem existiert noch die von Alfred Fairbank gezeichnete *Bembo Condensed Italic 294*, von der Stanley Morison sagt, "it looked happier alone than in association with the Bembo roman." Obwohl die Bembo *als Buchdrucktype geschaffen* ist, hat sie dank ihrer ausgeglichenen kräftigen

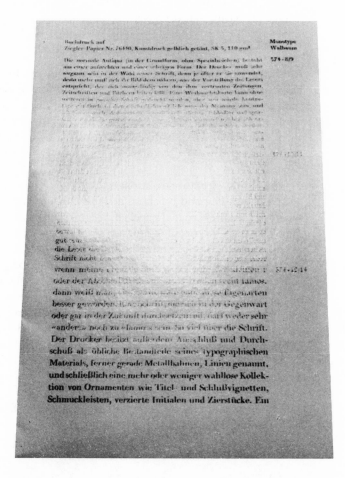

The blinding effect of light on print on coated high-gloss paper.

A comparison of two text types orginally designed for letterpress printing from metal types and converted for film typesetting and offset printing;   (left page) set by Monotype and printed letterpress on uncoated paper;   (this page, left) set by Linotron 202 and printed by offset lithography on paper sized for offset.

[In this book, both are printed by offset lithography. —ED.]

(digital typesetting). All of these faces are examples of attempts to clarify the technical requirements of the method of reproduction before the new typeface is designed.

Photo-typesetting offers the opportunity to create special types for offset and gravure reproduction. Letterpress printers can get along with fewer faces than general printers who also produce offset and gravure printing. The latter need to offer a number of typefaces to accommodate the specific requirements of various printing methods if they want to do justice to the task. There are hardly any faces that are equally suitable for all three printing methods, and none that can be used on all kinds of paper. However, this statement applies only to text type sizes from 6· to 12·; the larger sizes are far less susceptible to the specific disadvantages of a particular paper surface or printing method. Therefore, this discussion is limited primarily to text typefaces.

Influence of Paper Surface on Typographic Reproduction

A number of typefaces which were designed for printing on handmade paper (for instance Centaur or Caslon) undergo such a change in appearance when printed on coated paper that even an expert has to look twice in order to recognize them. Such is the extent to which a well-known typeface can be distorted when used on a different (or wrong) kind of paper.

The almost structureless surfaces of glossy, satinized, and coated papers demand typefaces designed to suit their idiosyncrasies. As these coated papers have a much higher blinding effect than do machine-finished natural papers, the eye has difficulty in distinguishing the fine subtleties of a typeface —the hairlines and very fine serifs; these get lost in the glare. The result is reduced legibility and, consequently, eye fatigue. It is absolutely necessary to use a face with a strong design for printing on finished or glossy paper. Some faces that are completely unsuitable for printing on coated papers are Caslon, Didot, and certain delicate versions of Bodoni and Walbaum. Nor does a fine sans serif face, if used in text typesetting, belong on coated paper. The reader has great difficulty in prolonged reading of small sizes of these faces when printed on coated paper. Machine-finished papers tend to produce less fatigue since the dazzling effect is slight or absent.

Influence of Paper Tint on Legibility

Legibility is also greatly influenced by the tinting of papers. During the last thirty years, unfortunately, it has become fashionable to artificially brighten and bleach bookpapers. This has more effect on legibility than even experts are willing to admit. Moreover these optical brighteners add to the cost of the paper.

Publishers and readers have by now become so spoiled that they judge the quality and value of a paper according to its whiteness, even paper used in publications with no halftone illustrations. White, bright white, and ultra white papers are fashionable. The gentle, slightly yellow tint which is much better suited to the human eye and necessary for optimum legibility is not much in demand, often even taboo. Though our eyes are suffering from the excessive use of bright white papers with their blinding effect, this undesirable trend continues. In textbooks there is the danger of creating two image levels: one level formed by the printed lines, the other by the very cold, shimmering paper whose glare swallows the fine hairlines and serifs, subtracting substance from letters, and making it difficult to recognize them. The type and paper no longer become one homogeneous unit, as occurs with gently tinted papers; instead the type stands alone and unconnected on the paper. Pure white paper can certainly be recommended for the printing of multi-colored or black and white halftones in order to heighten the brilliance and luminescence of the images. However, bright whiteness is not necessarily a sign of quality or durability in paper.

Structure and Opacity

Book papers should not be transparent; their surfaces may well be of fine structure or sometimes even have a matte, velvet sheen. It is, however, barbarous for the eye to have to read long texts printed on shiny coated paper. Paper that may be appropriate for a science or art volume, requiring optimum reproduction of pictures with some text, is not advantageous for the printing of a book with substantial amounts of text whose reader demands quite different qualities from the paper.

Normally speaking, offset papers are manufactured with a tighter surface structure than machine-finished book papers, increasing the impression of glossiness and coldness, especially if unsuitable light typefaces have been used and the paper has been bleached. Weight, volume, and opacity of paper have to be taken into consideration when a typeface is chosen. Typefaces which tend to print rather heavily (Times Roman or Plantin) should be avoided on more transparent paper, yet they reproduce perfectly well on coated or glossy paper.

Ink and Inking

It is important also to take into consideration the appropriate choice of ink. Not every shade of black is right for every kind of paper; it is up to the printer to choose the proper color and, if necessary, experiment with it. There are printers who mix some gray into their book inks. When large type sizes are used, this gray tone may be desirable; however, for smaller sizes the color may turn out to be too weak and the contours of the characters may lose their sharpness. The most experienced book designers insist on pure black ink for text printing. At the same time, they look for perfect printing pressure and even color. Stanley Morison hit the nail on the head when he said: "I think black is a good color." Well-balanced color is of the utmost importance: too much ink will smudge the print, filling in small counters and creating blotches and fattening the finer strokes of the type. The image of the typeface can be so distorted that one can no longer recognize it. On the other hand, if too little ink is used, the print becomes faint, legibility is impaired, and, in some cases, irregularities in the paper structure become visible and cause spotty printing quality. Whether too much or too little ink has been used, legibility is diminished in either case. The inking of machine-finished paper is an art which has to be learned. Truly, it is the beginning and end of perfection in printing.

Conclusion

The book as "fine printing" requires not only—as is generally acknowledged—the right typographic layout of lines and paragraphs, but also that components be selected to form a well-balanced entity: an appropriate typeface—legibility has to be a primary consideration; a paper that will give optimum reproduction quality with the printing process selected; the printing process most appropriate to the reproduction of the type; an ink appropriate for the paper selected; and, a paper tint easy on the eye.

A printed work that fulfills these five criteria can surely be considered perfect by the producer/designer as well as the reader. This, in the end, is the theme of this essay: neither type nor paper can be an end in itself. Both serve the whole: the printed work.

BIBLIOGRAPHY

Barthel, Gustav, Rahmer, Albert, and Stähle, Walter: *Gestalt und Ausdruck der Antiqua*. Stuttgart, Staatliche Ingenieurschule für Druck, 1970.

Caflisch, Max: *Fakten zur Schriftgeschichte*. Privately printed, 1972.

Frutiger, Adrian: The evolution of composition technology. In *IBM journal of research and development,* Volume 12, Number 1: The IBM selectric composer. New York 1968.

Jammes, André: *La réforme de la typographie royale sous Louis XIV : Le Grandjean.* Paris, Librairie Paul Jammes, 1961.

Kapr, Albert: *Schriftkunst*. Geschichte, Anatomie und Schönheit der lateinischen Buchstaben. Dresden, Verlag der Kunst, 1971.

Morison, Stanley: *First Principles of Typography*. New York, Macmillan, 1936; 2nd edition, Cambridge, University Press, 1967.

Simon, Oliver: *Introduction to Typography*. London, Faber and Faber, 1945, 1953 (revised); Penguin Books, 1954.

Tschan, André: *William Morris*. Berne, The Monotype Corporation Limited, 1962.

Tschichold, Jan: *Im Dienste des Buches*. St. Gallen, SGM-Bücherei, 1951.

——"Die Leserlichkeit verschiedener Schriftschnitte auf verschiedenen Papieroberflächen in Buchdruck, Offsetdruck und Tiefdruck." Basel, *Kupferschmid-Blätter* 10, 1953.

Vervliet, H[endrik] D. L.: "The Garamond Types of Christopher Plantin." In *Journal of the Printing Historical Society*, Number 1. London, 1965.

Vervliet, Hendrik D. L., and Carter, Harry: *Type Specimen Facsimiles II.* London, The Bodley Head, 1972.

Veyrin-Forrer, Jeanne, and Jammes, André: *Les premiers caractères de l'Imprimerie Royale*. Etude sur un spécimen inconnu de 1643. Documents Typographiques Français. II. Paris, André Jammes, 1958.

Warde, Beatrice: *Type should have "Fitness for Paper."* An Experiment and Comment. London, The Monotype Corporation Limited (no date).

The Rediscovery of a Type Designer: Miklós Kis

HORST HEIDERHOFF

THE HISTORY of the Janson-Antiqua types has been associated with two names: Anton Janson, a Dutchman (1620–1687), and the Hungarian Miklós Kis (1650–1702), a native of Miszttótfalu. For some time it had been suggested that Anton Janson was designer of the type, as reflected in the modern name. New facts and information show that the true designer is Miklós Kis. Let us try to solve the Janson puzzle by laying out and sorting all the Janson information we have, thus showing that there are no grounds for associating the two type designers. Janson and Kis both issued type around the same time; however, the more far-reaching activities and interests of Kis make him the more prominent of the two.[1]

Anton Janson was born in Wauden (Friesland) on 17 January 1620, the son of a well-to-do farmer. On his teacher's advice he was apprenticed in 1635 to an Amsterdam typefounder, probably Christoffel van Dijk, a goldsmith who later took up the art of lettercutting. Even this information may be questioned, though, because in 1635 van Dijk himself was rather young to be Janson's master. According to Gustav Mori, a German type scholar of the 1930s, Janson left Amsterdam in 1651 to go to Frankfurt where he worked at the typefoundry of Johann Luther. In 1656, after the death of Luther, Janson moved to Leipzig to work for the printer Timotheus Ritzsch. Later, in 1659, he established a typefoundry of his own which existed for nearly thirty years. His first known typeface specimens are dated 1671.

Anton Janson died in Leipzig on 22 November 1687. A funeral discourse held four days after his death and published in printed form in 1688, of which one copy has come to us, praises Janson as a "well-known typefounder." Writing in 1955, Jack Stauffacher characterizes Janson as "a worthy tradesman but no great artist."

In 1689, Johann Carl Edling, a typefounder and native of Strasbourg, married the widow of Anton Janson and carried on his typefoundry. Edling died in 1702, two years after his wife's death, and the typefoundry was then taken over by Wolfgang Dietrich Ehrhardt, a

typefounder and Edling's foreman of many years. In 1720 the business had already descended to Ehrhardt's heirs, who carried on the typefoundry as *Ehrhardtische Giesserey*. The same year, a specimen was issued by the Ehrhardt foundry of Leipzig, showing a complete roman and italic under the heading Verzeichniss derer *Holländischen Schrifften*. Although these types resemble the types that Janson himself issued, they differ in characteristic features. In this connection, Harry Carter, the famous printing historian, and the artist George Buday observed that "while Janson's types descended to the Ehrhardt family there are no grounds for associating the Dutch types of their foundry with him."

By 1868, the punches, matrices, and strikes of the *Holländischen Schrifften* of the Ehrhardt foundry were in the possession of the Drugulin foundry, established in 1831 by the Leipzig printer, Wilhelm Drugulin. Around 1870 he incorrectly referred to these specimens as *Renaissance Holländische*; they belong, in fact, to the group of transitional types. The original copper matrices for these types were bought by the Stempel typefoundry in 1919 and were called by them *Janson*; these matrices are still the property of D. Stempel AG.

Type scholars later misinterpreted these facts. Helmut Presser stated in an article in 1955: "The great resemblance between the specimen issued by Janson in 1678 and the *Holländischen Schrifften* [of the Ehrhardt specimen of 1720] suggests that Janson was the intellectual originator of these types. Perhaps he had these letters of Dutch character cut by Kis, the typecutter then living in Amsterdam." And Georg Kurt Schauer in 1957 tried to establish as fact that "Anton Janson, who had become an important tradesman in Leipzig, was the intellectual originator of the types named after him, which were cut for him by Nikolaus Kis, the typecutter congenial to Janson."

However, the assumption of a connection between Janson and the *Holländischen Schrifften* of the Ehrhardt foundry can no longer be sustained. The research of Carter and Buday has shown that in their dimensions and shape these types, so-called *Janson*, are typical of the Dutch roman types of the late seventeenth century. There is an unmistakable relationship between these characters and those which we find among the work of a Willem Janszoon Blaeu, for instance, or in other Dutch

1. For much of the following information I am indebted to Mr. József Molnár in Munich, whose extensive work on Miklós Kis has already appeared in magazines in the Hungarian language.

specimens such as those issued by Bartholomäus Voskens or Jan Adolph Schmidt. In this connection, an important clue is that the son of Bartholomäus Voskens, Dirk Voskens, was the master of Miklós Kis. Type designs usually do have their roots in history and tradition, following the models of the past. The *Janson* types, in particular the italics, are, however, clearly distinguishable from their ancestors. Tibor Szántó once wrote: "The Janson Italics are the best designs of this epoch, and they have an independent style of their own."

Carter and Buday also found the so-called *Janson* types among other faces in an undated specimen issued by the widow of Johannes Adams of the type foundry of Adamszoons and Ente in Amsterdam between 1700 and 1715. In a later study of this specimen, Harry Carter recognized twelve faces as identifiable with Kis types. By contrast, the types are not found in type specimens Janson issued in his lifetime.

Gustav Mori reproduced an octavo specimen of Anton Janson's showing, among others, a Mittel Antiqua and Cicero Antiqua issued in 1672 and 1673. Jan Tschichold, writing in a letter to D. Stempel typefounders in 1955, states: "Although Mori's essay throws some light on Janson's life, it does not provide new information on the 'Janson puzzle.' In other words, it is only one among several proofs that the types were *not* designed by Janson. Naturally, it had seemed strange to me before that Mori's reproduction showed *no* resemblance whatsoever with the Janson, however, probably like many others, I did not follow the matter up. Thus the suggestion made by Jack Stauffacher to henceforth call the Janson types 'Dutch Old Face' is well founded but can probably not be put into practice; well founded because in its style this typeface cut by Kis truly is a *Hollandische Antiqua* and was called such by Drugulin...."

While in Holland Kis learned to cut letters and he cut the types in question in the style then prevailing in Holland; at the time, there existed no native, long-established type style in Hungary.

In view of the above, we must seek the origin of the so-called *Janson* types in Amsterdam rather than Leipzig, for there are no grounds for attributing them to Janson himself. Nor is there any proof that Janson ordered the types to be cut by Kis, as assumed by Schauer, especially if we consider that Kis finished his apprenticeship in 1683 and that Janson died in 1687. In other words, any such contact between the two would have been possible only within a period of four years, and even this is further reduced by two years if we consider that in the Hungarian Bible which was printed by Kis between 1683 and 1685, the types he used are not those we know as the Janson types. Kis himself wrote that the reason he did not use the types was "... that I had cut the matrices myself when I was still an apprentice." In fact, József Molnár has established that the running headlines in Kis's Bible only show the first, still unstable form of the Janson design. Even if we assume there was a contact between Kis and Janson, we cannot give any reason why types said to have been produced by Janson were not shown in a specimen until that issued in 1720

by the successors to Ehrhardt, and did not appear in the specimen of 1689 by Edling nor those issued prior to 1687 by Janson himself.

A reconstruction of the path traveled by the matrices for the Janson types until they became the property of D. Stempel AG shows that there is only one proof of a link between the *Holländischen Schrifften* shown by the Ehrhardt foundry in 1720 and Kis as the cutter of the punches for these types; it is a single type specimen broadside. In 1942, Lajos Keleman, keeper of the archives, informed the famous Hungarian printer, Imre Kner, of the existence of this specimen. Kner, in turn, immediately informed Pál Szentkúty, who wrote about it in issue No. 4/1942 of the *Ungarische Bücherschau*. The specimen, presumably issued by Kis in Amsterdam in 1684/85, when his Bible was done, was among the documents and papers of the Hatfaludi family from Siebenbürgen, which were kept in the national archives at Budapest. The specimen is now kept in the archives at the National Hungarian Museum in Budapest.

Carter and Buday reported that this specimen supplies the solution to the Kis-Janson puzzle: "We owe a knowledge of this broadside to G. W. Ovink of Amsterdam, and the best surviving photograph of it to the librarian at Budapest, for the original was destroyed in the late war [not the case]. The fourteen sizes of roman and italic are recognizable with some difficulty, due to the poor quality of the printing and of the photograph, as the *Holländischen Schrifften* of the Ehrhardt foundry. The legend in Dutch at the foot means: 'If any man desires strikes or matrices of these types newly cut by Nikolas Kis, let him address himself to the afore-named master dwelling in Amsterdam on the Achter Burgwall over the brewery at the sign of the Swan in the house of Warner Warnersz.' There are displayed on this sheet, besides the Ehrhardt types, a set of small notes for psalms, a Median (Pica) Greek and three sizes of Hebrew." The specimen broadside described above clearly links the so-called Janson types to the name of Miklós Kis. That he is the only creator of the types becomes even more obvious from his biography.

Miklós Kis (Tótfalusi Kis Miklós) was born at Alsó-Miszttófalu (now Romania) in 1650. At the age of twenty-seven he left the theological college at Nagyenyeder to work as a schoolmaster in Fogaras and later as director of the school. However, he spent only three years in Fogaras as it was his intention to take a course in Calvinistic theology in Holland. The Calvinist Bishop Tofeus ordered Kis while in Holland to have the Bible printed in Hungarian by Daniel Elzevier and proposed that he should be one of the correctors. As he never received any money to have the Bible printed, he decided to do the printing himself in Amsterdam, at his own expense and without help. His friend Páriz (Papái Páriz Ferencz), a medical doctor and writer, whose *Pax Corporis* Kis was to print later in Kolozsvár (1698), persuaded him that he would serve his country best by becoming a printer rather than a preacher ("of them, thank God, we have plenty"). Kis arrived in Amsterdam in the autumn of 1680. He entered the Voskens typefoundry, and during the three years of his apprenticeship to Dirk Voskens he learned all the skills of the cutting and casting of letters. In his *Mentség (Apologia,* or perhaps more precisely, *Defense),* which he wrote and printed in 1698, Kis wrote that his master's father had been adept at cutting German types (as Bartholomäus Voskens, Dirk Voskens' father, was). "My master cut Roman and Black Letter fairly well, but not Italic. He made me cut all the italics and also new matrices if replacement was needed of defective matrices." This shows how talented Kis must have been, for Voskens was considered a highly reputed lettercutter in his time.

After three years of apprenticeship, Kis set up shop on his own in 1683 and started printing the Hungarian Bible with his own type. The Bible was to become the centerpiece among all his works commissioned by people from many countries. At this time, Kis had two masters and up to twenty men working for him in the printing of the Bible, which he finished in 1685. He went on to print the Psalms (1686) and the New Testament (1687). For many years afterwards, his Bible was considered the best of its kind, especially for accuracy of text and spelling.

From 1683 to 1687, to finance his printing, he was cutting types of many kinds for other typefounders and printers. He also recorded negotiations for the cutting of Chinese type. It is interesting to see that the Greek he cut had no ligatures, which seems to be evidence of the influence of his Utrecht friend Jan Leusden. Kis had contracts with people from Poland, England, Germany, Sweden, and Italy, as well as with Armenians living in Amsterdam. He also cut the first Georgian types.

In his *Mentség* Kis writes that two envoys came to Amsterdam from the Grand Duke of Tuscany, Cosimo de Medici, to order punches, matrices, and other material for a typefoundry, and to ask him in the name of the Medicis to come to Florence to set up the new typefoundry and teach disciples how to use the equipment. Although Kis did not accept this offer, it attests to the international reputation he had gained. Jószef Molnár has in his collection two books printed in Florence in 1693 and 1728 and a number of copies from books printed and published in Florence between 1693 and 1790. There can be no doubt that the types used are the so-called *Janson Antiqua* and Italic cut by Miklós Kis.[2] In 1965 Berta Maracchi Biagiarelli, in her article *Il privilegio di stampatore ducale nella Firenze Medicea,* described a document showing that Tempi and Finetti, envoys of the owner of the new printing establishment of Filippo Cecchi in Florence, visited Kis in Amsterdam about 1687/89. In other words, they were not sent by the Grand Duke Cosimo III, as Kis believed. However,

2. According to Molnár, there are two nineteenth-century reports about this acquisition by the Florentines of type, punches, and matrices in Amsterdam, viz., in Francesco Cambiagi's 1846 book about the Stamperia Granducale in Florence, and in 1881 by Salvatore Landi in *La Stamperia Reale di Firenze.*

the Cecchi printing establishment was in fact later merged with the old Stamperia Granducale. It is recorded that they bought fourteen complete sets of roman and italic type as well as Greek and Hebrew, the same number of types shown on the single Amsterdam type specimen we have of Miklós Kis's from 1684/85. For more than a hundred years, these types were used for printing in the Stamperia Granducale in Florence.

Since the time of Daniel Berkeley Updike's *Printing Types* (1922), it was commonly known that the types in use at Florence in the printing shop of Giovanni Filippo Cecchi at the end of the seventeenth century were the same as those used in the Ehrhardt typefoundry in Leipzig thirty years later. This mystery puzzled type experts for a long time without any successful solution until March 1954 when Henry Carter and George Buday, in their article in *Linotype Matrix 18,* attributed the so-called Janson types to their true creator, Miklós Kis.

His first large order probably came from Poland, commissioned by a Polish Jewish merchant, Salomon Benedictus, who made a deposition before a notary in Amsterdam in 1684. The order was for roman and italic types as well as Hebrew, and Kis bound himself to deliver the types by May 1685. Whether the merchant Benedictus was able to sell the types in Poland or elsewhere is not known. In any event it seems certain that the Hebrew type was meant for use in Poland, for in this contract Benedictus promised that the Jewish community could assure a safe-conduct through Poland should Kis ever wish to return to his home country.

Kis also had business relations with Sweden where his types played a part in the transition in Sweden from black letter to roman. They were shown for the first time in 1703 in a specimen printed by Johannis H. Werner, successor to H. Keyser III. Sten G. Lindberg reported this in a letter to Ödön Szabó, who had been asked by József Molnár to undertake research.

As far as we know, only one roman with italic found its way to England, where it was used for the first time in John Shower's *Mourner's Companion,* printed in 1692. It also appears in the Oxford University specimen book of 1695, in the 1698 *Specimen Book of the Heirs of Anderson* in Edinburgh, and, in the same year, in James Orme's specimen book. While the type historian A. F. Johnson recognized the italic only as a "Pseudo Janson," Stanley Morison and Harry Carter report that "... founts are shown of Nikolas Kis's two-line English Roman and Italic and of a Brevier Greek." We do not know how these types came to England, but there can be no doubt that the italic was first used in London in 1692. Harry Carter also tells about a receipt found in the archives of Oxford University which confirms that the London foundry of Robert Andrews paid for such types in 1695. Kis himself writes about a visit to England. Jószef Molnár believes that he visited England about 1687/88, i.e., after the Hungarian Bible was done. Molnár also tells of a letter which Kis wrote to Jakob Bogdan, painter in London, from which we learn that Kis expected money from England. So there are grounds for

Groot Canon Romein

Intramus mundum
Intramus mundum au

Clein Canon Romein

Dominus ille omnium
liberrimus, ſumme bo-

Dominus ille omnium liber-
potens, & ſummè ſapiens, in

12 pt. Kis-Janson Antiqua & *Kursiv*

ABCDEFGHIJKLMNOPQRSTUVWXYZ

abcdefghijklmnopqrſstuvwxyz &QuÆŒæœ

1234567890 ﬀﬁﬂßſſt £$?!†*§.,;:'»«)]

ABCDEFGHIJKLMNOPQRSTUVWXYZ

abcdefghijklmnopqrſstuvwxyz && QuÆŒæœ

1234567890 ﬀﬁﬂßſiſtſſt £$?!†§.,;:'»«)]*

ABCDEFGHIJKLMNOPQRSTUVWXYZQU

Acute accent é   Asterisk *   Ampersand &&

Cedilla Çç   Circumflex ô   Dagger †

Diaeresis Umlaut ü   Diphthong Æ æ Œ œ

Eszett ß   Grave accent è   Ligatures ﬁ ﬂ ﬀ

Section mark §   Tilde ñ

"*Let our people come to respect Books, so their reading will allow knowledge to spread throughout Transylvania....* Once an old woman asked me if she could look at one of my books, and while leafing through the pages, asked if there were any with thicker letters.... *This is my profession, to see to it that in this country books are plentiful & cheap.*" From Kis' *Mentsége* [Apology 1698]

Groot Canon Romein

Intramus mundum
autore, inhabitamu
arbitro, derelinqui-
mus judice ſummo

Aſcendonica Curſ

Ipſe quidem erat ab aeterno
in ſe ac per ſe ſatis beatus, cui
nihil omnino ad complemen-
tum omnimodae beatitudinis
deſideraretur; propoſuit nihi-
lominus ante tempora ſecula-

Longe aut.
cognitionem
nu depromps
ſolum, ſed g.
articulum in
dubitatum h.

Profeĉto no
convenient
theatrum di

Specimen of the Kis-Janson types and ornaments (D. Stempel foundry), arranged and hand set by Jack Stauffacher at the Center for Typographic Language, Greenwood Press, San Francisco.

assuming that he went to England on business and that he took sets of type with him.

In his *Mentség*, Kis also tells about types delivered in Germany. In this connection, we find an interesting passage in A. F. Johnson's *The Goût Hollandois*: "The only printer I have found of the seventeenth century whose use of pseudo-Janson can be compared with that of Cecchi [in Florence] in extent is Ulrich Liebpert, typographer of the Electors Frederick William and Frederick III of Brandenburg, at Berlin. Of dated books showing the type I know of nothing earlier than 1696, e.g., various works of the numismatist Laurentius Beger. …Liebpert had the Tertia and Mittel sizes, and other examples of his use of the type may be seen in an edition of Bidpai in Greek and Latin, 1697, and in a *Specimen versionis Coranicae*, 1698. That the two printers before 1700 who most favored this design were working respectively at Florence and Berlin does not help us to trace the home of the founder." To date we have no clue as to how Kis's matrices found their way to Berlin.

For nine years, Kis worked as a punchcutter in Holland. In autumn 1689 he left Amsterdam to return to his home country, Transylvania. On his way home he meant to leave a set of matrices in Leipzig with the intention of selling them, probably to Anton Janson. He could have heard about Anton Janson during his stay in Amsterdam from Voskens, since Janson had lived there, too. However, he could only have met Janson's successor, Johann Carl Edling, since Janson had died two years before. It would seem that he did not come to terms with Edling, because in his *Mentség* he says that "the matrices had not been bought in Liepzig as there were some defects in them."

But then, according to Jószef Molnár, Kis was inadvertently imprisoned as a heretic by a Polish nobleman who seized all his belongings. Naturally this caused financial problems for Kis. Kis appealed to the king of Poland requesting his help in regaining his personal belongings and goods, including many bibles and valuable books. In those days, the king's influence did not reach far, but as is often the case in times of greatest despair, help came from rather unexpected quarters. Robbers were making repeated raids in that part of Poland and the Polish count suspected that they were sent by the Hungarians. The count gave Kis back most of his possessions on the condition that he promise "not to send the robbers again" (*Mentség*, p. 100). Probably, Kis's joy at the sudden release of his belongings caused him to return directly to Transylvania in order to raise money by selling his Hungarian bibles. The matrices were left in Leipzig, where Kis was hoping they might, with Edling's help, be sold, despite their defects. Later Kis

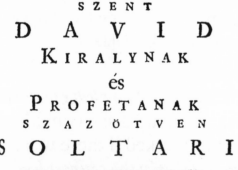

Psalter, Amsterdam, 1687. The second book printed by Miklós Kis following his Bible of 1685. Kis later decided to add this to the Bible despite his reluctance to increase its 1200 pages. All known copies of the Bible are bound together with the 104-page Psalter. (György Haiman, *Nicholas Kis.*)

Apologia Bibliorum, Kolozsvár, 1697. A polemical treatise in which Kis defends the emendations and orthography of his Amsterdam Bible (1685) against those who disapproved of him as a "typographer-scholar" and who disliked his modern orthographic principles and his educational publishing. (György Haiman, *Nicholas Kis.*)

meant to have them sent to Hungary, but this was never accomplished. Efforts were continued after his death in 1702 to get the matrices from Leipzig. An inventory set up at the explicit request of Kis's widow contains a note asking "that the Reformed church should have the matrices collected at their own expense."

As regards the aforementioned specimen issued circa 1715 by the typefoundry of the widow of Adams and Ente in Amsterdam showing the "Janson" types, Molnár suggests the following explanation. Mrs. Adams's late husband had been a partner in the typefoundry of Dirk Voskens; possibly they were brothers-in-law. In 1683, Adams parted from Voskens. After his death, his widow carried on the typefoundry with Abraham Ente. As we know from Kis's *Mentség*, his relations with his master, Dirk Voskens, were sometimes not the best, perhaps because Kis was too ambitious. Kis speaks about his master's qualifications with cautious reserve, which suggests that he might have left a set of matrices with Adams in Amsterdam rather than with Voskens. According to Kis he left a set of matrices in Amsterdam for safety's sake. "I left the set of matrices in Amsterdam in order to have them sent in case my death or other reasons should prevent me from cutting even better types for my home country, as is my intention." Kis intended to have these matrices collected later and sent to Kolozsvár. However, as we read in his *Mentség*, part of these matrices were either defaced or had completely

M. TÓTFALUSI K. MIKLOSNAK
maga ſemélyének, életének, és különös tseleked-e-tinek

MENTSÉGE.

Mellyet az Irégyek ellen, kik a' közönſéges
Jónak ezaránt meggátolói, irni kénſerít-
tetett.

KOLOSVÁRATT,
1698. Eſtendöben.

ELöLJÁRÓ BESZÉD.

IGazán mondják a' Theologusok, hogy Isten az Övéit (azért, hogy megidegenitse minden világi jóktól) abban ſokta meglátogatni, a' mit legnagyobb javoknak tarta-nak világ ſzerint. Nékem Belgiumban ollyan állapatom vólt, hogy ha pénz gyüjtésben gyönyörködtem vólna, és czélúl fel nem töttem vólna azt, hogy hazámat, valamint lehet, ſegítsem e' ſzerint: *Publica privatis anteferenda bonis.* Az-az: A' közönſéges jót eleibe kell tenni a' magánosnak, an-nyi idő alatt könnyen 40000 vagy talám 50000 forintot-is gyüjthettem vólna, és ha eddig ott maradtam vólna, azt merem mondani, kevés Erdélyi Úr vólna, a' kivel tserélnék pénz dolgából. Amazt colligálhatom ebböl, hogy mineku-tánna az én könyveimnek nyomtatásoknak gondjától meg-ſzüntem, és egéſzen magamat a' munkára adtam (noha még akkor-is vólt foglalatosságom és idöm töltéſe a' könyveknek köttetések miatt) az utólſó két eſtendömben keresetem én többet 15000 az-az tizenöt ezer forintnál (mellynek 11000 A forint-

Apologia, Koloszvár, 1698. Kis's second important polemical treatise, in which he defends his life's work, including his punchcutting, typography, and book publishing. (György Haiman, *Nicholas Kis*.)

disappeared and Kis brought several unsuccessful actions against the person sent to collect the matrices. His matrices reappeared between 1710 and 1715 at the typefoundry of Adamszoons & Ente.

This throws a new light on the Janson puzzle. The fact that Kis left a set of matrices, which had some defects, in Anton Janson's town does not establish a relationship between Kis and Janson. There is absolutely no proof of any contact, be it personal or through a contract, between the two during Janson's lifetime.

What then were the reasons why Kis's types did not reappear until as late as 1720 in the Ehrhardt specimen? Why did they not come to light earlier among the types used by Edling or Wolfgang Dietrich Ehrhardt? The latter must have known that these *Holländischen Schriff-ten* had only been left in Edling's care, not in his type-foundry's possession. József Molnár is perhaps right in assuming that Edling's encounter with Kis was an epi-sode of just a few hours. Johann Christoph Ehrhardt's heirs didn't take possession of the types until 1720 and then showed them in the specimen mentioned previ-ously. The fact that they were called *Holländischen Schrifften* is an indication that it was known the types had come from Holland. The fact that Anton Janson's name is not mentioned in this context makes it even more unlikely that the types were associated with him.

Kis returned to his native Transylvania and in 1694 set up a printing press and a typefoundry as well as a punchcutting shop in Kolozsvár, where he worked under difficult circumstances. He used the matrices he brought with him from Amsterdam and those produced in Kolozsvár to cast the types he wanted to use in his printing. The *Pax Corporis*, which was set in Kolozsvár, was partly set in the so-called Janson types. The irregu-larities which the characters show were due to the fact that Kis probably brought with him to Transylvania the earlier cut punches and matrices. He did not find the time to cut new and better types, as he had planned before he left Holland. His countrymen did not under-stand or appreciate his art, and as a printer he had more enemies than friends because of his high standards. Kis died in Kolozsvár on 20 March 1702, at the age of fifty-two.

While Anton Janson was the settled tradesman, who, by the way, mostly cut and cast German and Schwa-bacher (black letter), and was closely connected with the development of the typefounding trade in Leipzig, Miklós Kis was a cosmopolitan, a universal genius, called a "scholarly punchcutter" by Harry Carter and George Buday. He spoke several languages, was a poet and composer and, in particular, was a pioneer in fighting illiteracy in his home country. In the personality of Kis we find a synthesis of cosmopolitanism and nationalism. His reformation of Hungarian grammar and spelling was of far-reaching importance. The range of books he printed and published was broad: religious books and popular prose, medical books for the general public, as well as textbooks and cookbooks.

Imre Kner, in speaking about Kis's types as seen in the specimen kept at the National Library in Budapest, says: "The types are very beautiful and ahead of their time. There had been much experimentation and change [in type design] since the time of Garamond. Still, confusion existed until Bodoni, Didot, and Walbaum. The Transitional is buried in the Old Style. Kis's types took a considerable step forward, his italic even more than his roman."

The types, called Janson types by D. Stempel AG in 1919 and known as the Janson types since then, but designed and cut by Miklós Kis, have had a decisive influence on the typographic scene for many years, especially in the area of book design. Sensitive typographers, with a feel for the achievements of past masters and for classical sources in modern trends, still find many typographic applications in which the flair and unusual charm of Janson are seen to particular advantage. Time and again, prize winning books from the annual *Best Books of the Year* competition in Germany are typeset in Janson. A listing by *Stiftung Buchkunst* of the most frequently used typefaces in the years 1951 to 1975 shows Janson ranking fourth after Garamond, Walbaum, and Bembo. Because of its excellent design, Janson has been able to adapt to the demands of mechanical, photographic, and digital composition. The laudable history of the Janson types proves Kis to be one of the outstanding type designers of all time.

BIBLIOGRAPHY

Biagiarelli, Berta Maracchi. *Il privilegio di stampatore ducale nella Firenze Medicea. Estratto dall' "Archivio Storico Italiano"* Issue III, 1965, pp. 364–66. Florence, 1965.

Buday, George. "Some more notes on Nicholas Kis of the 'Janson' types." In *The Library*, pp. 21–35. London, 1974.

Buday, George. "Notes on Miklós Kis of the Janson Types." In *The New Hungarian Quarterly*, no. 62. Budapest, 1976.

Carter, Harry and George Buday. "The Origin of the Janson Types; with a note on Nicholas Kis." In *Linotype Matrix* 18, p. 7. London, March 1954.

Carter, Harry and George Buday. "Nicholas Kis and the Janson Types." In *Gutenberg Jahrbuch*, pp. 207–12. Mainz, 1957.

Haiman, György. *Tótfalusi Kis Miklós. A betümüvesz és a tipográfus*. Budapest, 1972. (This definitive biography of Kis has recently been published in an English translation by The Greenwood Press, San Francisco.)

Johnson, A. F. "The 'Goût Hollandois.'" In *The Library*, 4th Series, vol XX, no. 2, pp. 180–96. London, 1939.

Mori, Gustav. "Anton Janson, der Begründer des selbständigen Leipziger Schriftgiessergewerbes (1620–1687)." In *Altmeister der Druckschrift*, pp. 97–102, Frankfurt, 1940.

Morison, Stanley. "Anton Janson Identified." In *Signature*, no. 15, pp. 1–9. London, December 1940.

Presser, Helmut. Die Janson-Antiqua. Rätsel um eine Druckschrift. In *Imprimatur*, vol. XII, pp. 62–70. Munich, 1954–55.

Schauer, Georg K. "Janson–Antiqua, Amsterdam–Frankfurt–Leipzig." In *Börsenblatt für den deutschen Buchhandel*, no. 4, pp. 39–43. Frankfurt, 1957.

Stauffacher, Jack Werner. *Janson, A Definitive Collection.* San Francisco: The Greenwood Press, 1954.

See also Baudin, Fernand. *Nicholas Kis: A Hungarian Punch-Cutter & Printer, 1650–1702* by György Haiman [a review of the book]. 14pp. San Francisco: Greenwood Press, 1985.

Conference on the Tercentenary of the Amsterdam Edition of the Bible by Nicholas Kis Tótfalusi, Debrecen, Hungary, 25–27 April 1985. [In Hungarian, with a few articles in English.] Debrecen, Hungary: Library of Lajos Kossuth University, 1985.

This article has been translated from the German by Gertraude Benöhr. It has been set in ten and eleven point Intertype Janson by Walt Olofson at Mackenzie-Harris Corp., San Francisco.

Metal Type: Whither Ten Years Hence?

PAUL HAYDEN DUENSING

IN 1974, when *Fine Print* was launched, commercial type-casting in the United States and Canada had already swung from the predominantly hot metal operation of a decade previous to a largely photographic mode. The Intertype Fotosetter had been eclipsed by Mergenthaler's VIP, Monotype's Monophoto, Alphatype, and the Photo-Typositor. As technology moved from the 1970s to the 1980s, progress centered on the development of digitized electronic imaging at ever-accelerating rates of character generation. As the curve of composition speed ascended, the curve of metal typefounding activity descended, and the flow of hot metal equipment onto the secondhand market became a flood.

As the focus of commercial typesetting came to rest very largely with photographic and then with electronic technology, traditional typefoundries began to experience an attrition characterized by a wave of mergers and closings, and, in a few cases, by diversification into other lines of manufacture. During this period the materials from the Weber Type-foundry in Stuttgart were divided between D. Stempel of Frankfurt and Johannes Wagner of Ingolstadt near Munich, and most of Berthold's stock in Berlin also went to Wagner. Haas in Switzerland became the repository for matrices from Deberney & Peignot, Berling of Sweden, Olive of France, and a small foundry from Denmark. The famous Bauer foundry moved from Frankfurt to its former subsidiary, Neufville, in Barcelona, and then absorbed several smaller foundries and finally, in 1984, the matrices and materials of Typefoundry Amsterdam.

In the United States the attrition has been mostly among Monotype houses, since most true foundries were merged at the end of the previous century when American Type Founders was formed. Today there are a limited number of firms offering metal type in fonts: Castcraft (Typefounders of Chicago), Mackenzie-Harris, Los Angeles Type Founders, Barco/Acme, Quaker City Type, and American Type Founders. In addition several individuals have purchased Mono-type equipment and are now casting fonts or offering composition service: Harold Berliner's Type Foundry, The Out of Sorts Letter Foundery (sic), and several others.

In the face of this rather generalized catabolism, one may well ponder the future of fine printing, which is so heavily dependent upon metal type as a prime element in its activity.

As the level of orders to the foundries declines, the metal type designs which will remain available will almost certainly not be those which make fine printers' hearts go pitty-pat; the survivors will be the sans serifs of industry and commerce, not the stuff for setting poetry to make the soul soar.

If the traditional sources dry up, what then shall the fine printer of ten years hence do? There are, it seems to me, five avenues to the resolution of this problem. First, it is likely that sources for metal types will continue for some years to come. One or two European foundries will remain, as will foundries in India and the Orient. The printer may be faced with having to seek these out, although there may also be commercial type importers willing to handle this traffic. Castcraft has imported and stocked European types as well as carrying on their own casting program. Recently the Oedipress has also embarked upon an import program, and there is a German dealer who refonts and sells used foundry type in considerable quantity.

Secondly, fine printing's face may alter considerably as metal faces that are not traditional book faces begin to be used for book typography. The use of Franklin Gothic by Claire Van Vliet, or Promotor, used by Roswitha Quadflieg, come to mind, and we may well anticipate the use of Craw Modern, Stymie, Univers, Helvetica, and even (oh horrors!) Chelten-ham. While the mere mention of some such faces gives this reporter severe mental indigestion, a considerable part of their total effect is dependent on *how* they are used; with which faces they are combined, how they harmonize with the illus-trations, colors, papers, open space, etc. In the hands of sen-sitive and adroit typographers, many non-traditional designs can look quite acceptable (and yes, one must admit there are a few typefaces which are indeed beyond salvage, if not also beyond satire). If there is a positive side to the shrinking of the typographic cornucopia, it is perhaps to encourage us to look more closely at our typographic resources and to reconsider the potential of the type designs we do have.

Thirdly, the rising number of amateurs with mechanical typesetting and typecasting ability augurs well for the future. As this equipment has become available on the secondhand market at attractive prices, those willing to expose their lungs to metal fumes and their epidermis to squirts of molten metal have enjoyed the satisfaction of seeing beautiful new types pour forth from the casting machine. A number of printers have acquired Linotype and Intertype machines (and a few have also installed Ludlow equipment) for the setting of slug composition. Others have acquired Monotype composition machinery or Thompson, Display, Giant, or Super Casters for the production of single types—either for their own composition or to supply fonts to others in a small way. The increased use of this equipment, perhaps in conjunction with foundry type, or perhaps even with the development of the capacity for matrix generation (either replicas of foundry faces or original designs) is perhaps close to an ideal answer to the problem of continuing the letterpress tradition. It allows for the personal involvement of the printer/compositor in the typesetting process; in spacing, line-end decisions, typographic refinements of kerning over periods and commas, cutting-in of awkward letter combinations, and the myriad other decisions which contribute to the craft's fascination. Whether the supply of type metal survives, and the amateurs maintain interest in making type, and fine printers without letter casting capacity connect with and patronize the casters—in short whether the whole infrastructure will work—remains to be seen.

A fourth possibility is that letterpress fine printers may well use state-of-the-art technology to generate film negatives from which letterpress plates may be made by any of several methods (Dycril, Nylaprint, and—not far away—laser etching). Such methods would open up a wide range of newer designs and of course bring, effortlessly, the advantages of kerning, revising, formatting, modification, etc. Perhaps the largest disadvantage is that the printer would probably not control the inputting as an in-house function and this would raise costs and lower both the personal control and satisfaction. There can be no question that a very large part of the fine press tradition resides in the sense of personal satisfaction arising from hands-on involvement in assembling the letters, making decisions, and using the best of one's tastes and talents to create a superior piece of printing.

Finally, there is a distinct possibility that fine printing will gradually shift from letterpress to offset and/or electrostatic imaging. So far we have seen little of this beyond a few avant garde efforts, but with continuing improvement in planographic and electrostatic methodology and their potential for both calligraphic and illustrative purposes, I cannot believe their increased use is anything other than inevitable.

If we consider the type designs available among the possibilities mentioned above, the use of foundry faces doubtless suffers because many foundries are no longer in business, those that are offer few book faces or text sizes, and custom castings are prohibitively expensive. In Barcelona, Fundición Tipográfica Neufville produces the splendid Bauer cutting of the Bodoni designs (the most elegant and inspired of all the Bodoni versions), Weiss, Horizon, and others in a complete range of sizes, if not always on the Pica system. D. Stempel still has Palatino, Optima, Sabon, and Garamond in their casting program and Haas has cut the Basilia design in recent times which, though little known, seems well suited for book work. This foundry, though small and stretched to capacity, possesses a huge inventory of matrices, a treasure house of great types, most of which are unfortunately not in their current program. Stephenson Blake continues to cast the venerable Caslon series, Lectura (acquired from Typefoundry Amsterdam), Perpetua, and other traditional faces. Johannes Wagner has the beautiful Hiero Rhode and its superb calligraphic italic with shortened capitals, and matrices for Delphin, Codex, Walbaum, Post Roman and Post Antiqua, Trumpf, etc. Ludwig & Mayer have matrices for Dominante, Firmin Didot, Rhapsodie, and—for the adventurous—Matheis Mobil. The selections from American Type Founders are currently almost exclusively in advertising and display faces, although they still have matrices for the Benton design of Garamond (to my mind one of the most consistent designs ever made, including the italic), Bulmer, Whitehall (née Benton), and the venerable Oxford.

Among the Linotype and Intertype faces one still encounters are Electra, Waverly, Caledonia, Fairfield, Granjon, and the excellent Monticello. But the selection of book faces from Monotype (both the scaled-down American operation, and the English Corporation, which excelled in producing type designs for book work) seems to me to be the most fruitful of all: names such as Bembo, Bell, Dante, Spectrum, Lutetia, Van Dijck, Berling, Sabon, Plantin, Baskerville, Centaur, Emerson, Poliphilus from England; and Italian Old Style, Janson, Granjon, Deepdene, Bulmer, and Californian from the United States come readily to mind. The ability not only to keyboard texts but also to cast fonts for hand composition by others augurs well for the future of this source. Monotype's wide assortment of accents and special swashes, as well as the possibility of investing in the custom cutting of a new character now and then, makes it a very attractive medium.

Without doubt the short term evolution of the field of fine book printing will preserve the traditional methods, letterforms, printing surfaces, and illustration techniques. The more dramatic, long term changes will begin as high technology equipment comes on the secondhand market at prices attractive and affordable to the small shop. In the final analysis, human nature being the infinitely adaptive phenomenon it is, we may expect to find a mixture of all these possibilities—from the anachronistic artificer who makes the type and paper and binds by hand, to the twenty-first century whiz kid who uses the very latest materials and processes. Like the artists and printers of both our times and of times past, the crucial point is not the superficials and the hardware, but whether the mind and spirit have contributed to the tasteful and appropriate interpretation of the text for the printer's ultimate audience—the reader. Considering the kind of individuals who are attracted to the fine printing field, I remain firmly optimistic for the future.

Addresses for a number of single type sources are listed below. I have not included Enschedé, Oxford, and Cambridge, The Smithsonian, and some others, as they are not actively engaged in casting type for sale. Of the various types mentioned above, their costs and availability must be ascertained by correspondence with their producers; specimens of these faces may be found in Jaspert, Berry, and Johnson's *Encyclopaedia of Type Faces*, and of course, in catalogues of the various foundries.

Current Suppliers of Metal Type

American Type Founders Inc., 200 Elmora Avenue, Elizabeth, New Jersey 07207

Barco (Acme) Type, 237 South Evergreen, Bensonville, Illinois 60106

Harold Berliner's Type Foundry, 224 Main Street, Nevada City, California 95959

Castcraft (Typefounders of Chicago), 1100 South Kostner Avenue, Chicago, Illinois 60624

The Dale Guild, Inc., 2205 Route 9, Southard, Howell, New Jersey 07731

Fundición Tipográfica Neufville, S.A., Travesera de Gracia 183, Barcelona-12, España

Golgonooza Type Foundry, Box 111, Ashuelot Village, New Hampshire 03441

Haas'sche Schriftgiesserei, Gutenbergstrasse 1, Münchenstein, Switzerland

Robert Halbert, Box 848, Tyler, Texas 75710

Hansestadt Letterfoundry, 261 East Fifth Street, St. Paul, Minnesota 55101

Richard Hopkins, Box 263, Terra Alta, West Virginia 26764

Mackenzie-Harris Corp., 460 Bryant Street, San Francisco, California 94107

The Monotype Corp. Ltd., Salfords, Redhill RH1 5JP England (matrices only)

The Oedipress, 3503 Rodman Street NW, Washington, DC 20008 (importer)

Out-of-Sorts Letter Foundery (sic), 25 Old Colony Drive, Larchmont, New York 10538

Quaker City Type Foundry, Route 3, Box 134, Honey Brook, Pennsylvania 19344

Sellner KG, Fr.-Ebert Strasse 48/58, 6301 Grossen Linden (Giessen), West Germany (used type)

D. Stempel Letter Service, 106–114 Hedderichstrasse, 6000 Frankfurt am Main-Süd, West Germany

Stephenson Blake & Co. Ltd., Sheaf Works, Maltravers Street, Sheffield S4 7YL England

Sterling Type Foundry, Box 50096, Castleton, Indiana 46250

Type-Studio SG, Goethestrasse 21, 8000 München 2, West Germany

Joh. Wagner Schriftgiesserei, Römerstrasse 35–37, 807 Ingolstadt am Donau, West Germany (type and matrices)

A New Civilité

Paul Hayden Duensing

A Short Review of Civilité History

"One day Robert Granjon came upon the completely natural idea of imitating the handwriting of his time in printing type; he cut punches, drove matrices and cast letters which matched his writing: that was in the year 1556. . . . The first book he printed with his new types was *Dialogue de la Vie et de la Mort* (1557)."* From that point onward, the story of the flowering and decay of the Civilité letterform becomes a tangled web, with fonts being used in a variety of locations, new fonts cut by other punchcutters, casual mixing of portions of this and that Civilité, and replacement sorts by still other hands.

The handwriting style upon which Granjon based his type had developed in France as scribes wrote more rapidly and with occasional flourishes and heavy pressure upon their split-nib pens, and indeed, Granjon referred to the style as *lettre française* (No. 1). When the English version of this script was considered by John Baildon in 1570, he called it "Secretary." "Civilité" is actually something of a nickname. The type seemed to the printers of that day to recommend itself particularly to certain kinds of printing, among which were poetry and belles-lettres, music, and texts dealing with morals.

1. A French cursive hand; manuscript leaf, 1494 (Bancroft Library, University of California, Berkeley).

Erasmus wrote one of these latter called *De Civilitate Morum Puerorum Libellus* which was translated into French as *La Civilité Puerile* (Lyons, 1558); thus the name Civilité. As the title indicates, the book set rules of etiquette and social behavior for children. Christophe Plantin used the Civilité in the same year to do another version of much the same topic, called *L'ABC*,

* Maurits Sabbe and Marius Audin, *Die Civilité Schriften*, Vienna, 1929.

2. Civilité cut by Robert Granjon for Christophe Plantin in 1557 and now in the collection of Joh. Enschedé en Zonen, Haarlem (lent through the kindness of Sem Hartz, former general art director of Enschedé en Zonen).

ou instruction pour les petits enfans. . . . Now whether all this had any effect upon the children is doubtful, but the net result was a useful addition to the typographer's selection of typefaces.

After Granjon's version of 1557 (No. 2), we believe other fonts were cut by Danfrie, 1558 (No. 3); Ameet Tavernier, 1559 and 1560; Granjon again about 1562–1568; Van den Keere, 1570; Wolsschaten, 1601; Cottrell about 1765; Rosart, 1768; and an unknown cutter of a copy of Breton's Gros Romain in 1811. A number of the punches and matrices remain today in the collections of the Musée Plantin-Moretus at Antwerp, Joh. Enschedé en Zonen, Haarlem, and the Deberny-Peignot collection at the Haas Typefoundry in Switzerland.

The Civilité design gradually died out as a type for general use, although there were occasional small volumes set in it in France, Belgium, Switzerland, and the Netherlands through the 1800s.

In the United States, a font of Civilité was cut by the Dickinson Type Foundry of Boston sometime between 1883 and 1894 in 18 point, under the name of Cursive Script (No. 4). It is shown in the Boston-Dickinson-Central catalogue of 1894 on page 378, and in the ATF Collective Specimen Book of 1894, and was subsequently picked up by the Hansen Type Foundry in their 1909 book. Several years ago my own small foundry came into possession of a set of matrices for this face, with a view of revising some characters and producing a viable font. Upon close inspection, however, the number of characters needing recutting was too formidable to contemplate and the project has languished.

It was not until 1922 that American Type Founders started Morris Fuller Benton upon designs of their Civilité (No. 5). Because of its wide availability and range of sizes (from 10 to 48 point), it became virtually the only version of this letterform known to most printers in the United States. The first matrices were cut 18 July 1923 and the last size (10 point) was completed 26 March 1924. Various alternate characters were cut until late 1924, including some latticed ornamental figures. In December 1924, a bolder version was cut in the 18-point size,

3. Deberny & Peignot Civilité descended from the Danfrie cutting of 1558 (from the Grabhorn Collection now in possession of the Arion Press).

but was never released. Ironically, over the years, the more authentic forms of *E H K d h l p* and *s* have been eliminated and the more debased forms have survived—presumably because they were more "normal" or at least less exotic in design.

4. Cursive Script cut by the Dickinson Type Foundry between 1883 and 1894 (from the collection of Paul Hayden Duensing).

These last two designs, the Dickinson Cursive Script and the ATF Civilité, were both badly misconceived renderings, drawn by artists not conversant with the history and traditions of the Civilité heritage. Many of the loops and flourishes were eliminated in favor of accommodating the automatic typecasting machine; the earlier fonts were, of course, hand cut and made for casting with hand molds. Some years ago a Swiss publisher asked Enschedé en Zonen to cast a font of of their Civilités for him. The foundry balked, but finally furnished an estimate of the cost, and to their surprise, the publisher accepted. When, however, the font was completed, the cost ran to three or four times the original estimate because of the difficulty in casting the long kerns and fragile hairlines and the great delicacy of the matrices. The incident calls to mind the words of Harry Carter in *A View of Early*

Typography: "Assertions of opinions that certain kinds of letters or whole scripts were avoided or handicapped in typography because they made difficulties for punchcutters and typefounders should be discounted. That printers fought shy of kinds of type that were expensive or troublesome to handle is true; but to a large extent they had to use them nevertheless. The comparative numbers of readers, printers and typefounders are such that the convenience of the least numerous gets very little consideration."

Zapf Civilité

As early as 1940 Hermann Zapf began sketches for a new typeface based on the historic Civilité model first cut by Robert Granjon in Lyon about 1558. These sketches were studies he had done starting in 1938 in connection with a Civilité for his *Pen and Graver*. In surveying the developmental history of letterforms, Zapf sketched out a delicate alphabet in July 1940, which was envisioned for production in perhaps 16- or 20-point Didot for the setting of poetry and other texts of an appropriate degree of fantasy and delicacy. The proposal was submitted to the D. Stempel Typefoundry of Frankfurt am Main, but the idea was dropped, most likely on the basis of its probable limited market. Typefoundries are, after all, devoted to the premise of mass production, and the very large expense attendant upon the development, cutting, trials, production, and promotion of a new metal type design precludes the realization of those designs without a wide base of demand. Thus the designs of industry and the marketplace receive first priority and the types for belles lettres come quite far behind. In this first design there is a close modeling upon traditional prototypes, although there are unmistakable nuances of the Zapf touch evident in the cohesiveness of the overall design and concept.

Some five years later between late October and mid-November of 1945, calligraphic trials were completed for a new Civilité form to be used in Manuscript No. 50, of Johann Wolfgang Goethe's *West-östlicher Divan*. This work was done in the style of an early Persian illuminated manuscript, written in gold and silver upon purple Japan paper. In this second design a greater progress toward freedom and individuality was evident in the formation of the characters.

For the first volume of the *Pen and Graver*, in 1949, Professor Zapf designed two pages using as *leitmotiv* the Civilité genre. These were cut by hand into lead plates by the brilliant Stempel punchcutter and Zapf's longtime friend and associate, August Rosenberger (1893–1980) (Illus. b, c).

5. The American Type Foundry Civilité, from an extensive specimen issued early in 1924. Note the variety of alternate forms.

Showing of the
complete font
of the alphabet,
cut in 24 point
on Didot system
by Paul H. Duensing
in Vicksburg,
Michigan

FIRST SPECIMEN OF ZAPF CIVILITÉ

A NEW TYPEFACE DESIGNED BY HERMANN ZAPF

THE PRIVATE TYPEFOUNDRY OF PAUL H. DUENSING

VICKSBURG/MICHIGAN·USA 49097

ert. möglich als Ligatur

frankfurt quod/psalm 105 stop the

zero my give de and per um yet

pfe and where know can ja retina

padova here besser wath stop every 3

yes mix thy & michael ? erg um 2

The first modern exhibition 1971

A h G B Q S E R U Y m

weite Zurichtung, Fette wie diese
Zeile in blauer Farbe

Lugdunum England The Shakespeare

Niedrige Versalien und grosse Ober- und Unterlängen

First sketches with
a broad-edged pen
on Japanese paper
for Zapf Civilité 1971
to test the weight,
the spacing, and to
compare alternate
letters for the
new type face

Ligatures marked
with asterisks.
Not all of
the proposals were
selected for the
final art work
to be cut in type
by Paul H. Duensing

a

The Civilité page
(No. 23)
from the 1952 edition
of *Pen and Graver*
published by
Museum Books, Inc.
New York,
with pencil sketches
of characters to be used
as a type face

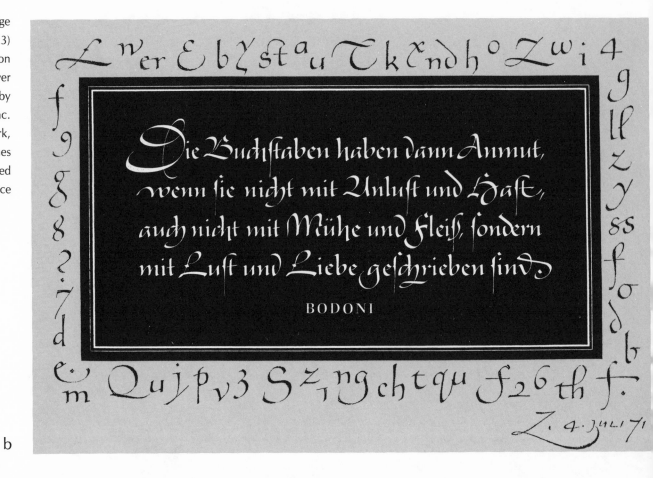

b

The Civilité alphabet
shown on page 22
of *Pen and Graver*.
Originally designed as
calligraphic examples,
but never intended
to be used for a type

The 25 pages of
Pen and Graver were
cut by hand
by the punch-cutter
August Rosenberger,
Frankfurt/Germany
(1893–1980)

c

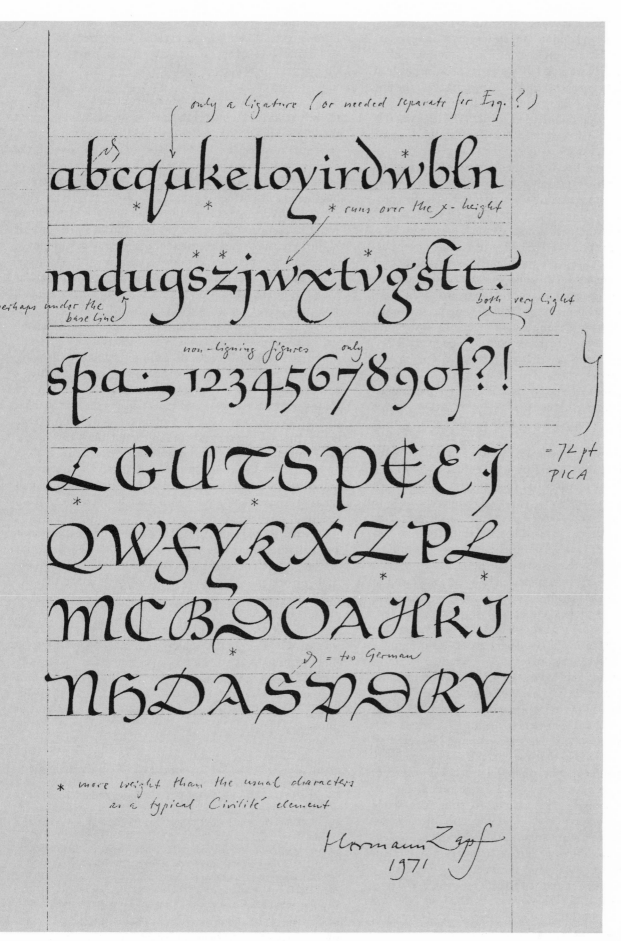

Retouched drawings done with the broad-edged pen of the final characters for the Civilité type. Executed in 1971 in 72 point size

Several proposals for ligatures, finials and for special swash letters to emphasize the calligraphic impression of Zapf Civilité

d

In the summer of 1971, the Association Typographique Internationale met in London. One steamy evening at a cocktail party at the flat of John Dreyfus, Hermann Zapf pulled me aside and said, "I want to talk with you, because I have in mind an idea for a typeface. I think there is a place [in the fine printing field] for a Civilité and I would like to know if you would agree to make the matrices for it." The idea was discussed briefly and it was decided that Zapf would do some sketches that were based on the historic Civilité but incorporating a slightly more free and contemporary feeling; I would repair to my private typefoundry and consider whether my competence in matrix making was overmatched by this proposal. (I eventually found it was, but by then it was too late.)

In due course the preliminary sketches arrived in Kalamazoo, Michigan (Illus. a). They were reviewed from the aspect of the limits of the pantograph engraving machine (with respect to the fineness of hairlines—in the present size the hairlines are held to .003″) and the requirements of the typecasting machine (in terms of the limits of kerns being worked through the delivery channel, etc.). In one or two minor instances, suggestions were made about the design of a letter, with reference to the differing perception of English and European language readers. The intent in every case, however, was to preserve the calligraphic freedom of the original design and the masterful interpretation of its creator, with a minimum of compromise occasioned by the matrix-cutting process (Illus. d).

Some matrices were generated in 1972 and proofs of the trial casts were sent to Frankfurt on 4 February, 1973. After a number of further matrices had been cut (interspersed with long periods of inactivity), I decided for technical reasons to scrap everything except the design and start over again. This was done; new patterns were made of the entire font and new matrices engraved. Proofs from trial casts were sent to Germany for review. By November 1983 the nearly completed font (two or three matrices remained to be cut) was taken to Zapf's studio in Darmstadt. The following month, a proof with corrections was received at my private typefoundry's new home in Vicksburg, Michigan and the work of revision extended into the spring of 1984. The work of "justifying" the matrices, as a final step before casting a full font, is the most exacting, laborious, and tedious step in the entire process. Each character must first be positioned on the body to align vertically, and secondly, left-to-right so that in any combination, there is an optical evenness to the fitting of letters with respect to their neighbors; exact records must be kept of all machine adjustments so that the character can be precisely repositioned in subsequent castings. This process is made very difficult in the present case by the fact that some characters have vestigal joining strokes on one or both sides, while others have no such strokes. Also, a difference of only .003″ in alignment is readily apparent to the practiced eye. In aggregate, the justification of the 105 characters in the present font consumed over 184 hours at the typecasting machine.

With the completion of the corrections, a small trial font was dispatched to the typographic laboratory of Professor Walter Wilkes at the Technische Hochschule in Darmstadt, where the accompanying specimen has been printed.

The first use of this type in the United States will be in Hermann Zapf's publication "Poetry through Typography"
to be printed by his friends Jim Yarnell, Wichita; Walter Hamady, Mt. Horeb, Wisconsin; Jerry Kelly, New York City; and Walter Wilkes, Darmstadt. Only seventy-five copies of this unique printing will be offered for sale.

Some Design Considerations

In the Civilité of Hermann Zapf, the designer has embodied the spirit of the historic letterform, while imparting a warm, contemporary feel to the individual letters. In general, the counters are more open and there is greater uniformity of letter width than in the historic model. The sudden shift from hairline to a heavy blob is gone, as are also the heavy and distracting diagonal strokes to the *d* and *v*. If the classic form could be compared to Bodoni or Didot in its stark contrast of thicks to thins, then the present design may be thought of as Garamond in its smooth shifts between weights of strokes.

Because of the prevalence of the first-person-singular pronoun in English, a "romanized" form of *I* was designed. The presence of variant forms of *b d g l A B D E H R* etc., several ligatures, and a nice selection of finials provides the font with considerable latitude for variety (page 37). The finials have been provided with "built-in" periods (which can, of course, be tooled away for line endings not needing a period). As the typographer chooses one or another form of these variants, the texture and appearance of the text changes subtly, becoming more dense or open, more familiar or exotic, rhythmic or staccato. In some letters such as *Q P G g z*, the contemporary feeling is quite strong, and a few such as *M N* and *Y* have an unexpected flippancy. The arabic numerals are, of course, a contemporary addition, and the small ear at the upper right corner of the zero differentiates it from the lower case letter.

The matrix maker of Zapf Civilité acknowledges the honor and educational experience of working with Professor Zapf on this project, and marvels at his great patience through the trials, errors, and long delays. It can only be hoped that the public reception of this design will justify the labors of its production.

In one of the Civilité plates in *Pen and Graver*, a text from Bodoni was used as the vehicle to display the calligraphy (Illus. b). In translation, this text says "Letters have grace only if they are not written with disgust and in haste, not with pain and laboriousness, but written with delight and with love." That is Hermann Zapf's thought in the creation of this type.

Carter, Harry. *A View of Early Typography up to about 1600*. Oxford: Oxford University Press, 1969.

Carter, Harry and H. D. L. Vervliet. *Civilité Types*. Oxford: Oxford University Press, 1966.

Corey, D. Steven. "On Type: Civilité," *Fine Print*, Vol. III, No. 3, 1977, pp. 71–73.

Sabbe, Maurits and Marius Audin. *Die Civilité Schriften des Robert Granjon in Lyon und die flaemischen Drucker des 16 Jahrhunderts*. Vienna: Bibliotheca Typographica, 1929.

Zapf, Hermann. *Pen and Graver*: Alphabets and pages of calligraphy by Hermann Zapf. Cut in metal by August Rosenberger. New York: Museum Books, 1952.

For a more extensive bibliography of books and articles about the history of Civilité types, mostly in French and Dutch, see the footnotes on pp. 1–10, Sabbe and Audin, op. cit.

Terpsichore and Typography

KRIS HOLMES

THIS YEAR THE FIRM DR.-ING. RUDOLF HELL, a manufacturer of computerized graphic arts equipment in Kiel, West Germany, will release a new script typeface family, Isadora, designed especially for digital composition. Isadora is a roundhand script in the pressure-pen style perfected by English writing masters of the seventeenth and eighteenth centuries, yet its forms are an expression of modern calligraphic ideas.

Fine Print has asked me to write about the design process of Isadora, to provide a view of how a type designer works in the modern era. Is type design different today from what it was in the "golden" (really, "leaden") age of Monotype, Linotype, and foundry type? Is the artist oppressed or aided by the computer in this post-Orwellian epoch? As a designer, I can only answer such questions subjectively, but I hope that an explanation of how I worked on this one design will allow readers to form their own more objective conclusions.

For me, the most important aspects of Isadora are that the design is *original*, and that it is derived from *pen-written* forms. Originality is unfortunately rare in type design today because the lack of copyright protection for typefaces has permitted plagiarism to become endemic in the typographic industry. Hence, many equipment manufacturers prefer imitation to inspiration. Yet, original type designs may always have been scarce. Stanley Morison wrote (anonymously) in the *Fleuron* in 1928 that the appearance of Jan van Krimpen's Lutetia "created something of a sensation, not only for its singular beauty and clarity of form, but because the face was in no recognizable way purloined from ancient times, but instead rose freshly from the reasoned canons of type design."

The pen is important because it was the tool with which I learned the art of letter design. More than a tool, the pen has been a means of understanding the guiding principles of the scribal arts. When I examine the writing of another scribe, whether a famous modern calligrapher like Hermann Zapf or an anonymous medieval monk, I feel a kinship of spirit through the traces of the pen. This feeling is not limited to Western scribes. In his treatise on calligraphy, *The Rose Garden of Art,* the Persian calligrapher Qadi Ahmad writes:

> The *qalam* [pen] is an artist and a painter.
> God created two kinds of *qalam*:
> The one, ravishing the soul, is from a plant
> And has become a sugarcane for the scribe;
> The other kind of *qalam* is from an animal,
> And it has acquired its scattering of pearls
> from the fountain of life.

Yet a typeface is not pen writing, but a mass-produced, industrial artifact. Today, letters can be replicated billions of times by sophisticated technology. The Arts & Crafts calligraphers and printers taught us to be true to materials, but they were thinking of pens, ink, foundry type, and handmade paper. Today the lettering artist is faced with computers, lasers, and cathode-ray tubes. How can we be true to these things? What would it mean to be false?

Isadora was conceived in the materials of handwriting and realized in the materials of high technology, but it expresses a single *design.* Where does a type design really begin? With handwriting? With ideas? With sketches? With proofs of trial characters? The roots of Isadora began early in my study of calligraphy, and as important as skill with a pen were the people who taught me the writing hands and conveyed in that teaching their ideas, their visions, and their dedication.

I studied calligraphy at Reed College with Lloyd Reynolds and Robert Palladino. Reynolds was a charismatic teacher who influenced several generations of West Coast calligraphers and teachers. His broad interest in Asian art and religion, in poetry and mythology, in American values and social change influenced many of his students beyond the acquisition of penmanship, though transmission of the italic hand was often accomplishment enough.

Lloyd was direct. He taught you true principles as he believed them. To get his message across, he was by turns erudite, rhapsodic, sermonizing, or critical. Often he was gruff, though the word can barely convey the full intensity of the man when, from over your shoulder, his piercing gaze would spy some infraction on your practice sheet, he would growl at you to move over, and he would grasp your pen in his gnarled hand and show you really how to *write*. To me, a farm girl who had come north from California's Central Valley to an avant-garde college, Reynolds was sometimes terrifying, though I have never forgotten his lessons.

My other teacher, Robert Palladino, had been a student both of Father Edward Catich, the expert on Roman inscriptional writing and carving, and of Reynolds. In addition to his majestic brush-written Roman capitals, Palladino had a command of medieval and classical scholarship that led me to take real pleasure in learning and using the less common but still beautiful scribal hands.

The path to Isadora began one day when I stopped by the rustic Reed College calligraphy studio after hours, as I often did, and found Lloyd there, practicing with his big Coit pen on a roll of butcher paper. He knew I was captivated by letters, and he suddenly put down his Coit, pulled his pipe out of his mouth and said, "If you're really interested in calligraphy, get interested in modern dance." Typically, he recommended not some new brand of pen, but a new mode of artistic expression. He believed that the power that guides the pen in its rhythmic dance across the page also guides the dancer, and he emphasized the first canon of Chinese painting, "Heavenly breath's rhythm vitalizes movement."

I began the study of modern dance at Reed with Judy Massee, herself a student of Martha Graham, and later I went to the Graham School in New York City. Dance became for me a lifelong practice as well as an inspiration for my work as a designer. For me, letters are a dance on the page, moving through space like spoken sounds move through time. Each of my designs is a new exploration of the rhythm that vitalizes motion. With Isadora, this exploration takes its most literal form.

But the typeface Isadora would take another sixteen years. I served a long apprenticeship, much of it trial and error of my own devising, since there are no schools for type design. Lloyd, and his simple wooden studio, and even his calligraphy program at Reed have all passed away, but letters still flow from the bamboo pen he cut for me.

My first work in type design was as part of a team with Hans Eduard Meier, a Swiss lettering artist, Dell Hymes, an American anthropological linguist, and Charles Bigelow. Working with Meier's Syntax typeface, Bigelow, Meier, and I created new designs for special characters to be used in typesetting Native American literary texts that Dell Hymes had newly shown to have originally been composed in verse form. Next, Bigelow and I designed a set of initials for the Arion Press's new edition of *Moby-Dick*. Working closely with the press proprietor, Andrew Hoyem, we developed a font of subtly "pictorial" letters whose design features seemed to convey (perhaps only in our imagination) some of the tension of taut ropes and billowing sails, of wicked harpoons and undulating whale flukes. The face was christened "Leviathan" and is now available for trade photocomposition on Berthold equipment. Later I went to work as a staff type designer at the Compugraphic Corporation which had just installed a fascinating computer software system for type design and production. Called Ikarus, it had been developed by Dr. Peter Karow in Hamburg, West Germany. At Compugraphic I gained experience both in computer-aided type design and in the day-to-day demands of industrial type production.

My association with the Hell firm began in 1980 when I started as a freelance designer. I proposed the Isadora design to the Hell type development committee, which included Hermann Zapf, Max Caflisch, and Peter Käpernick, manager of the Hell type production office. With Caflisch's advice and direction, Hell had begun an exciting program to produce original designs for digital composition, and had already released several fine new designs by Hermann Zapf and by Dutch type designer Gerard Unger. (For examples of work by Zapf, see *Fine Print*, January 1985; by Unger, April 1981; by Caflisch, April 1982.)

I presented my first design ideas in keyword form. Normally, a complete typeface alphabet should not be designed all at once, for usually the first proofs of a design will show that one has made some global miscalculation—for example straight stems that are too thick for the round bowls—which then must be laboriously corrected and modified throughout the whole alphabet. Sometimes more subtle visual problems will appear: the design will seem to have too much "sparkle," or perhaps not enough "spirit"; it is "awkward" or it is too "mannered."

To avoid some of these problems (though it seems they can never be entirely avoided without trial and error) the cautious designer chooses a few key letters and tests many design features on them before attempting a full alphabet. I presented the word "Hamburgefons" (a nonsense word that contains typical letterforms) in two weights of a new script type that I proposed to call Isadora. The keywords were approved by the Hell committee, and I started the long effort to turn designs of twelve test letters for each weight into a complete typeface of 146 characters. The keywords had been drawn in a few inspired weeks, but the finished types would take five more years.

The idea to design a new script for digital technology came while I was lettering the title of the July 1980 cover of *Fine Print*. In attempting to turn those letters into type, however, I found that I couldn't use the wildly cursive letter shapes of the cover because they couldn't be tamed to combine harmoniously in arbitrary arrangements without needing retouching or design modifications by a lettering artist. The type designer must give up the freedom of calligraphy or lettering that encourages each letter shape and space to be uniquely adjusted to the particular moment and task. Typefaces are systematic in their features and structures, and must be developed rationally. The task then becomes, how to make the letters work together as a team, without creating a rigid bureaucracy?

Frederic Goudy said, "The old fellows stole all of our best ideas." Although I wanted a new script that came from my own writing hand, I felt that a successful script typeface would require deeper understanding of the historical roundhand styles. Since my calligraphic education at Reed had concen-

Script letters written in preparation for the design of Isadora

Rough pencil sketches of Isadora

Original pencil drawings from the enlarged sketches (see next page)

WIDEN BOWL 1 PX.

Bit maps showing the positions of the individual bits that constitute the character images of letters *g* and *b*

Rough pencil sketches drawn to the approximate size of the proposed type

Enlargement of rough sketches to approximate Hell drawing size

Schriften ändern sich in ihrem Stil mit der Zeit und der Technik. Nicht nur die Technik der Schriftschöpfer, sondern auch die der Setz- und Druckmaschinen beeinflußt das Aussehen der Schrift. So ist es auch heute im Lichtsatz. Der Digiset setzt seine Schriftzeichen aus vielen kleinen Lichtlinien zusammen. Dabei entwickelt der Kathodenstrahl seine eigenen Gesetzmäßigkeiten, wie sie bei jedem technischen Vorgang auftreten. Wir überlassen die Gestaltung eines Zeichens nicht dem Zufall der linienweisen Aufzeichnung. Besonderheiten der Auflösung und des runden Lichtpunktes

nen Lichtlinien zusammen. Dabei entwickelt der Kathodenstrahl seine eigenen Gesetzmäßigkeiten, wie sie bei jedem technischen Vorgang auftreten. Wir überlassen die Gestaltung eines Zeichens

Setz- und Druckmaschinen beeinflußt das Aussehen der Schrift. So ist es auch heute im Lichtsatz. Der Digiset setzt seine Schriftzei-

Specimens of Isadora in 16-point, 24-point, and 28-point sizes

trated on the broad-edged pen of the Humanists, not the flexible, pointed pen of the later English writing masters, I pored over the rare script writing books in the Harvard Houghton Library. There I came to admire the work of many masters of the pressure-pen scripts, especially that of Joseph Champion, who published *Penmanship Illustrated* in 1759 and *The Penman's Employment* in 1763.

I was particularly enchanted by Champion's occasional use of a double line in the stem of lowercase *p*. I thought this delicate detail was especially appropriate for the precision of digital composition and felt that it could be extended over the entire alphabet to create a brilliant pattern in words and lines, and an exciting texture on the page. I also thought the tension of the thick stem and the thin hairline following and then emerging from it created an engaging visual rhythm. From the historical alphabets in the writing books, I made only sketches, not photographs, and later put the research sketches out of sight as well, so as not to be too influenced by the personal styles and ideas of the "old fellows." As a result, Isadora is a modern design based on certain principles of scripts, but is not an imitation of any one historical script.

I wanted a script for contemporary typography—big on the body, with a large x-height and relatively short ascenders and descenders. For clarity and strength, the capitals were to be proportioned like the classical Trajan capitals but with a dancelike rhythm that the Romans did not permit in state inscriptions, even when celebrating a victory over the Dacians. I wanted the capitals to compose well with the lower case but especially to be exciting in their own chorus. In the end, they were more closely based on the brush-written majuscules advocated by Catich and Palladino than on the sinuous shapes of the mercantilist pointed-pen cursive.

I wanted a lower case with a relatively simple joining scheme, because the tracery of complicated joins can sometimes obscure the letterforms themselves. Digital typesetting can provide extremely precise alignment and overlap, so there were no severe technical limitations, but I observed that routine joinery seemed to make the text pattern monotonous. After months of experiment, I decided to create a more syncopated rhythm, first emphasizing the direction and polarity of the letters by having asymmetrical joining strokes extending from the right side but not the left, and second, interrupting the linkage occasionally by designing some letters without joins. Reynolds had taught a formal italic hand without joins and an informal italic handwriting with joins, though he emphasized that some joins were "safe" and some "unsafe." I applied similar ideas to Isadora.

The name Isadora came to me during my drawing because Isadora Duncan had brought dance into the twentieth century and started the series of innovations that became the modern dance. According to accounts by her contemporaries, Isadora's dancing was strong as well as graceful and delicate; her formal inspiration was classical, but her ideas were modern, liberating, and sensational. I wanted my Isadora script to have the same qualities: inspired by classical forms but energized with a modern tempo. To keep the forms constantly alive in my mind, I wrote everything in script! My drawing table cover became a mosaic of grafitti, covered with experimental capitals and swashes. I wrote shopping lists and valentines, memos and correspondence, all in proto-Isadora. I

wrote in different colors and in different sizes, with different kinds of pencils and pens. Some forms emerged as favorites, but others I abandoned or filed away in an archive of designs that were not yet ready to be brought into the world.

When I finally had some small size letter shapes that I understood with my hands as well as my eyes, shapes that seemed to work well in text combinations, I had them photographically enlarged to the approximate size that Hell needed to do the digitization and production of type. I knew I was on the right track with Isadora when the assistant at the photo shop looked at the sketches and said, "This is great! Where can I get this type?" I thought of a line from a San Francisco Mime Troupe comedy that seemed to suit my aspirations for Isadora: "Here she is, that Tiny Titan of Terpsichore!"

I loved the texture and drama of those photo enlargements, but was shocked when I laid the Hell digital grid on top of them and saw that my dance would have to be disciplined. Hairlines had to be thickened, or they would disappear at 12 point and below. The gap between thick stem and delicate join line would have to be increased where the two were parallel, or it would fill in and coarsen the letter. Parameters had to be established for the whole design to make it work as a system of stem and round and hairline measures, of precise alignments and parallelisms, so that the Ikarus system could attempt to rationalize the letter elements in the discrete pixels (picture elements) of the digital raster. The letter-spacing, the letter shapes, and the letter joins had to be coordinated so that the joins would connect properly in every combination, and so that letter pairs without joins would appear to be properly spaced.

With all these features in mind, the keyword was extensively modified, redrawn, and then digitized with Ikarus and proofed on a digital typesetter. The first tests showed that many of the design concepts were well founded, because the odd words of text, made out of the letters available in the keywords, seemed to have some of the liveliness and grace that I had desired. Yet many problems that can be seen only in real composition in text sizes became evident as well, and the letters again underwent metamorphosis on my drawing board. When the keyword at last seemed right, I went on to draw the rest of the character set which includes capital and lower case alphabets, lining figures, old style figures, punctuation, foreign accents, ligatures, diphthongs, and assorted signs and symbols (total 146).

When these at last returned from their processing into patterns of computer bits and ultimate reconstruction as letters in pages of test text, I felt like a choreographer facing a class of delinquents. Certain letters refused to join the dance or somehow broke the rhythm—some were too fat, some too weak, some were wildly waving to everyone, and others were plodding and sullen. I had striven to keep their individual spirits alive, but now I would have to drill them into a working troupe. And so, more rehearsals, more exercises, more work at the barre, more work on the floor, until the letters step by step relinquished their individuality and began to form words, and the words became lines, and the lines, pages, and throughout them all was a pattern, a texture, a theme that I had glimpsed so long before, but could now at last see clearly. And so could anyone, for it was now a typeface, and no longer a vision.

The Dante Types

John Dreyfus

ABCDEFGHIJKLMNOPQRSTUVWXYZ abcdefghijklmnopqrstuvwxyzffffiflffifffl

ABCDEFGHIJKLMNOPQRSTUVWXYZ abcdefghijklmnopqrstuvwxyz ffffiflffifffl

ABCDEFGHIJKLMNOPQRSTUVWXYZ 1234567890$ & .,-;:!?"/()[]"?!:;-,. & $1234567890

synopsis in Monotype fourteen Didot

FINE PRINTING is impossible without fine types, as readers of *Fine Print* will readily agree. Yet most readers remain blissfully unaware of a *fine* type having been used, simply because its features do not interpose themselves distractingly between text and reader. So it is likely that few readers will be familiar with either the criteria or the techniques involved in designing and creating a new type. I will therefore try to illuminate some of the basic problems involved, while explaining how the late Giovanni Mardersteig (1892–1977) managed to make such a success of his Dante types.

Mardersteig was exceptionally well fitted to tackle all the problems which the task entailed. He had developed a fastidious taste for type through experience in publishing and book production, and also through his use of Giambattista Bodoni's historic types on a handpress which Mardersteig set up at Montagnola in 1922 and named the Officina Bodoni.[1] He had enough lettering skill to make very accurate drawings of the kinds of letters he later ordered to be made as fonts of type; and he had the good fortune to discover an exceptionally talented Parisian punchcutter, Charles Malin (1883–1955). Malin cut replacements for some of the original Bodoni punches borrowed by Mardersteig, and later cut punches for nearly all the new types Mardersteig designed for use at the Officina Bodoni. During a collaboration which lasted from the mid-1920s until the mid-1950s, Malin became a close friend of Mardersteig and a great admirer of his work.

Such advantages would have been of little use unless Mardersteig had first established in his own mind a crystal-clear idea of the kind of type he needed. By the time that he set about the task of making drawings for Dante, he had already used so many of the best available types that he knew exactly which characteristics would best suit his needs, both for hand composition at the Officina Bodoni and for mechanical composition at his Stamperia Valdonega (established in 1949) where he printed mechanically composed texts on power-operated presses. He had in mind a variety of uses for a new type which would differ from those he had hitherto used, and which would be superior in legibility and elegance. The new design was to comprise a roman and an italic, and the pair were conceived in a manner intended to make them work together more harmoniously in color and proportion than they do in either Monotype Bembo or Monotype Centaur, to cite only two of the many types he had previously used.

Dante italic owed a great deal to his fascination with the earliest fonts of italic cut between 1499 and 1516 by Francesco Griffo, a Bolognese craftsman about whom Mardersteig wrote with deep knowledge and insight.[2] In particular, the design of the lower case *g* in Dante italic reflects Mardersteig's study of Griffo's italics. The enlarged reproduction of the Dante italic *g*

g

makes it easier to pick out three features which combine to make this letter so pleasing and efficient. First, notice the balance and contrast between the shapes of the upper and lower bowls. Next, observe the unusually straight linking stroke between the two bowls, which nevertheless sweeps down gracefully into the broader curve of the lower bowl. And finally note how the distribution of weight between thick and thin strokes,

1. For a full account of this press, see Giovanni Mardersteig, *The Officina Bodoni: An Account of the Work of a Hand Press 1923–1977*, edited and translated by Hans Schmoller (Verona 1980), reviewed by me in *Fine Print* (October 1981).

2. See his essay "Aldu Manuzio e i Caratteri di Francesco Griffo da Bologna" in *Studi di Bibliografia e de Storia in Honore di Tammaro De Marinis* (Vatican City 1964) Vol. 3, pp. 105–47.

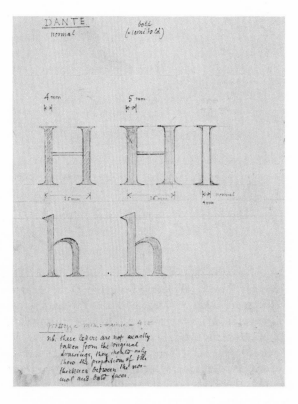

Sketch drawn by Dr. Mardersteig in 1961 indicating the weight and serif treatment to be followed by Matthew Carter in cutting four experimental punches for Dante Semi-bold, before the series went into production at the Monotype Works. Dr. Mardersteig's comment reads: "N. B. These letters are not exactly taken from the original drawings, they should only show the proportions of the thickness between normal and bold faces." The original was sketched with black and red pencils on a cream-colored sheet of wove paper measuring 8⅜ x 5⅞ inches; the marks of the pencils have become slightly rubbed through the sheet of paper having been folded first horizontally and then vertically, and the surface has become stained and soiled through use. The ratio between the normal and the semi-bold weight was set at 4:5.

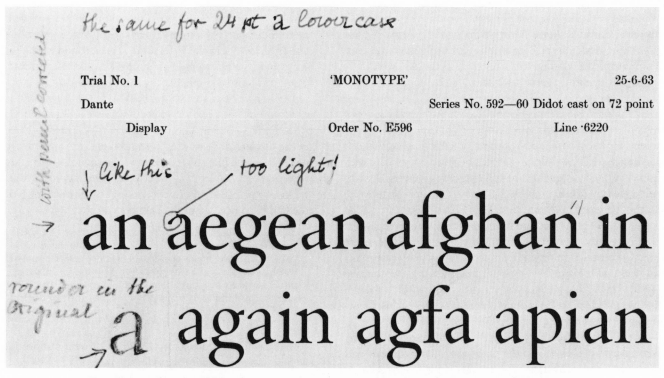

First trial proof produced by the Monotype Corporation on June 25, 1963 showing the 60 Didot size of Dante cast on a 72 point, with manuscript comments by Dr. Mardersteig indicating how he wanted the lower case *a* to be modified. This was the largest of the sizes created for production with the Monotype Super Caster. Because it was three times greater than the biggest size of original handcut Dante, it required sensitive interpretation by the type drawing office in the Monotype Works. This size received particularly close scrutiny by Dr. Mardersteig, who found that fine details, which had scarcely been visible earlier in the smaller sizes, immediately caught his eye when rendered on this much larger scale.

DANTE

Charles Malin, Paris

abcçdefghiıjklmnopqrstuvwxyzæœ ff fi fl ffi ffl ß   1 2 3 4 5 7 8 9 0 — ? ! ' , ;

A B C D E F G H I J K L M N O P Q R S T U V W X Y Z Æ Œ   *A B C D E F G H I J K L M N*

Madame & Monsieur Charles Malin
présentent au Docteur Giovanni MARDERSTEIG
et à sa famille leurs meilleurs vœux & souhaits de

abcdefghiìjklmnopqrstuvwxyz ʒ æ œ ç &   fi fl ff ffi ffl ß ä é è ö ü

ECHO BOCCACE OIEH Æ Œ

combined with the comparative straightness of the linking stroke and the careful placing and design of the ear at top right, help to create a letter which never jolts the eye as it traverses a line of text. In many other forms of italic *g*, the imbalance of the bowls, or the directional emphasis given to lines in the letter, which interrupts the natural movement of the reader's eye moving from left to right, turn this letter into a discordant element. As the pioneer of italic type, Griffo made several alternative forms for this tricky letter, and in one of them can be found a very similar balance of bowl shapes, and a similar treatment too of the link stroke between them. Dante roman also owes something to Griffo, who cut the superb roman used in Aldus's edition of Cardinal Pietro Bembo's dialogue *De Aetna* (Venice 1495), recut as Monotype Bembo in 1929; during the same year, Malin completed Mardersteig's design named Griffo which was based on the same source as Monotype Bembo, but which stayed closer to the fifteenth-century original.

By the time Mardersteig came to design Dante, he had got out of his system any previous desire to re-interpret earlier type designs. He had also gained a deep knowledge of what makes a type design lively, legible, and attractive. Working closely with a punchcutter had taught him to avoid excessive regularity as can be seen by comparing the top serif on the italic *d* of Dante and the top serifs on the letters *b*, *k*, and *l* in the same font. The specimen of Dante printed on page 222 of this issue gives readers an opportunity to observe how Mardersteig handled three aspects of type design which I consider to be particularly important. First, his treatment of serifs (or finial strokes); second, the way in which he contrives the transition from thick to thin strokes; and third, the handling of counters (the enclosed portions in letters such as *a, e, g, b, d*).[3]

Lines of types often have to be set without extra space being inserted between them. Under such conditions, the eye will read a line more easily if the type has been designed to create an impression of "tram lines" between which it can travel confidently and without distraction. These implied lines will empha-

size the base of the lower case characters and also the line formed by the tops of these characters when ascending strokes

punchcutter

in letters such as *b*, *f*, etc., are ignored. Two methods can be used to strengthen these lines. The baseline can be more clearly defined not only by the form of serifs at the feet of letters such as *h, i, k, l, m, n, r, u*, and *x*, but also by horizontal stress given to the rounded parts of letters such as the top of the lower bowl in *g*, and the top arc in the letters *b, d, h, m, n, p*, and *r*. The length and weight given to the bar of the *t* is also important; the Dante italic *t* is strengthened by brackets beneath its crossbar.

Dante owes its name to the book in which it was first used, an edition of Boccaccio's *Trattatello in Laude di Dante* published by the Officina Bodoni in the autumn of 1955. This short treatise on the life of Dante was set in the 10D and 12D sizes, with displayed lines and initials set in 20D and 30D capitals—all produced from punches cut by Malin between 1946 and 1952. Mardersteig was very generous in describing how important Malin's role had been in making the Dante series of types:

> . . . Charles Malin deserves credit for its success. Despite the many corrections I made after the first cutting, he always patiently helped me to achieve the balance and harmony I was looking for and he showed keen pleasure in the many improvements brought about by minor changes. Small revisions of this kind are always necessary, because it is difficult to visualize the effect of a tenfold reduction in letters drawn to a height of three to five centimeters."[4]

Malin's death in 1955 almost coincided with publication of the first book printed in Dante. In the 198 editions Mardersteig printed at the Officina Bodoni, he used this type more often than any other typeface. Dante appeared in forty-nine of the

---

3. Readers who require a compact and lucid explanation of what type design involves should study Hermann Zapf's *About Alphabets* republished by the M.I.T. Press as a paperback in 1970.

4. See *The Officina Bodoni* (Verona 1980), p. 104; Mardersteig included on pp. 229–34 a moving tribute to Malin, incorporating a memoir supplied in 1954 by a friend living in Paris who tried with limited success to extract biographical details and explanations of working methods from the reticent old punchcutter.

editions printed on the handpress at Verona. He often used a version cut by the Monotype Corporation, which manufactured Dante in a greater number of sizes than Malin had cut by hand. In addition a set of titlings and a semi-bold were made in the Monotype range.

Since the mid-1920s Mardersteig had been friendly with the Monotype Corporation's first typographical adviser, Stanley Morison. The two men had worked together on several typographical publications, and their correspondence was resumed after the end of World War II. Mardersteig also had previous experience of collaborating with Monotype staff in manufacturing a typeface from his own drawings. While working in the mid-1930s for the Clear-Type Press owned by the Scottish publishing house of William Collins, he had designed a proprietary typeface which was made for Collins at the Monotype Works. So Mardersteig gladly agreed to a suggestion from Morison that Dante should be adapted for Monotype composition. The idea was first put forward about a year before the handcut version was first seen by the public in 1955.

After I joined Monotype in 1955 as its second typographical adviser, we managed to persuade Mardersteig that Dante would stand a greater chance of success with Monotype users if it were to be provided with a semi-bold version. By that time Malin was dead, and as Mardersteig put it: "When the inventive powers of Malin came to an end, so did my pleasure in type designing."[5] Mardersteig was therefore reluctant to make a complete set of new drawings for a semi-bold; furthermore he had no interest in using a type of this kind in his own printing. Luckily I soon began to enjoy more frequent meetings with him because I had also become involved in his work for the Limited Editions Club of New York, for which I was serving as European consultant. Realizing how much he had grown used to the stimulus and flexibility of collaborating with a punchcutter, I suggested that if he would simply make a sketch indicating how he would like the semi-bold to be related to the normal Dante font, I would find a punchcutter to make four trial letters in order to establish an agreed basis on which the Type Drawing Office at the Monotype Works could prepare a complete set of ten-inch working designs for Dante semi-bold.

At this point I must explain that a letter cut on a punch by hand can be relatively easily and quickly modified to meet suggestions from a designer for minor improvements; whereas almost any alteration to a pantographically-cut punch used in manufacturing Monotype matrices entails the making of a new pattern, as well as cutting a replacement punch. Furthermore, a skilled hand punchcutter contributes his own interpretative skill in creating a type design; he can also make beautifully sharp smoke proofs direct from his punch as the work proceeds, and he can often do wonders by partially regrinding a punch that has already been cut, instead of starting again from scratch.

By 1961 I had become a friend of one English punchcutter who was in his early twenties, but who had enough skill to cut the four punches we needed for Dante semi-bold. Both Mardersteig and I already knew his father, Harry Carter, from whom he inherited great typographical talents. Matthew Carter (born 1937) had cut a fine set of numerals for the Westerham Press to use with Monotype Van Dijck. He had previously studied

5. See John Barr's catalogue *The Officina Bodoni* published for the British Library (London 1978), p. 58.

punchcutting at the Enschedé foundry in Haarlem, Holland, under an old German craftsman who had cut experimental punches that had been used in creating Monotype Van Dijck. Working from Mardersteig's sketch (see illustration, page 218), Matthew cut punches for two capitals, *H* and *E*, and for the lower case versions of the same letters. Examining proofs of these trial punches made it possible for Mardersteig to decide that he wanted heavier and less stubby serifs, and also to settle for a heavier weight of cross-bar in the *H*. These decisions naturally affected the structure of serifs throughout the font, and also they affected cross-bars in other letters such as *E* and *F*.

Progress on the normal weight could be made with fewer uncertainties because sizes already cut by Malin could be used as prototypes. The first proofs to be submitted to Mardersteig were of the 12D Monotype cutting. This was produced at the outset for two reasons: because it was urgently needed in Verona, and because it was easy to compare with Malin's version. Monotype based its working drawings on its analysis of Malin's 12D and 10D fonts. A few days after Mardersteig had enough time to study the first proof of the Monotype 12D cutting, he wrote on 3 May 1956 to the Monotype Works in England saying: "It is a great pleasure for me to be able to tell you that the result seems remarkably good and I would ask you thank all your colleagues to whose care and painstakingness I owe such a decisive contribution. If I have a few objections, I am sure that you [he was addressing the assistant general manager] and your collaborators will understand that perfection can never be achieved at the first attempt. In any case, my suggestions for improving the face are comparatively minor ones."

Comparatively minor they may have been, but none the less Mardersteig's first group of suggestions alone affected a total of seventeen characters. Many different factors were involved. In a few letters, he spotted irregularities of weight—the top serif in *N* was too light, and so was the extremity of the foot of *R*. A few other letters had been made too wide for his liking, in an attempt to use up available unit values. Occasionally he saw ways to improve on his original design as cut by Malin, so he set about providing new italic drawings for *B* and *r*. Later, as sizes never cut by Malin were added to the Monotype range, he perceived through photographic enlargements that a simple proportional increase from a smaller size would produce too coarse a result, so that a great many letters had to be modified.

Monotype's task in carrying out so many improvements was complicated by the fact that much of the work had to be done in its Frankfurt matrix-making department. This had been opened in an attempt to increase the Corporation's ability to fill the higher level of matrix orders received during the 1950s when a large number of new scripts had to be cut for developing countries, as well as servicing orders from customers in the Western world. Several key members of Monotype's staff traveled frequently between England and Frankfurt, but distance and the difference of language added to the difficulties of maintaining a consistent result. Matrices for the display sizes were later made at the Works in England, where the staff were direct inheritors of skills that had been practiced there since 1900.

To be fair to Mardersteig, I must add that his objections, criticisms, and suggestions were always expressed clearly and constructively; and in a few cases, he sensibly changed his mind about the design of an individual letter if he perceived a more satisfactory way of drawing it. Moreover, he knew from his

16 point

ABCDEFGHIJKLMNOPQRSTUVZ *ABCDEFGHIJKLMNOPQRSTUVZ*

abcdefghijklmnopqrstuvz *abcdefghijklmnopqrstuvz*

1234567890 *bdfghjklpqyffffiflffiffl* 1234567890

experience as a Monotype user about the limitations imposed on any design by the 18-unit system, and was perfectly ready to modify letters so as to make it easier to produce a really harmonious and evenly matched set of Monotype matrices for each size.

Eventually the range of sizes and varieties cut for the Dante family by the Monotype Corporation extended thus (using the contraction 6/7 to signify a 6 Didot point design cast on a 7 Anglo-American point body):

Dante Series 592:
6/7, 7/8, 8/9, 9/10, 10/11, 11/12, 12/13, 13/14, 14/16 (composition matrices); 18/20, 24/30, 36/36, 48/60, 60/72 (display matrices)
Dante Semi-Bold Series 682:
6/7, 7/8, 8/9, 9/10, 10/11, 11/12, 12/13, 14/16 (composition matrices)
Dante Titling Series 612:
16/18, 20/22, 28/30, 36/36 (display matrices)

In Verona, Mardersteig extended his collection of foundry sizes to include a 16-point Didot size cast in roman and italic. He also had alternative characters cast for several lower case letters in roman and even more numerous in italic for sizes from 14 to 16 point (as well as a complete 20-point italic, with variants). The 16 point type is shown above. They were manufactured by the Ruggero Olivieri foundry in Milan. The entire corpus of typesetting equipment now available for Dante shows how great a debt the printing trade owes to the activity of a private press. Discriminating printing houses in several European countries soon installed Monotype Dante. In England the first sets of matrices were bought by the Curwen Press, and others such as the Westerham Press soon followed suit. The matrices have also been used with great distinction in Germany, notably in publications of the Maximilian Gesellschaft.

Dante was the outcome of a lifetime devoted to fine printing. The type came into being not solely because Mardersteig had such a deep artistic and scholarly understanding of type design, but because he was also a *masterly* master-printer whose presswork was always magnificent. But it must be emphasized that his books were printed by letterpress; and it must be remembered that the technique of rolling ink onto types cast in relief differs from the technique of inking an offset plate onto which the image of types has been transferred photographically. Similarly, the technique of impressing a letter into the surface of a sheet of paper differs from the technique of transferring a film of type by offset onto the surface of a sheet of paper. Dante having been designed with the express intention of impressing its letters *into* and not *onto* paper, Mardersteig was opposed to its being adapted for photocomposition and offset printing. But since his death, a few craftsmen have become as skilled at modifying metal types into forms suitable for the new computer technology, as Malin was skilled at converting large two-dimensional drawings into much smaller three-dimensional punches.

Having examined a few examples of Dante set in hot metal but printed by offset from reproduction proofs, I believe that by sensitive interpretation, Dante could be successfully adapted for photocomposition. In the meantime I regard Dante as a double-barrelled success, because it hit the target first as a handcut design, and hit it again when reproduced by mechanized techniques in an extended range. Without Giovanni Mardersteig's watchful, patient, and courteous eye in control of both shots, the results could never have been of such superb quality.

This article has been set in Dante types at the type foundry of Michael & Winifred Bixler in Skaneateles, New York. Roman and italic are shown in nine- and ten-point type; nine-point semi-bold is also used.

The Punchcutter
in the Tower of Babel

PAUL HAYDEN DUENSING

BEFORE THE FIRST TYPE PUNCH was cut by Johann Gutenberg or one of his contemporaries, the letterforms of the time (the Gothic blackletter) were engraved on woodblocks to create a printing surface. The language of the text may have been Latin, or Dutch, or late Middle High German, but in any event the cutter was required to provide the "sorts" peculiar to the host language: accents, diphthongs, and long vowel marks, quite in addition to the myriad signs of contraction (the line over certain letters to indicate an abbreviated ending).

Some typical Latin abbreviations cut in type. The tradition was inherited from scribal practices used to produce justified columns as well as to save parchment.

When type punches were first cut for driving into copper to form matrices, the same requirements caused the punchcutter to add these sorts to his inventory of forms. In the very earliest of times this necessitated cutting a new punch for each different accent on the same letter, and we can see in the types of the 36-line and 42-line bibles the minor variations

Types from the 42-line Bible attributed to Johann Gutenberg showing variations in the basic letter as the accent changes, and therefore indicating that a new punch was cut for each accent. A number of characters were also cut in several widths to aid in justification of lines. (From Aloys Ruppel, *Johannes Gutenberg: sein Leben und sein Werk*. Berlin: Verlag Gebr. Mann, 1939. page 145.)

which verify that a totally new punch was generated each time. It was some years before an unknown punchcutter (some scholars identify Granjon, others Garamond), while perhaps impatiently cutting the third or fourth version of an accented *e*, thought of the expedient of the "stepped" punch.

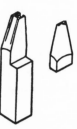

The "stepped" punch showing the recess cut to accommodate the accent. Thin shims behind the accent punch brought it up to the plane of the face of the punch, and heavy twine held it in place while being driven. (From L. Legros & J. Grant, *Typographical Printing-Surfaces*. London: Longmans, Green and Co., 1916, page 195, figs. 145–48.)

This clever innovation allowed—for the most part—each vowel to be cut only once, but punched repeatedly with the addition of an array of interchangeable "floating" accents (the exceptions were, of course, letters such as the Ç or ç, where the cedilla is *attached* to the character, or Ø, g or Ð where the lines intersect). There are a few cases where sorts of a given language must be cut specially in any case: ð, ß, Þ. From the punchcutter's point of view, the stepped accents also had the added advantage of enhancing the consistency of the letters, since the *e* was always the same *e* and not a near copy.[1] As the technology of typefounding has changed over the years, the methods of adding accents have also altered. The first major change was the introduction of separate piece-accents which were either added to the interline spaces in the case of capitals, or fitted to the space above a filed-down lowercase sort. Now these units worked well enough in sizes above the equivalent of Great Primer (18 point), but became nettlesome to use as text sizes became smaller, and there the stepped punch continued to be used.

1. A few months ago I cut a series of Middle High German accents for William Rueter's edition of the poems of Walter von der Vogelweide.

I cut an accent both above and below each vowel and then trimmed half of the cast letters at the top and the remainder at the bottom. Obviously only a few dozen of each were needed, and I doubt any commercial or reputable founder would operate this way.

The second solution came with the introduction of the electrotyping process in the 1800s. This invention allowed the assembly of a type character with a carefully fitted piece-accent to be placed in the electrolytic depositing tank. The resulting matrix then allowed the casting of the letter plus accent on one body, and obviated recutting. When Linn Boyd Benton invented the punchcutting pantograph, the time needed to generate a new character was greatly reduced, for the same character pattern could be used with various accent patterns. For the more common European accents, this method was universally used by both typefounders and manufacturers of composing matrices. In the case of more exotic or unusual accents, the matrix maker could often engrave the accent into a previously punched matrix. (Having done this on a number of occasions in my own small foundry, I can attest that it sounds far easier than it, in fact, is: the difficulty lies not in the cutting, which is a purely mechanical act, but in positioning the matrix properly under the cutter so the accent will be centered left and right and at the proper distance from the letter. An error of .003″ is readily detectable to the eye in many cases, particularly with ń, ḥ, ê, and č. The problem is greatly compounded in optically placing accents over italic characters. The latest wave of technology—digitized electronic character generation—has largely eliminated these concerns, if the system is properly programmed, by allowing virtually any accent to be added to any character (see also the generation of Kanji, page 105).

In examining the chronology of how language was adapted to the typefounding process, it is interesting to see what happened shortly after the invention of printing from movable type. As would be expected, each major geographic extension of the new technology brought additional linguistic adaptations, a development which was propelled, first, by the novelty of printing (once, that is, people got over the notion that it was an invention of the devil and stopped burning or jailing printers and typefounders) and by the economic incentive for those bringing the business of printing and publishing for the first time to a new location. Secondly, there was the "social" prestige accruing to the prince or church official who had a printing office in his realm (but again, this occurred only after the bias for hand-lettered texts and against mechanically produced volumes had abated). Obviously if a governing ruler sensed that the arrival of a press in his lands was inevitable, he would rather have it "in-house" where he could better control it. A third powerful influence was, of course, the need of the Catholic Church to both control the output of information to the faithful and to generate materials in other languages for conversion of the unsaved. The latter use of the press was, however, much slower in coming, for the earliest reaction of the clergy was alarm, and the desire, not so much to control, as to close off the dissemination of information to the masses. It was not until after Martin Luther had demonstrated the power of the press to communicate, and the literacy rate had begun to rise, that the Church began to use the press for its own purposes in a really vigorous program of proselytizing and conversion.

Of the three forces that accelerated the adaptation of printing and typemaking to foreign languages, the force of religion was by far the strongest. Not only the presses of the Propaganda Fide in Rome, which was the largest, oldest, and most prolific, but also the bible societies in every major country were very active in this area. The Dutch and English with their far-reaching empires were especially industrious in producing such materials. One need only skim the pages of *The Book of a Thousand Tongues* (London: United Bible Societies, 1972) to become aware of the volume and range of bible translation and printing throughout history. We see a particularly graphic example of both religion and national pride as motives in the story of Nikolas Kis who first translated and printed the bible in Hungarian (see *Fine Print*, January 1984), and while he may have expected to make an adequate income in addition to earning the thanks of his fellow countrymen, he was greatly disappointed in both areas. The lack of financial rewards for bringing the necessary accents to a type font to adapt it to another language was not the greatest of the disappointments suffered by the progenitors of such endeavors, however. In her book *The Printing Press as an Agent of Change*, Elizabeth Eisenstein relates the results of introducing vowel points to the Hebrew language and the reaction of the laity

נִמְצָא חֶרֶב וַחֲנִית בְּיַד כָּל־הָעָם אֲשֶׁר אֶת־שָׁאוּל
לְשָׁאוּל וְלִיוֹנָתָן בְּנוֹ : וַיֵּצֵא מַצַּב פְּלִשְׁתִּים אֶל־מַעֲבַר

Pointed Hebrew types. Some seventy characters have interior or superior accents; twenty-three inferior accents may be set under the plain or accented characters as well.

when they were able to properly assess the degree of indecision among translators of the Old Testament:

> Spanish Catholics . . . condemned a supplementary treatise added to Plantin's Antwerp Polyglot. This treatise explained problems associated with translating from the Hebrew and had already alarmed friendly censors in Louvain who advised its author to cut it out.
>
> If the faithful were to learn that a 'literal' translation from the Hebrew could be one of several possibilities because this language lacks vowels and several literal meanings could be taken from a single word, the authority of the Vulgate would be entirely undermined. In fact, the censors' fears were justified, for this very treatise was to be censured severely in Rome. [p. 332]

Nonetheless religion continued to be the prime mover of the expansion of the press (in the publishing context) and naturally of the adaptation of alphabets through the inclusion of accents and special characters as well as whole non-Latin fonts, as increasing numbers of vernacular languages were added to the typographic repertoire. In some cases the motive was to bring the bible to those who had previously been denied it, but there was also a concomitant and parallel movement to publish polyglot bibles of all the earliest texts in the original, that scholars might compare the various renditions in their quest for The True Word. In this latter field, no example could better illustrate than the famous Antwerp Polyglot Bible printed by Christophe Plantin in 1572. A considerable number of special sorts and indeed whole fonts were cut, huge quantities of type were cast, reams of paper made, hundreds of hours of tedious setting, proofing, correcting, printing, and distribution were amassed to make this project a fit tribute to its patron, King Philip II of Spain. At the crucial moment, His Majesty came up a little short of cash and thus drove Plantin to the brink of bankruptcy.

Following the first great waves of bibles for both the conversion of the laity and for the reverification of texts by scholars, there was a hiatus of nearly a century. The great fonts had been cut and were now used in publishing not only liturgical texts, but an ever-increasing number of commercial documents needed to reshape the world for the coming of industrialism. The esoteric fonts of the earlier periods became battered and were worked over from time to time by different hands. When they no longer answered the requirements, individual fonts were occasionally recut, but seldom with more than a remote harmony to the other sizes the printer might already possess. The energy of a renaissance, the impetus of a great groundswell of activity was lacking. During the eighteenth century there was a long, slow diminuendo of the production of exotic types.

In 1821 a young French army officer stationed in Egypt, Jean François Champollion, made known his success in finding a key to the translation of the writing systems of the ancient Egyptians: the text of the Rosetta Stone was translated! The text was less than earth shattering for its own content (some priests were honoring the young monarch Ptolemy Epiphanes on his ascension to the throne in 196 BC), but the news quickened the imagination of both the lay and the scholarly public. Not only were types cut to recapture the trilingual (hieroglyphic, demotic, and Greek) inscriptions of the Stone itself, but now that the key was known, to reassess

Hieroglyphics have been cut in both solid and outline forms; a complete font comprises well over 3,000 characters. Demotic script was more like an everyday script for ancient Egyptians, being less monumental and quicker to write than the pictograms.

and retranslate earlier texts. Scholars studied other exotic languages—both classic and contemporary—and, of course, needed new fonts to tell the world of their latest discoveries. By reason of national interest in their countryman's achievement, the French were vigorous in their pursuit of foreign language studies, and the pedantic English and Germans were not far behind. Indeed, the public, or at least the portion of it with literary interests, became quite fascinated with the novelty of strange jumbles of symbols which might mean a great deal to one reader familiar with the language and nothing to another unversed in it. "Hieroglyphics" became a buzz-word for the mysterious, ineffable, and supernatural. The novelty of polyglotism was evident in 1798, when

> Dr. [Edmund] Fry put forth proposals for publishing the important philological work on which he has for sixteen years been engaged, and which, in the following year,

Illyrian and Indian scripts probably cut on wood for Fry's *Pantographia* of 1798.

was issued under the title *Pantographia*, with a dedication to Sir Joseph Banks, President of the Royal Society. This important work, which displays great learning and research, was favourably received. It exhibits upwards of 200 alphabets, amongst which are 18 varieties of the Chaldee and no less than 39 of the Greek. Many of the letters were cut by the author expressly for the work, under the direction or with the advice of some of the most eminent scholars of the day, and not a few subsequently found a place among the specimens of [his] foundry. (Talbot Baines Reed, *A History of the Old English Letter Foundries*. London: Faber & Faber, 1952. p. 305)

Three of the numerous Greek fonts represented in Fry's *Pantographia*. Some of what were represented as different alphabets were, in reality, only minor geographic variants interpreted by various scribes.

As this fad built over time, there was a tendency to increase the number and variety of languages and writing systems represented. The text—because of the largely religious impetus to the expansion of exotic fonts—was frequently The Lord's Prayer. It was short, widely known, and available in a huge number of tongues; sometimes it was virtually the only thing available in a given language, where an accurate English translation was also available. The silliness reached some kind of climax in the 1850s when Prince Louis-Lucien Bonaparte, a nephew of the emperor, published a book which purported to render accurately one of several biblical verses in an impressive array of 300 languages and a wide variety of scripts. The book was a great success and much admired in its author's social circles. It was, however, more the product of showmanship than scholarship, and was to be found more often in the fashionable salon than in the scholar's study.

In the first third of the nineteenth century, mechanical

typecasting became a reality. The need for vernacular scripts increased with the accelerated tempo of business and the rise in literacy. Around the middle of the century the feasibility of "growing" matrices electrolytically greatly speeded the production of new type designs. In Europe and the New World, this meant a great proliferation of the so-called Gay Nineties faces, characterized by decoration, ornamentation, and excesses of every kind. In other parts of the world, and particularly in the Orient, with its problems of producing huge numbers of matrices for each size of type, the process was ideal. Characters could be quickly and cheaply cut by hand in soft metal, and placed in the plating bath with little further care other than eventual justification of the matrix. The process was much quicker, cheaper, and easier than cutting the character by hand on the end of a steel punch, a process perhaps also including counter-punches, and then hardening, drawing, and driving the punch, followed by justification. Good or bad, typefaces proliferated.

At the turn of the century, three inventions added even more velocity to the proliferation of type fonts: the invention of the punchcutting pantograph by Linn Boyd Benton, the Linotype by Ottmar Mergenthaler, and the Monotype by Tolbert Lanston. The first literally made possible the commercial viability of the other two, for without a large supply of matrices produced quickly and cheaply, there was little hope for any mechanical type composing system. Perhaps equally important was the ability of the pantograph to generate for a broken punch a replacement which was indistinguishable from the original. The printer of 1734 may have been relatively unconcerned that the lowercase g in his font of Great Primer ordered this year did not perfectly match that supplied last year, but to the owner of a Linotype or Monotype it mattered rather a great deal, particularly in the latter machine where the unit values or set widths of the characters have to be within very close tolerances.

As might be expected, the early use of these machines was concentrated on the production of roman and italic types for the European languages. As the Western markets became saturated, Linotype, Monotype, and Intertype began to attack the problem of the non-Latin alphabets. They solved the problem of setting Arabic and Hebrew (both of which are read from right to left) by the ingenious expedient of punching the characters upside down on the matrices, and then adding simple mechanisms which either turned the slug around during delivery, or reversed the direction of delivery of the lines upon the galley. (The Monotype Corporation Ltd. also developed a clever three-bladed mold which could either cover or expose the accents punched below and/or above the

الطابع اذا اراد حفظ بعض مجموعات فقـد يتيسر

Arabic as cut by Linotype & Machinery Ltd. In the Linotype system, each accent combination was represented by a separate matrix. Mixer machines and a considerable number of side sorts were necessary for composition.

central character, saving a huge number of nearly duplicate matrices and simplifying the setting procedures for Arabic in particular.)

As the punchcutting pantograph was adapted to the engraving of matrices instead of punches, it was avidly adopted by the typefoundries. Semi-skilled labor was able to produce three to eight times as many characters as a skilled hand punchcutter. The languages of the Near East became well represented both as type and as matrix systems, and the manufacturers now tackled the scripts of the Indian subcontinent: Devanagari (for Hindi) came first, followed by Tamil, Gujurathi, Kannada, Oriya, and others. Most of the languages of Africa were reduced to representation in the Latin alphabet augmented by varying numbers of diacritical marks, since most were without an endogenus writing system. (A definitive linguistic study has yet to be made of what subtle differences in phonomes may have been lost by laying the grid of the roman alphabet over the sound systems of these languages, particularly in the case of certain African dialects which use clicks, lip smacks, humming, or whistling sounds [rising, falling, or steady] as linguistic elements. Since, in quite a few cases, the original assignment of symbols was made by those more adequately trained as theologians than as scientific linguists, the accuracy of their transcription may be seriously called into question, but the true sounds may never be recaptured.)

Following World War II, the United Nations was particularly important as a force to further literacy in developing countries. The impact of their intentions had scarcely begun to manifest itself in the production of new type fonts, when the feasibility of setting type first photographically and then electronically became commercially viable.

The new modality brought with it the answer to a number of vexing problems inherent in earlier composition systems. Photographic typesetting meant that character exposures could overlap (which, of course, meant that the bane of metal typefounders—true joining scripts—now became not only

Ἐξ ὅλων τῶν μεγαλυτέρων καὶ πλέον χρησίμων
ἀνακαλύψεων, ὁ Πλάτων, τὴν ἀνακάλυψιν τῆς
Ἐξ ὅλων τῶν μεγαλυτέρων καὶ πλέον χρησίμων
ἀνακαλύψεων, ὁ Πλάτων, τὴν ἀνακάλυψιν τῆς ἀλφαβη

The setting of accented Greek is made more complex by the presence of up to twenty-three variant breathing marks and accents over or under characters. This is Gill Sans Upright Greek 572 cut by the Monotype Corporation.

وفى خلال بضع سنوات ـ بعد عام ١٩١٨ ـ
بدأ صنع ماكينة المونوتيب وأدواتها اللازمة جميعها فى
مصانع إنجلترا ، ومن ثم أعد برنامج جبار لم يسبق
له مثيل فى تاريخ الطباعة ولم تقم بمثله شركة أخرى ،

Monotype Arabic, set using a three-part mould blade to allow casting or masking of upper and/or lower accent marks.

possible but easy). The joining of letters in Arabic and Manchurian alphabets to form words could now be seamless and smooth; the tiny white spaces between characters would be seen no more. A considerable number of "floating" accents

仰休任件 冴准冶

Because the basic forms are stored in computer memory, they may be called up for either right, left, superior, central, or inferior positions to form compound Kanji of Chinese characters.

could be double exposed over any given character (which reduced the problem in setting Greek, with its accents and breathing marks, to relatively simple procedures); a range of sizes could be set from one set of master film negatives (admittedly with some loss of design quality until computer-aided refinement programs came on stream), and even the complexities of setting Chinese and the Chinese-derived Japanese Kanji have been simplified. Instead of thousands of individual characters on the keyboard, the radicals or sub-assemblies of the characters are stored and combined as superiors and/or right-and-left components to create the full character.

The level of activity surveyed in this overview may seem concentrated and frenetic when compressed into the compass of a few paragraphs, but chronologically it spans many centuries, thousands of characters, huge numbers of man hours, thousands of books, pamphlets, newspapers, bibles, types, and matrices . . . and not a few unheralded failures along with several triumphs. The future may well contain optical scanning devices, translation programs, and other things undreamed of, but the accomplishments of these dedicated, patient, and skilled workers who were the first to deal with the problems of recording the world's thoughts in type will be evident as long as books survive.

BIBLIOGRAPHY

Augustin, J. J. *Schriftproben: Orientalischer Typen wie auch phonetische Akzente.* Glückstadt & Hamburg: J. J. Augustin Co., 1933.

Bloomfield, Leonard. *Language.* New York: Henry Holt & Co., 1950.

Brill, E. J. *Specimens of Type Faces.* Leiden: E. J. Brill, Printers, 1953.

Budge, Sir E. A. Walles. *The Rosetta Stone and the Decipherment of Egyptian Hieroglyphics.* London: The Religious Tract Society, 1929.

Cambridge History of the Bible. 3 vols. Cambridge: Cambridge University Press, 1963–70.

Daley, P. V. "Phonetics and the Printer," *The Monotype Recorder.* Vol. 37 No. 1, Spring 1938, pp. 15–18.

Eisenstein, Elizabeth. *The Printing Press as an Agent of Change.* 2 vols. Cambridge: Cambridge University Press, 1979.

Fry, Edmund. *Pantographia; containing accurate copies of all the known Alphabets in the World, together with an English explanation of the peculiar Force or Power of each Letter; to which are added specimens of all well authenticated Oral Languages; forming a comprehensive Digest of Phonology.* Type Street [London]: Edmund Fry, Letter-founder, 1799.

Hendricks, Donald. "Profitless Printing: Publication of the Polyglots," *J of Libr Hist II,* April 1967, pp. 98–116.

Imprimerie Nationale. *Cabinet des Poinçons de l'Imprimerie Nationale de France.* Paris: Imprimerie Nationale, 1948.

——— *Spécimen des Types Divers de l'Imprimerie Nationale/Types Ètrangeres.* Paris: Imprimerie Nationale, 1878.

Lyons, John. *Language and Linguistics.* New York: Cambridge University Press, 1984.

[Rooses, Max, ed.] *Index Characterum architypographiae . . .* Paris: Editions du Musée Plantin-Moretus, 1905.

Monotype Corporation Limited. *The Monotype Recorder* [Special issue: "Easing the Adventure into Literacy"] Vol. 42 No. 3, Winter 1962–63.

——— *The Monotype Recorder* [Special issue: "Languages of the World"] Vol. 4 No. 42, Summer 1963.

Nakanishi, Akira. *Writing Systems of the World.* Rutland, Vermont: Charles E. Tuttle Co., 1980.

[Plantin, Christophe] *Index sive specimen characterum Christophori Plantini* [reprint of 1924]. Anvers: Christophe Plantin, 1567.

Veyrin-Forrer, Jeanne, & André Jammes. *Les Premiers Caractères de l'Imprimerie Royale. Étude sur un spécimen inconnu de 1643.* Paris: 1958.

West, Fred. *The Way of Language.* New York: Harcourt, Brace, Jovanovich, 1975.

Notes on Frederic Warde and the True Story of His Arrighi Type

HERBERT H. JOHNSON

WHEN an impoverished Frederic Warde[1] died on July 31, 1939, the last of a line of Wards, who had settled in Rhode Island in 1673, he was quite alone, with no wife, no children nor any other immediate family. His typographic achievement seemed destined to go unrecognized and unrecorded. He was a major American typographer and type designer, a star who rose quickly above the horizon, shone brilliantly—albeit briefly—and slowly, painfully faded. His intimate friends were few, for Warde was not given to making easy friendships nor to confiding in others. But he chose his intimates well; they formed his "family,"[2] and how fortunate we are that they chose to memorialize this hitherto largely unrecognized star in the typographic firmament. Under the sympathetic leadership of Alfred C. Howell, Warde's "family" gathered together his personal papers and books and commissioned Will Ransom to write the superb biographical portrait which appeared in *Print*.[3]

Ransom had full access to the Warde archives and to both oral and written communications with the family and other friends. Warde's intimates vetted Ransom's manuscript with two notable results. One is the lack of factual errors—there is just one, of little significance.[4] The other result is the deliberate omission of mention of Warde's marriage to and subsequent divorce from Beatrice Lamberton (Becker) Warde.

This essay is part of a larger work on Frederic Warde which the author intends to dedicate, when published, to Paul Standard and to the memory of Franz Hess.

Reference to and quotations from the following letters are given with the permission of The Carl and Lily Pforzheimer Foundation, Inc.: Miscellaneous Manuscripts 3371, 3372, 3378, 3373, 3374, letters from Frederic Warde to Bruce Rogers, and 3419, a letter from Stanley Morison to Bruce Rogers.

1. Warde began altering his given name, Arthur Frederick Ward, in 1918 by dropping his Christian name and adding the terminal "e" to the family name. Shortly thereafter he experimented with two variants of Frederick—Frederique and Frederic—before settling on the latter in 1926. During the "Frederique" period, his wife Beatrice affectionately addressed him as "Kiou."
2. Other "family" members included Crosby Gaige (1882–1949), Sherman Post Haight (d. 1980) and his wife Anne Lyons Haight (1895–1977), Henry Watson Kent (1866–1948), and Bruce Rogers (1870–1957), among others.
3. Vol. II, No. 1, May–June, 1941. Ransom's biography of Warde is prerequisite reading for this article.
4. Warde's father died in 1903, not 1900.

In fact, Ransom did record these events but removed them at the request of Henry Watson Kent who, in deleting the offending paragraph from his copy of the draft manuscript, commented, "Is this necessary?" Kent's editorial pressure was most unfortunate and the offense to Beatrice entirely inappropriate. The Wardes had attempted to create an open marriage in which each was free to lead his and her own life. That the marriage failed was far less important than the implication that Beatrice was more to blame than Frederic.

Twenty-five years later the Warde archives were donated to the Grolier Club by Howell's son, Alfred H. Howell, a past president of the Club. In the spring of 1985 Jerry Kelly and George Laws, both calligrapher-designers, honored Frederic Warde by mounting a revealing exhibition of his work at the Grolier Club. The multifaceted Warde was shown as superb typographer, insightful writer and critic, and outstanding calligrapher, and as the designer of the Arrighi types. There were numerous examples of Warde's sensitive book work and his preference for understatement rather than elaboration. He was quite innovative in his use of fleurons, but he deliberately abandoned this talent in favor of precise lines of caps and small caps, classically positioned and spaced, giving a somewhat reserved quality to many of his title pages. His color design sketches—or *marques*, as he preferred to call them—are often things of rare beauty and, when compared to the printed volumes, clearly demonstrate the inherent superiority of pen and brush and ink. The display of Warde's Italian running hand, which he developed sometime before 1917, added another distinctive element to this beautifully mounted exhibit.[5]

5. In an unusual step, Kelly and Laws included a large amount of Warde's personal papers never before exhibited. These discoveries from the largely unexplored archives tended, however, to diffuse the focus of the exhibit, raising more questions about Warde than they answered. Yet this bold, intentional step was taken in order to display some fascinating nuggets which, it is hoped, would elicit comments about Warde from those who knew him and those few who have studied his *oeuvre*, his life, and his times. The result, I am told, was most gratifying and there is every reason to believe the Grolier Club will mount a comprehensive exhibit in 1994 to celebrate Warde's centenary.

The lovely invitation for the exhibit was sympathetically designed and beautifully printed by George Laws in a way that would have pleased even Warde. As one who has studied Warde's work for the past ten years, I applaud Kelly and Laws, the Grolier Club, and the Club's incomparable librarian, Robert Nikirk, for their splendid efforts.

Arthur Frederick Ward was born July 29, 1894 in Wells, Minnesota. Little is known of his life before October 24, 1917 when he entered the United States Army Air Service, except for an intriguing photograph of New York's "Polyclinic Hospital Surgical Class, 1915" in which he appears as Dr. A. F. Warde. We have a record of his military service showing his enlistment at San Diego, California, and Aviation Cadet training with the 35th Squadron, United States Army School of Military Aeronautics at the University of California, Berkeley. He was honorably discharged on January 10, 1919.

In his unpublished notes of an interview with Beatrice Warde in 1965, Paul Bennett recorded her memories of first meeting Frederic Warde at her mother's home the night of the false Armistice, 1918. A friend of her mother had brought him. "He had the finest voice I'd ever heard in a man. I was attracted to him at once. He was in uniform, a second lieutenant with wings, a handsome man. We got along well. Mother never cared for him but she didn't forbid me to see him, though she did dominate my life." The eighteen-year-old Beatrice was smitten, and she and Warde continued to see each other until his return to San Diego. After mustering out of the Army Air Service in 1919, Warde hurried back to New York to continue his affair with Beatrice; "Mother called me Freddie's concubine."[6]

May Lamberton Becker, Beatrice's mother, children's book critic of the New York *Herald Tribune*, pulled strings to land Frederic a position with the MacMillan Company. The peripatetic Warde was soon after employed as supervisor of Monotype composition by The Printing House of William Edwin Rudge, first in New York in 1919 and later at the new plant in Mount Vernon, just north of the city. In 1920, during his earlier period with Rudge, he spent some time at the Lanston Monotype Company's school in Philadelphia learning the finer points of machine operation in order to better supervise the stringent composition requirements of Bruce Rogers, who had just begun working with Rudge.

The first of many BR benefactions to Warde was an introduction to William A. Kittredge, formerly of the Riverside Press, then art director of Franklin Printing Company in Philadelphia. The two men formed a lasting friendship which continued through personal visits and voluminous correspondence for the rest of Warde's life. By 1921 Warde had achieved a well-deserved reputation as a man of great technical expertise and one who could be depended upon to produce composition of the highest quality. Though still very much reserved, he began to draw closer to BR and his circle of friends. When Beatrice graduated from Barnard College in June, she needed only to get Warde to ask BR to write to his longtime friend Henry Lewis Bullen, and the job as Bullen's assistant at the American Type Founders Company library was hers. "Frederic and I married in 1921. He was twenty-seven and I, eighteen [sic]. We agreed each would not interfere with the other; each would live his own life."[7]

Warde began to accept public speaking engagements in 1922, both in New York and Philadelphia. After much coaxing from Kittredge and others, Warde applied for the position of director of printing at Princeton University Press. He was appointed in July and began work the first day of August. One of his Princeton colleagues attested to Warde's well-known reputation for perfection. He described him as "ruthless" in his quest for fine printing and "unreasonable" when his goals were not met. But the quality of bookmaking there improved dramatically. The firm foundation laid by Warde later enabled P. J. Conkwright to rise to preeminence as a typographer at Princeton.

Warde wrought even greater gains in his career over the next two years. His essay, "Book Printing in America as One of the Fine Arts," appeared in *The New York Times Book Review*.[8] Three books he designed were selected by the American Institute of Graphic Arts for the 1924 "Fifty Books of the Year" exhibition and four others were selected a year later. Samples of his work received notice in both *The Inland Printer* and *The American Printer*, sometimes accompanied by photographs or illustrations. He arranged his first exhibit, "Survivals in the Fine Art of Printing" in June 1924, at the art museum of Princeton University. A handsome catalogue which he wrote, designed, and printed was available for sale. He was also at this time corresponding with Stephenson Blake and Company of Sheffield, England, regarding the cutting of a new roman typeface which he had designed (it was never cut). By the autumn of 1924, Frederic decided to spend the following year abroad, and even though it was not a particularly appropriate time for Beatrice to leave American Type Founders (Bullen was still in Europe on a year's sabbatical), the two of them resigned their respective positions in December. They sailed for France on the *Aquitania*, arriving in Cherbourg on January 7, 1925, to begin a new and potentially more exciting typographical adventure.

They were met in Cherbourg by Stanley Morison, who had studiously cultivated the Wardes' friendship while in America, and had made many promises to them of gainful employment.[9] As gentle as doves, the Wardes were not as wise as "the Serpent,"[10] which was Beatrice's nickname for Morison at the time. From the beginning, plans were made for the Wardes to write for *The Fleuron*. Frederic would write a lengthy appraisal of the work of Bruce Rogers, getting BR's cooperation and approval. Warde's notebook for the period shows an outline and rough draft of some portions of the text. In reporting to BR on their first month in Europe, Warde writes of spending a week in Paris, moving to Ebury Street in London, visiting BR's old friends in Cambridge, and working on an article about BR which would be finished in about two weeks. A glance at BR's revisions on his set of galley proofs indicates that he was not entirely pleased with Warde's performance. In later years, Beatrice often "confided," *sotto voce* and not for publication, that she wrote the *Fleuron* article for Frederic,[11] but Warde's notebook seems to indicate otherwise.

Warde's work for *The Monotype Recorder* began almost immediately, too, for his rather interestingly designed cover full of type ornaments appeared on the March–April 1925 issue.[12] He may not have been responsible for the ghastly yellow ink

6. Bennett interview, June 4, 1965.
7. *Ibid.*

8. December 23, 1923.
9. Nicolas Barker, *Stanley Morison*. Cambridge, Massachusetts: Harvard University Press, 1972. Pp. 163 and 182–183.
10. In a letter from Beatrice to her mother, 7 November 1925.
11. *Op. cit.*, Bennett.
12. No. 206, March–April, 1925.

"...the artistic quality of a type-letter is determined by its degree of grace of line and proportion.

The standards of grace & proportion are to be looked for in the natural motions of the pen."

W. A. Dwiggins

"...the artistic quality of a type-letter is determined by its degree of grace of line and proportion.

The standards of grace & proportion are to be looked for in the natural motions of the pen."

W. A. Dwiggins

The original Arrighi (top) and Vicenza variant, type set courtesy of The Press in Tuscany Alley, San Francisco.

"...the artistic quality of a type-letter is determined by its degree of grace of line and proportion.
The standards of grace & proportion are to be looked for in the natural motions of the pen."

W. A. Dwiggins

Monotype Arrighi

The design for Arrighi passed through three distinct phases. The principal differences occur in the upper serifs of ascending letters. In the original Arrighi, they were pear-shaped and extended to the right. In the second version, these serifs extend to the left and are set at a sharp angle. The variant was used, for the first and perhaps only time, in Plato's *Crito*, printed for Warde by the Officina Bodoni at Montagnola in 1926, and it was there called Vicenza. The capitals for both are roman. When Warde adapted it for Monotype, the ascenders were shortened, the serifs made horizontal, and the weight of the entire face was slightly increased.

on medium blue stock, which transformed one of the more satisfying *Recorder* designs into an unappealing cover. But the point is that full-page reproductions from Arrighi's *Coryciana* (1524), and the *Writing Book of Gerardus Mercator* (1540) both appear as samples of calligraphy for Beatrice's first *Recorder* article, which appears in this issue. Warde at this time most likely began his search for a punchcutter for his new italic type, which was based upon the types of Arrighi as shown in the *Coryciana*.

For most of 1925, Warde spent about ten days each month in Paris, and by May 29 he was confident enough in what he had seen of the city to write Rogers suggesting that they set up a press in France. He boasted of knowing all "the worthwhile printers, typefounders, and papermakers." More importantly, he writes of his new type: "The thought occurred to me that there must be a real old-fashioned punch-cutter somewhere in the city. Working on that notion, I discovered him—a wonderful fellow. A type face (italic) is now being cut by him, and he has surmounted the most difficult problems in cutting the punches. . . . He's a real craftsman, he keeps to a rigid diet and goes to bed early every night in order to keep his hands steady and his head clear." Warde does not give the name of his punchcutter, Georges Plumet, but each Arrighi punch has Plumet's stamp impressed in its shank. Warde goes on to give costs for punches and matrices and offers to supervise the cutting of any types or ornaments which Rogers might design.

This, in 1925, is the earliest mention I have found thus far of Warde's Arrighi type. This letter, therefore, is of great importance, in view of the unnecessary controversy that has subsequently arisen regarding the type's design and ownership. The controversy was precipitated by a claim first made

in 1950 by Stanley Morison that he, Morison, was responsible for the creation of Arrighi type.[13] The claim had lain dormant for seventeen years until it exploded in 1967 with the publication of *The Elegies of a Glass Adonis*.[14] The printer of the book, Will Carter, included a "Typographical Note" which had as its premise the validity of the following statement written in 1953 by Morison: "The punches were cut by Charles Malin in Paris. . . . I think I was solely responsible for the negotiations and began the discussion with Malin . . . and handed the matter over to Warde when he later arrived in this country [Warde arrived in January 1925]. This was because I found he knew more about these matters than I did."[15]

There are three, possibly four, untruths in this short paragraph: First, that the punches were cut by Malin, when they were, in fact, cut by Georges Plumet of G. & H. Plumet, 174 rue Vercingetorix, Paris xiv. (See illustrations.) Second, that Morison knew of the work on Arrighi type before June, 1925. It was only in June that he first learned of Warde's type. Morison then rushed to arrange with the poet Robert Bridges the first use of the new type for a first printing of Bridges's poems in

13. John Carter, *A Handlist of the Writings of Stanley Morison*. With some notes by Mr. Morison. Cambridge: Privately printed, 1950, p. 11. Morison writes, "First modern use of Arrighi's italic, re-cut, at the instance of S.M., by the punch-cutter Charles Malin of the Rue Didot, Paris, to whom he had been introduced by F. Thibaudeau of G. Peignot & Fils, typefounders. Malin also cut the first sizes, capitals and lower case, of *Perpetua*. The detailed supervision of the *Arrighi* re-cutting was undertaken by Frederic Warde, for whom was written the introduction, now superseded by James Wardrop's celebrated article on Arrighi in *Signature* of July 1939."
14. Poems by C. A. Trypanis. New York: Chilmark Press, 1967.
15. As printed in *Elegies*.

Frederic Warde used his Arrighi types in this book printed under his supervision at the Officina Bodoni.

Page from the introduction by Stanley Morison.

Facsimile page from the book showing the original italic type of Ludovico degli Arrighi. Warde's type was based on a lighter version that appeared in Arrighi's *Coryciana*, 1524.

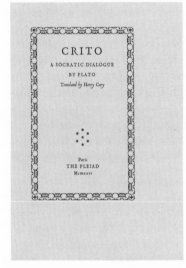

The second book printed at the Officina Bodoni used the Vicenza variant of Warde's Arrighi type.

Page spread from the *Crito*.

Both Frederic and Beatrice Warde attended the "bon voyage" luncheon for Henry Lewis Bullen on December 11, 1923 at the ATF Library. Frederic is second from the right, middle row, seated; Beatrice is obvious. Besides Bullen (seated front row center with bow tie), other notables include Robert W. Nelson, ATF's president (on Bullen's left), and Bruce Rogers (seated second row, left), peering over the shoulder of Linn Boyd Benton. Morris Fuller Benton is standing to the left of his father. Photograph from *Inland Printer*, January 1924.

The books reproduced above are courtesy of the Gleeson Library, Special Collections, University of San Francisco.

The Tapestry.[16] Warde was duped into believing that Morison had *already* committed him and his type to the Bridges volume. When Morison—with the Wardes in tow—first went to visit the poet and his wife on June 28, no such commitment had been made. In fact, the Bridges were not even expecting the Wardes.[17] But, writing to Bruce Rogers from the Mitre Hotel, Oxford, June 27 [28], 1925, Warde again mentions his italic type. He, Beatrice, and Morison had just returned from a visit with Robert Bridges at his home near Oxford. "As you know," Warde reports, "the poet is a crank about calligraphy, and he is much pleased to have this book of his [*The Tapestry*] in this new type, which is calligraphic—but not so much as the Blado." In a later letter to BR, March 18, 1926, Warde was still deceived: "Morison had committed himself to old Bob Bridges to use my type—and that caused him to be more interested in coughing up a few poems—I suppose." Third, work on the Arrighi began not before Warde arrived in January 1925, but in April or early May 1925, when Warde, not Morison, gave Plumet the commission. The typefounders, P. Ribadeau-Dumas, 25 rue Julie, Paris XIV, began casting type in July. And fourth, there was nothing in Warde's background to suggest that he knew more about cutting punches by hand than Morison did. It appears that Morison was trying to circumscribe Warde's role in the initiation and design of Arrighi by limiting his responsibility to supervising the punchcutter.

There are three letters which sum up the Arrighi story very nicely. The first is from Bruce Rogers to Morison, February 19, 1926, in which he makes, as he admits, "an impudent and cheeky request." Bruce Rogers sought permission to use Arrighi type in a John Drinkwater volume[18]—and he wanted permission to enlarge the type and print from photoengravings[19]—and he also wanted to substitute sloped capitals from another unspecified typeface—and he also wanted, of course, Morison and Warde to set the type for him. The operative sentence appears on the last page of this letter: "I wouldn't have bothered you at all with this request had I not heard from F.W. that he is in Lugano, for an indefinite stay, printing a book." This indicates that BR considered Warde, not Morison, responsible for the type. BR did not know that Warde had a second font of the Arrighi with him when he arrived at the Officina Bodoni in Lugano. Morison's reply, dated March 17, is curiously cavalier: "By all means do whatever you jolly well like with the caps," but he does not respond to BR's other requests, no doubt because he knew he did not have the proprietary right to do so.

But Warde, writing from Switzerland, March 18, 1926, has the last word:

Dear Bruce Rogers:
I have just received Morison's letter [with BR's own letter enclosed] about your request to use some of "*my*" Arrighi type. I say "MY" to make it clear that the punches, matrices and type are, and have been from the beginning *entirely* mine and fully paid for.

The idea was mine—that of first finding the punchcutter and having the fount cut—and *all* the work preparing the designs and in cooperating with the French punch-cutter has been done by me alone.

The work of Frederic Warde carried him throughout Europe in 1925, 1926, and part of 1927. He did a large amount of research and worked with a number of fine printers in France, Germany, and Holland. His most important connection was with the Officina Bodoni in Montagnola di Lugano. The Officina Bodoni had been established in 1923 by Dr. Hans (later, Giovanni) Mardersteig and within three years had earned its reputation as a fine hand press. It was here that Warde brought his Arrighi and "Brevi"[20] types in early 1926. Mardersteig has written of their relationship:

Warde's intention was to establish a hand press and produce bibliophile editions for a few American publishers who had shown interest. He was therefore keen on studying my printing methods at Montagnola. We agreed that he should come with his new type and that between us we would produce two books: he would do the composition and I was to look after the printing. Our joint work began at the end of January 1926 with [the] facsimile edition of Vicentino's writing book, in which the introduction by Stanley Morison was set in the newly cut italic. We became good friends in the course of our stimulating collaboration; only rarely in later years did I similarly enjoy working with a colleague. We used to have fun building castles in the air, thinking up neglected titles for future publication, and making lists of suitable type-faces. We even had plans to establish the perfect small machine-equipped press in Florence, to which a printing-school, grandly called the 'Academia Typographica,' was to be attached.[21]

Warde returned to the United States in October 1927. He had already begun publishing under The Pleiad imprint and was looking for an American co-publisher/distributor. He talked to Princeton University Press, but before any decision had been made, BR persuaded him to return to Rudge's. But soon BR had another plan and I do not doubt that he discussed it with Warde when they met in November. "New problems arose when the Monotype Company in Philadelphia asked me to let them cut the [Centaur] design for their machines," wrote BR in 1949. "For various reasons, but chiefly because I was going back to England for a year or two, it was decided to have it made by the Monotype Company of London." BR now put his plan into action, ". . . an italic was desirable; but not feeling prepared or competent to design such a letter I prevailed upon Frederic Warde to revise his beautiful Arrighi to accompany the Roman founts."[22] In early 1928, Warde was on his way back to England.

---

16. *The Tapestry*. London: Privately printed, 1925.
17. See Morison/Bridges correspondence as quoted in *The Printer and the Poet*, by Nicolas Barker. Cambridge: privately printed, 1970, p. 17.
18. *Persephone*. New York: William Edwin Rudge, 1926. The Arrighi type was used, not the Vicenza variant.
19. Plates were used but the type was reproduced in its original size.

20. In one of his notebooks, Warde wrote out the colophon for Plato's *Crito* using "Brevi" as the name of his new variant, now known as Vicenza. In the printed volume he merely states, "being the first use of a new type."
21. *The Officina Bodoni: An Account of the Work of a Hand Press, 1923–1977.* Verona: Edizioni Valdonega, 1980.
22. *The Centaur Types*. Chicago: October House, 1949.

The Arrighi punches cut by Georges Plumet in 1925. Included are alternate forms and variant ascending characters for the Vicenza font. The lower case *e* (third from right, middle row) has a circumflex tied to its shank.

The Arrighi matrices struck by the Parisian typefounders P. Ribadeau-Dumas in 1925.

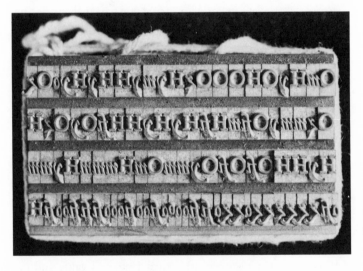

Plumet's device is stamped upon the shank of each of the Arrighi punches.

Trial characters of Arrighi cast for alignment by P. Ribadeau-Dumas.

A close-up of the alternate forms of lower case *g*.

Warde also commissioned Plumet to cut these six ornaments. The two on the left were used in Bridges' *The Tapestry*.

Morison was quick to communicate to his friend D.B. Updike what small news of their plans he had heard on the Monotype grapevine, probably from Beatrice:

> There is a little Monotype news which I would like to communicate to you in confidence. Mr. Bruce Rogers, it seems, has made an arrangement with Mr. Best[23] by which Centaur is to be cut as a Monotype face; but Mr. Rogers would not allow this to be done in the United States, having insisted that it be cut here. This has been arranged and I believe Mr. Rogers is about to leave the United States for this and such other countries as Europe has to offer. I gather that Warde is accompanying him on some sort of typographical *Wanderjahre*.[24]

If Morison had had any proprietary right to the Arrighi type, or the use of the name "Arrighi," he surely would have exercised his right at this time.

The marriage of Centaur and Arrighi was a great success aesthetically, but financially it was a disaster for Warde because very few sets of matrices were sold during his lifetime. Warde had been living on almost no money for nearly five years and he decided to return to the United States in 1929 to regain financial stability. He and Crosby Gaige established the Watch Hill Press at Gaige's country estate in upper Westchester County, but before they had barely begun work, the stock market crash destroyed their dreams.

The last years of Warde's short life were given over to sundry endeavors. He remained with the printing house of William Edwin Rudge until Rudge's death in 1932. Then followed an association with the Morrill Press and a partnership in McFarlane, Warde, McFarlane, Publishers, before joining Oxford University Press in New York as production manager. He designed a number of volumes for George Macy's Limited Editions Club, as well as Macy's *The Dolphin*, Number 1. (The story of Warde's role in the creation of *The Dolphin* has yet to be told.)

Warde devoted himself more and more to his avocations—landscape design, the culinary arts, perfume making, and the construction of intricate watches and chronometers. Both his finances and his bookmaking suffered and, when the end came in July 1939, I doubt that he could have been happy with the unfortunate twists and turns of his life.

In 1967, following the publication in *The Elegies of a Glass Adonis* of Morison's claim to the Arrighi designs, Paul Standard wrote a brilliant defense of the primacy of Warde's role in a review that appeared in *Publisher's Weekly*.[25] Standard wrote, "During Warde's lifetime no question was ever raised as to his [Warde's] capacity to design the Monotype Arrighi or the earlier foundry version. Any doubt on this point puts the burden of proof on the doubter—and such proof has yet to appear." Some printing experts on both sides of the Atlantic agreed with him, but no further documentary evidence was offered to refute Morison's claim. Therefore, those who read Carter's Note in *Elegies* without also having read Standard's

review believed that Morison had a role in the creation of the Arrighi type.

Two later books which deal with the subject in some detail, *The Printer and the Poet* (1970) and *Stanley Morison* (1972), both by Nicolas Barker, put forth elaborate defenses of Morison's 1953 statement. At the same time they inadvertently add more evidence which casts an unmistakable shadow on Morison's claim. Neither book presents any documentary evidence showing that Morison had ever met or corresponded with the punchcutter Georges Plumet. Every piece of correspondence with Plumet and the typefoundry Ribadeau-Dumas, including payment of invoices, are acknowledged to have been handled by Warde.

If only some friend had questioned Morison in 1953 about the discrepancy between his own statement and that of Ransom in the Warde biography (where Plumet is credited with the punchcutting), Morison could have retreated gracefully. But even then he probably would not have done so, because beginning about 1949, Stanley Morison began "recreating" his own typographic past. A little change of date here, a little memory enhancement there, and soon he had a background for himself more comprehensive than even a Morison could have experienced. I have no doubt that there were those in England who felt he had gone too far, but by 1953 Morison was an industry, and those who were writing about him and about the typography of the period were reluctant to tarnish his image. This was equally true in America. Those writers who rode the Morison line saw the impending crash when James Moran published *Stanley Morison: His Typographic Achievement*[26] in 1971. Moran first said what other printing historians were thinking: that Morison frequently took credit for the work of others, that he constantly revised dates to demonstrate that he had seen, heard, thought, wrote, or acquired something before his colleagues had.

Claims written by Morison about his career should not be accepted without documentation or independent corroboration. That many aspects of the work of a brilliant scholar and writer are now suspect is indeed sad. In his defense, I can only say that Morison continued to overstate his spheres of influence and achievement perhaps in an attempt to keep the publicity mill churning at Monotype Corporation.

It is appropriate to close this account with the story of the sale, "loss," and recovery of the Arrighi punches and matrices. Will Carter recounts part of the story of their sale to the Metropolitan Museum of Art in 1934; here are the details. Henry Watson Kent, recognizing the great historical value and intrinsic beauty of these artifacts, prevailed upon Warde to sell them to the Museum, together with his correspondence and other records relating thereto. The Arrighi punches and matrices were stored at the Museum Press along with the original type purchased by them in 1926. Kent had every confidence that the Museum Press had earned the right to be a permanent part of the Metropolitan, and, as a consequence, that the Arrighi would be preserved there as a memorial to himself as well as to Warde.

But after Kent's death in 1948, his successor as secretary to the Metropolitan declared the Museum Press redundant and ordered it sold to the highest bidder. Ostensibly, there were

23. Harvey D. Best was president of Lanston Monotype Company, Philadelphia.
24. *Stanley Morison and D. B. Updike: Selected Correspondence.* Edited by David McKitterick. New York: Moretus Press, 1979, pp. 162–63.
25. "Who Designed and Cut the Arrighi types?", November 6, 1967.

26. Published by Lund Humphries, London, 1971.

only a few items of real monetary value: several Monotype machines with matrices and several printing presses. The most valuable items were the hieroglyphic types (called Gardiner), specially cut and cast for the Museum, which were required for a continuing series of Egyptological studies. While Kent was turning over in his grave, a friend came to the rescue.

For some years prior to his retirement, Kent had employed the services of Huxley House Typographers in New York. One of their principals, Franz Hess, was a man of great culture and charm. Hess was born in Germany and came to the United States in the 1920s. About 1928, he set up a typesetting plant in New York which eventually grew to become Huxley House. He no doubt knew the story of the Arrighi treasure and of Kent's attachment to it. In September 1949, Huxley House purchased the entire composing room of the Museum Press for $1,900. The Museum stated in the sale agreement that the Arrighi and hieroglyphic "types" remained the property of the Metropolitan and could not be sold or destroyed, but that all other contents of the composing room were included in the sale. This included the Arrighi punches and matrices. When Huxley House was dissolved in the 1960s, the hieroglyphic types were transferred to the Press of A. Colish in Mount Vernon, where they are in use today. I have been unable to locate the Arrighi type, but I suspect that it was offered back to the Metropolitan and that they, not having used the type for years, ordered it destroyed. Fortunately, Hess did not allow the Arrighi punches and matrices to leave his possession when Huxley House's assets were sold. Instead, he purchased them himself and stored them at his home in Lime Rock, Connecticut. That he intended to find a permanent repository for the Arrighi artifacts was not in doubt, nor did he ever make a secret of his ownership of this material. He knew that the Arrighi punches and matrices, unlike the type, were unencumbered by the agreement with the Metropolitan.

Hess died before he could complete his plans. Shortly thereafter, his widow, Mrs. Flora Hess, invited to lunch her Connecticut neighbor, the eminent printer-typographer Joseph Blumenthal. The purpose of the lunch, besides the companionship of two gentle and gracious people, was to discuss the "old printing stuff" she had uncovered in Franz's study. A few days after their meeting, I received a most exciting letter from my friend Joe. To shorten an otherwise long story, I will only say that without the generosity, support, and good offices of Joseph Blumenthal, the Arrighi punches and matrices might now be lost or destroyed. Though I admit to a small part in this story, it was Joe who convinced Flora Hess of the historical importance of this material and the advisability of donating it to Rochester Institute of Technology as a memorial to her late husband. The Arrighi now rests in honored glory in the Cary Collection there, thanks to Joseph Blumenthal and Flora Hess.

And Frederic Warde? He rests in equally honored glory at Watch Hill Farm, thanks to the preservation of the records of his achievement.

Sidenote on Greek Type

Mark Livingston

THE QUESTION of what Greek characters *should* look like—and it is odd that the Greeks themselves, in arbiting so much else of our taste and very sense of form, should have responded to it so indifferently—is a complex study. What we know as lower case is a script form largely the invention of medieval scribes (whose worst tendencies toward crypticism found their way into the early Greek typefaces); while the capitals derive from incised, linear inscriptions far older and less stylized than, say, the Trajan capitals.

In twentieth-century Greek type design we find, after centuries of rather more separate than equal evolution, a movement to romanize the lower case letters by assimilating them with the upright forms evolved for Latin—and at the same time some regard stirring for the Greek capitals as entities in themselves, not merely modified romans. Reconciling Greek letters' split heritage (a duality not only historical, but also technical: founded in chisels, styli, and quillpoints) remains perhaps the single greatest hardship facing the Greek type designer—a challenge only heightened by the plethora of breathing and accent marks strewn through, above, and below the writing line.

Optima Greek was worked into type by Matthew Carter, from Hermann Zapf's designs, for issuance by Mergenthaler Linotype in the early 1970s. The design came as part of a campaign led by Linotype's Athens agent, Costas Chryssochoides, to popularize a range of traditional and modern roman-based faces, which included Greek "clones" of Baskerville, Century Schoolbook, Helvetica, Souvenir, and Times Roman. Zapf/Carter's skillful adaptation of the weight, color, and character of the roman, in Optima Greek, brooks little quibbling; for all the Greek letters' great commotion of curves, diacritics, and erratic finishings, the continuity is nearly seamless.

> Κοντὰ τρεῖς ἑβδομάδες ἔτσι κάμνει.
> Ἀρρώστησεν ὁ νοῦς του ἀπὸ λαγνεία.
> Στὸ στόμα του μείνανε τὰ φιλιά.

Happily, others of the best modern type designers also picked up the gauntlet—especially, it seems, during the 1920s and 1950s—doubtless with the sense of returning to the first water of their stock in trade. While pioneers' honors are due the early Greek hands and typefaces, our own century has

arguably innovated and advanced Greek type design as much again as all those preceding it—ironically, as the demand for Greek has dropped off.

Victor Scholderer's New Hellenic, developed for the Monotype Corporation with Stanley Morison's help, and issued in 1927 with much pomp and circumstance, goes far in setting formal standards for the "new classicism." Its upright forms; slight flaring in the limbs; minimized serifs, beaks, hooks, and loops (in the lower case), and broadened lobes, recall Edward Johnston's pivotal London Underground "gothic" letters, while retaining some sense of script. The types issued as Monotype Gill Sans Greek between 1954–59, and based on Eric Gill's great sans serif roman (of the same vintage as the New Hellenic), make a more radical effort to purify the letterforms according to Gill's graver's instincts, releasing incised forms of exemplary clarity and beauty. In weight and character the standard Gill Sans Upright (Monotype No. 572) reads perhaps more heavily and monotonously than New Hellenic, but the extreme form, the Light (No. 672), strikes a keen balance of spareness and legibility. Here, too, we encounter the novelty of an *inclined* lower case version, based on the *upright*, replacing what would formerly have been an independent, original script form—replicating backward, as it were, the evolution of italic as the consort of roman.

Hermann Zapf's Attika (Linotype nos. 6976, 6977) pares away some of the Gill types' idiosyncracy, squares and hunches its shoulders, and draws in the lower case's troublesome tentacles somewhat—all so as to regularize the x-line's horizontal band. (Still more so Linotype's Helvetica Greek aforementioned.) Adrian Frutiger's Univers Greek (Monotype nos. 889, 893, 989, etc.), issued in 1957, exhibits further straightening and compressing, probably with dense text composition in mind. While the visual logic of applying twentieth-century ideals of regularity to the familiar quirkiness of Greek letters may be open to dispute, these efforts all bear comparison with the warmed-over nineteenth-century types in which most classics students must face Greek now—in ever more disintegrated photoreproduction, which is worse still.

Shaded, serifed Greek types also advance in modern hands. Among them, Bremer Presse's calligraphic Greek (by Wiegand/Simons, 1923; see *Fine Print*, "On Type," April 1986) departs from the main track along a middle one: supplying a "missing" historical link—an uncialesque, upright scribal lower case—more a proprietary curio than a signpost. Jan van Krimpen's Antigone (1928) stylizes the upright, handlettered script form in a distinctly "reedy" manner, lighter in touch than the Bremer Presse Greek, which if anything accentuates the individual letters' characters. His Romulus Greek, a

This article was originally printed as an obiter dictum to the review of *C. P. Cavafy : A Selection of Poems* published by the Camberwell Press, which is typeset in Optima roman and greek. The author wishes to thank J. H. Bowman and Matthew Carter for their insightful criticisms, which are incorporated in this revised version.

Ἐξ ὅλων τῶν μεγαλυτέρων καὶ πλέον χρησίμων ἀνακαλύψεων. ὁ Πλάτων. τὴν ἀνακάλυψιν τῆς ἀλφαβητικῆς γραφῆς, δὲν τὴν εἶδε μὲ μεγάλην

Monotype New Hellenic

Ἐξ ὅλων τῶν μεγαλυτέρων καὶ πλέον χρησίμων ἀνακαλύψεων, ὁ Πλάτων, τὴν ἀνακάλυψιν τῆς

Monotype Gill Sans Upright

Ἐξ ὅλων τῶν μεγαλυτέρων καὶ πλέον χρησίμ ἀνακαλύψεων, ὁ Πλάτων, τὴν ἀνακάλυψιν ἀλφαβητικῆς γραφῆς, δὲν τὴν εἶδε μὲ μεγά

Monotype Gill Sans Light Upright

αβγδεζηθικλμνξοπρσςτυφχψω
ΑΒΓΔΕΖΗΘΙΚΛΜΝΞΟΠΡΣΤΥΦΧΨΩ

Linotype Attika

ὅταν δ ὁ δαίμων εὐροῆ, πεποιθέναι τὸν αὐτὸν εἰ δαίμον οὐρεῖν τύχην. ἐμοὶ γὰρ ἤδη πάντα μὲν

Monotype Univers

αἶψα δ’ ἐξίκοντο, cὺ δ’ ὦ μάκαιρα μειδιάcαιc’ ἀθανάτωι προcώπωι

Bremer Presse

Κόσμον τόνδε, τὸν αὐτὸν ἁπάντων, οὔτε τις θεῶν

Linotype Heraklit

ΑΒΓΔΕΖΗΘΙ
ΚΛΜΝΞΟΠΡΣΤΥ
ΦΧΨΩ

Stempel Phidias Titling

ΑΒΓΔΕΖΗΘΙΚΛΜΝΞΟΠΡΣΤΥΦΧΨΩ
αβγδεζηθικλμνξοπρσςτυφχψωϝ
ἡἠἡἠἡἦἡἤἡἦἡἦἡἠἡἡἡἦἡἦἡἦἡῂ

Monotype Antigone

Ἐν αρχη ην ο λογος, και ο λογος ην προς τον θεον, και θεος ην ο λογος. Ουτος ην εν αρχη προς τον θεον. παντα δι’αυτου εγενετο, και χω-

Enschedé Romulus

ΕΖΗΘΙΚΛΜΝΞΟΠΡΣΤΥΦΧ
αβγδεζηθικλμνξοπρσςτυφχψω

Officina Bodoni Griffo

formal face issued by Enschedé in the 1930s, on the other hand, stiffens and suppresses the Greek letters' quirks, to sort "logically" with the roman family of that name—a Procrustean bed, as it proves, for the Greek. (See *Fine Print*, "On Type," April & July 1981.) Romulus's open capitals are a welcome source of Greek initials.

Professor Zapf's Heraklit (Linotype nos. 3269–74, 1954) satisfies itself with refinements of the standard Greek cursive lower case. Zapf improves legibility by evening out the proportions, and the thicks and thins, as in several of his popular roman types. His Phidias Titling is fully conformable with the latter—in effect a Palatino/Michelangelo Greek capital alphabet. Giovanni Mardersteig's Griffo Greek also returns to the cursive of the early printers; with a slight modernizing—to be precise, a *Bodonizing*—in evidence.

A pleasure common to all these faces (which leaves them wide-open to preference) is the degree of freedom, even license, that each designer takes in interpreting the basic letterforms. Perusing a few of them, for instance, one notes Scholderer's satisfying departure, in rescuing the capital *xi* from its usual sore-thumb runic appearance—by assimilating it with the lower case form: a notion which Van Krimpen also takes up. (Scholderer's transfer of the *w*-form to the capital *omega*, on the other hand, flies in the face of tradition without compelling reason or reward.) Or note how, in each face, in both majuscule and minuscule, the goblet and bowl of *phi* and *psi*, respectively, sit on or are produced from the stem. Or how widely the proportions of stem- to x-height in these letters vary (in which Gill and Van Krimpen strike the extreme). The crookneck of the small *delta* seems to beg any easy solution, while inviting a wide range of attempts; similarly no one seems able, or willing, quite, to systematize the small *gamma*—or for that matter the lobes and loops of small *beta, zeta,* and *xi*. One might wish to combine particular letterforms or traits from three or four faces to suit one's own taste, but the gist of it is the joy of form, given a bit more than usual rein. The ride is a lively one even for us *barbaroi* (the old Hellenic epithet for nonspeakers of the mother tongue).

Unhappily, the availability of all these faces is curtailed further each year by the obsolescence of those technologies through which they were issued, and the attendant closings and mergers of their proprietary houses. At this point, some resourceful scholar or dealer would be performing an inestimable service in ferreting out and recording the current sources for Greek type, in all typographic media and at every scale of production.

It is not, fortunately, entirely a matter of *obits* and research, yet. I visited Kris Holmes and Charles Bigelow in their San Francisco typography office early one evening in the course of this writing, to peer over the shoulders of their staff as they busily readied the several fonts of their new digitized face, Lucida®, for licensing and distribution. Designed for use with the new generation of 300-lines-per-inch laser-typesetters (together with a sister face, Pellucida, adapted for coarser VDT screens), Lucida has been drawn using resolutions of 1000 lines per inch. With the same precision once applied through ink, engraving tools, and casting and printing tech-

Lucida is a registered trademark of Bigelow and Holmes.

nology, they labor, pixel by pixel, to translate their freehand designs into the most fluid possible programmable forms: a medium little more tractable, maybe, than hardened steel punches.

As a happy outgrowth of technical font needs, Kris Holmes has undertaken a complete Greek font. In the new Lucida Greek—an exaggeratedly inclined script form, com-

ἦν γάρ ποτε χρόνος ὅτε θεοὶ μὲν ἦσαν,
θνητὰ δὲ γένη οὐκ ἦν. ἐπειδὴ δὲ καὶ
τούτοις χρόνος ἦλθεν εἱμαρμένος

Bigelow and Holmes Lucida

bining cursive and "inclined" traits—we find a familiar refreshment of the letterforms. This can be seen, for example, in a delicate tapering and flaring of the limbs; calligraphic, oblique stem-finishing; and a distinctive "ichthoid" shaping of the lower case loops, which have been crimped closed and slightly shorn off. Though we may regret the relatively limited commercial life and use of these noble modern metal, and even phototype, faces, we may take heart to see Lucida and perhaps other faces arising, to give desktoppers and their phototype providers ready access to legible modern Greek, on their own terms—in the tradition of Aldus. Given the shabby state of classical text publishing today, careful popularization and experiment can hardly do harm.

Cutting Anglo-Saxon Sorts

STAN NELSON

THERE ARE SEVERAL WAYS to create a new piece of type. The original character can be carved in type metal and a matrix can be grown electrolytically onto it. Or a pantograph engraving machine can translate a pattern into either a punch or an engraved matrix. But the traditional approach, indeed the only technique used for about 400 years, is the hand cutting of a steel punch from which a matrix is struck and type cast. It is this time-proven method that I have been using in the creation of new types. It is this technology that I have used to make the Anglo-Saxon sorts for the Windhover Press *Forked Branches* by Ezra Pound (see review in *Fine Print,* July 1986), which was set in the 16-point Romanée designed by Jan van Krimpen in 1928.

Making letters to sort with an existing fount of type requires great care and attention to detail, since all of the qualities of the design must match.

Romanée is a beautiful, sophisticated type, intended by Van Krimpen to replace the lost, companion roman for an old italic design that survives at Joh. Enschedé en Zonen in Holland. In Van Krimpen's words, "I tried to provide for the missing of the roman by making a design that retained the proportions and many of the features of that roman without slavishly copying it. It is, once more, in the very last place for me to say how far the roman, judged as an independent type, is a success. As a companion for Van Dyck's italic I think it a distinct failure. . . ." (Page 41, *J. Van Krimpen on Designing and Devising Type,* Joh. Enschedé en Zonen, 1962). Van Krimpen was too modest regarding the success of this design, for its proportions, weight, and the quality of its line are at once modern, yet the design's roots are firmly planted in the best of the past because it is based upon a fine old Dutch face by Christoffel Van Dyck. The x-height is generous (as is true of many Dutch designs) though not excessive. The color of the design is even, without too much contrast between thicks and thins, and the counters are open. The fit is very even and throughout there is a crispness that shows the refined hand of Van Krimpen and his very talented punchcutter P. H. Rädisch. Considering the excellence of their work, matching letters to this design is a somewhat daunting task.

The process of hand cutting punches lends itself to the solution of this problem since each character is being sculpted in its actual size, and it can be measured and tried repeatedly to determine how well it will work with the rest of the design. Soot impressions, called smoke proofs, are made of the punch and then compared with the design. After making alterations, the character is proofed again. It is not necessary to scrap the punch if slips occur because it can be ground down and reshaped. Eventually the letter should be the same weight and

Tools used for punchcutting, specifically, a scribe, small files, and gravers, along with punches and matrices. Illustration by Stan Nelson.

size as the other characters and should have the same design qualities. In this case the Anglo-Saxon character edh is closely related to the capital *D* and a reversed *6*. The thorn is much like a lower case *p* and a capital *I*. The serif treatment is trim and neat and is not heavily bracketed.

After I had accepted the commission to cut the Anglo-Saxon characters, Kim Merker, director of the Windhover Press, supplied me with a specimen of the Romanée design and several Romanée types to serve as patterns, as well as sample Anglo-Saxon characters from a smaller Monotype face. Copies of printed examples of the needed sorts served as additional reference. From this material I prepared a *face gauge,* which established the dimensions of the typeface design, such as the x-height and the height of the capitals.

With this homework completed, I was ready to begin the actual punchcutting. The face gauge is used to lay out the overall dimensions of the design on the polished face of the steel punch. Further measurements of the sample types provided additional information regarding the width of the letters and the weight of the strokes. I then drew the contours

Smoke proofs of a preliminary "wavy" version of the thorn character, replaced early in the project.

Smoke proofs of an early version of the thorn character with heavier slab-like serifs.

Smoke proofs taken late in the cutting process, as the character neared its final shape.

These small files, which come in a variety of shapes, reach into the narrow angles and contours of the letters.

Once the punches were finished, hardened, and tempered, they were used to strike matrices. These matrices were carefully fitted so that when fixed beneath the mould and cast, they would produce types of the correct height and width. This process of fitting the matrices (also known as justifying the matrices) requires a mould in which sample types may be cast. These samples are measured and, based on the results, the matrices are altered until the cast types are perfect. Because Romanée is cast on a European body (16-point Didot) a special mould was required for this project. This 16-point

Finished characters cut to print with 16-point Romanée: (left to right) capital edh, lowercase edh, thorn.

of the letters onto the punch by hand using a sharp scribe. One letter was transferred from a sample Romanée type to the polished face of the punch by offsetting a soot impression onto a thin coating of slightly tacky varnish. After the soot transfer the character was outlined on the steel punch with the scribe and it was ready for cutting.

Before the outside contours of the letter are cut, the inside portions, called the counters, are formed (counters may be created either by scooping away metal with a graver or drill, or by counter-punching). In this project both methods proved useful, so two of these Anglo-Saxon sorts, the upper and lower case forms of edh (Đ and ð), were engraved, and the other two characters, versions of thorn (þ), were counter-punched. The counter-punch is a small, separate punch cut to the shape of the counter and hammered into the punch to create a cavity. The decision about whether to engrave or use counterpunching depends largely upon the size or complexity of the counter involved; where the counter shapes are simple, counter-punching is employed.

After forming the counter, the letter is filed to its final contours. Filing is quite a lot of fun, involving the use of progressively finer files, starting with one that is twelve inches long and ending with needle files as small as three inches.

Didot mould was made by altering an existing (though incomplete) 14-point mould. Special brass shims were created that increased the size of the mould. Such mould conversions were very common in past centuries since there were no fixed standards governing type bodies and heights. In order to satisfy the needs of many different customers, each frequently having his own standard, type moulds were altered just as in this case. This represented one of the interesting dimensions of this project.

Once the mould was ready and the matrices fitted, I cast a quantity of type by hand, pouring molten type metal vigorously into the mould with a small ladle. I then piled the solid types on a table and broke off the excess metal (called the jets). After smoothing the sides of the types and trimming their feet, I was ready to deliver the finished types.

Of course, throughout this narrative I have neglected to say the obvious: the success or failure of the process of creating new sorts for an existing typeface rests largely in the hands of the punchcutter, whose skill and patience, and whose willingness to keep working until the punch is perfect, determines whether the final product will be of any use. Many surviving examples of replacement or supplemental punches demonstrate failures to match faces successfully. I certainly intend to keep on trying.

Oldřich Menhart

Paul Hayden Duensing

The creation of typefaces is the area where, in both basis and purpose, the least change has occurred. It was, and still is, the bridge between author and reader, the servant of the word, and a graphic picture of the tongue, speaking across the boundaries of space and time.

OLDŘICH MENHART was a man for whom the making of letters—both calligraphic and typographic—was the most meaningful expression of the innermost soul. Over his sixty-five years he created hundreds of pieces of lettering, ornaments, shields and miniature drawings, as well as twenty typefaces. By some standards, Menhart was not a large producer, but the designs that came from his hand and mind were the product of years of study, of refining stroke, stress, and ductus, succeeding at last in creating letters which evoked a spirit that was peculiarly nationalistic, ethnic, and Czech.

The legacy left by Oldřich Menhart lies in three areas: type design, calligraphy, and typography. In the chronology that follows, his type designs show his development from a rather brash and prescriptive young artist who was so very proud of his first design, to the mature master of letterforms, who created some splendidly fresh typefaces for both text and display. Menhart's calligraphy was highly personal; it often eschewed the usual broadnibbed pen and chancery italic of contemporary calligraphers for the spring pen and a willfully rough and primitive "finish" to the roman or italic letterforms he wrote—an honest acknowledgment of the human being behind their creation. Menhart's contributions to typography can only be hinted at here, because to examine the topic adequately would require dozens of samples of his designs to illustrate the degree to which he succeeded. May it suffice to say that his work shows a masterful marriage of calligraphy with type;

N.B.: Throughout this article certain passages, printed in italic, have been taken from the text of a new work on the thoughts and working methods of Menhart, to be published in English for the first time by The Aliquando Press and The Private Press and Typefoundry of Paul Hayden Duensing. The source of these quotations is Tvorba písma a grafická úprava knihy (*The creation of types and the graphic design of books*), *Brno, 1958.*

the relationship is never forced, but is a natural flowing together of the right text, right format, and right design. His years of teaching have provided a generation of students who continue this legacy of sensitivity to both written and drawn letters, and to their use in the making of solid, tasteful books.

Menhart was born June 25, 1897 in Prague, the son of a master goldsmith who taught each of his four sons drawing, carving, and engraving. In 1911, young Oldřich entered an apprenticeship as a compositor in a Prague printing office. In 1915 he began five years of military service and at twenty-four he produced his first book with Karl Mrazek, *The First Czech School of Ornamental Letterforms*. In this work the author set out the "rules" he had "discovered" during his early study of type and calligraphy. His opinions covered the use of various design elements and their ability to convey emotional overtones of the message to the reader. In 1924 he received a stipend from the Czech Institute, and was able to visit Antwerp and Paris. During this trip he met O. Zahradník, a dealer for the Bauer typefoundry, who encouraged him to submit a design proposal to the foundry. In 1929 he left the State Printing Office with harsh words for its stifling bureaucracy and became a freelance book designer and calligrapher.

In the year following he worked out his first type design, Codex Antiqua and Kursiv—a strongly calligraphic letter with great energy, but little polish or sophistication. Through the good influence of Georg Hartmann, the director of the Bauer foundry, the design underwent several metamorphoses before it eventually emerged in 1936 as Menhart Antiqua and Kursiv. In a letter to the foundry which accompanied his drawings, Menhart wrote: "Like the attempts of [William] Morris and others (who had only slight success), my design tries to show how the refined hand of the [highly trained] scribe can come through with equal clarity in both drawn letters and in printing types built up strictly architectonically. Moreover, the difficulties which typographers have had in the setting of type up to now [uneven densities of certain letter combinations, awkward letterfitting, obtrusive diacritical marks, etc.] will not occur in the future."[1]

He went on to explain that he had thrown out every bit of excess typographic baggage, retaining only the eternal, clear, comprehensible, and elemental forms of the classic letter designs,

ABCDEFGHIJKLMNOP
QRSTUVWXYZÄÖÜÉ
abcdefghijklmnopqrstuvwxyz
1234567890&ÇŘàèéêçñôöüř
ABCDEFGHIJKLMNOP
QRSTUVWXYZÄÇÉÖÜ
abcdefghijklmnopqrstuvwxyz
1234567890äàçêéèôöñřüß

OLDŘICH MENHART'S TYPES & LETTERING

Menhart roman and italic, English Monotype Series 397, was cut in the 1930s. The even tone in text blocks was achieved by thickening the thin strokes, rather than the normal process of slimming down the thicks. Note especially the angularity of the italic and the harmony of the accents with the basic letter design. Cast from Monotype matrices in the author's collection.

Klidnost, kterou písmo krásně působí, není však ztrnulost a neživost, nýbrž organisovaný život. Jako u jiných umění spočívá v rovnováze pohybů. Tato klidnost tedy má dvě složky:

Hollar, designed in 1939 by Menhart as a personal favor for the Prague printer and publisher, Jaroslav Picka. The design shows a number of characteristics which were to infuse most of Menhart's designs, especially the calligraphic influences.

ABCDEFGHIJKLMNO
PQRSTUVWXYZ
abcdefghijklmnopqrstuvwxyz
1234567890-:;!?)""&

ABCDEFGHIJKLMNO
PQRSTUVWXYZ
abcdefghijklmnopqrstuvwxyz
1234567890-:;!?)""&

Figural and Kursiv, designed in 1940 and first displayed publicly in 1948. The roman is slightly reminiscent of the Haarlemmer face designed by Jan van Krimpen, but the angularity of the italic seems to have no precedent in western type design.

ABCDEFGHIJKLMNOP
QRSTUVWXYZ
abcdefghijklmnopqrstuvwxyz
1234567890-:;!?)„"&

ABCDEFGHIJKLMNOP
QRSTUVWXYZ
abcdefghijklmnopqrstuvwxyz
1234567890·:;!?)„"&

ABCDEFGHIJ
KLMNOPQRS
TUVWXYZ
1234567890
{-?.;,'$:}

(3) Nikdo nesmí být úředním orgánem vzat do vazby, leč
v případech stanovených zákonem; musí pak být nejdéle
do 48 hodin propuštěn nebo odevzdán soudu nebo úřadu,
kterému podle povahy věci přísluší provésti další řízení.

abcdefghijklmn
opqrstuvwxyz
+1234567890&+

The small lettered devices are samples of Oldřich Menhart's designs for ex libris, bindery logos, stationery, etc.

Manuscript was indeed one of the most original designs to come from the pen of Menhart and it closely follows the form of his personal handwriting.

Monument was designed in 1950 and cut in 20, 28, 36 and 48-point Didot sizes. The specimen shown is from a 24-point re-cutting on Pica body by the author.

Parlament was designed for the printing of the Czech constitution and other historic documents, and was then destroyed.

Unciala was the last major type to come from Menhart. It represents the distillation of a lifetime of study and evaluation based on the experiences of a practicing calligrapher. Virtually no other type can be used with this face because of its highly personal and unusual design. Cast from matrices in the author's collection.

and concluded by saying that "up to now it has never been possible for a type designer to achieve such simplicity and strict discipline in the making of a typeface."[2] All of this for his very first design! His later writings concerning his designs are far more conservative. The type that emerged was not such a revolutionary form at all, but a tranquil, largely unremarkable roman and italic, greatly influenced by the styles of Walter Tiemann and Peter Behrens. Only here and there did it show some hints of the Menhart *leitmotifs* which would occur again in his later designs: the serifs which are blunted and truncated on the left and sharpened and elongated on the right of the lefthand stroke of the *A*, the base of the *F, H, I, M, N* and *T*, and the tops of the *U, V, W, X* and *Y*.

In 1932, not long after the first few sizes had been cut at the Bauer foundry, Menhart wrote an article that appeared in the magazine *Vitrinka*, in which he described his methods of drawing a typeface. In it he said: "As a Czech, I use types which, set in the Czech language and printed in Czech books, awaken the impression of an apparent harmony, more comprehensive and more idiosyncratic than composition in any other language."[3] This became one of the man's lifelong goals: to share the richness of his culture with the world by creating designs that serve the endogenous Czech literature with an uncommon degree of "rightness" and also display the Czech national style to the rest of the world. Menhart was well aware that no letterform intrinsically expressed "Czech-ness," but he also understood that the particularly large number of accents used in the Czech language presented problems which were not satisfactorily addressed by most of the types of the time. He summed up his views by saying: "I believe that a Czech style of type comes above all from the spirit in which it was designed, which gives it its 'signature,' and not so much from decorative composition, and even less from the geographic location of its creation."[4]

Preissig's[5] experiments finally demonstrated that diacritical marks are not themselves letters, as are, for instance, numbers. They are only a subdued accompaniment of script which must not disturb the fluency of the basic letterforms or bring to the printed text excessive disquiet and confusion. Similar to punctuation marks, accents too ought to help the reader by making the text more legible, gently and unobtrusively bringing to his attention the change in pronunciation and the proper phonetic values of the letters. If the graphic function of the marks intended to clarify pronunciation exaggerates and elevates their importance to the level of the symbols of the Latin alphabet themselves, the fluency of even the best type design is destroyed, the calm perception disturbed, and the reading of the text made more difficult. The correct size, coloration, placement, and forms of accents are technically and aesthetically a significant part of Czech type design.

By 1934, Menhart had designed his second type called Menhart Series 397, for The Monotype Corporation Ltd. of England, by whom it was cut in 10, 14, 18 and 24 Didot sizes. (This article, and the others on Czech bookmaking in this issue of *Fine Print*, are set in Menhart Roman.) This is a rather light, open letter in which the accents dance gracefully over the characters as integral parts of the type design, not as unpleasant afterthoughts. In the handling of the design features he took the unusual tack of thickening the normally thin strokes, while leaving the thick

strokes in their normal weight. He thus created a type that assembles in a beautifully even texture on book pages. In spite of the handsome features of the design, it never caught the public fancy. Bill Turner, the late overseas sales manager for Monotype, once told me: "I cannot believe we have managed to sell more than four or five sets of matrices since the face was cut."

In 1939, with the rumblings of war on all sides, Menhart designed a type called Hollar, cut in only one size, for the Prague publisher Jaroslav Picka. It is a solid, dense type with strong calligraphic overtones. The squared forms of the lower case, and the swelled calligraphic strokes, are characteristics which would be seen four or five years later in his Manuscript font.

In the summer of 1940, Menhart designed a new roman which incorporated his ideas of what a contemporary book face should be. Eight years later, the design and a companion italic were displayed at an exhibition and subsequently were purchased by the typefoundry of the State Printing Office in Prague. It was cut in 1949 and named Figural. Although the roman is rather sedate, with only a hint of a calligraphic heritage, the italic gives way totally to the influence of the broad pen, and the spikey, angular quality of the lower case shows the full flowering of Menhart's artistry. (Eleven years later, when Menhart designed his last set of letterforms, it was a set of swash caps for the Figural Italic, issued in 1962, the year of his death.)

In the forms of letters it is necessary to know the difference between that which is organic, that which is the body, and that which is dress. Just as casual or ostentatious dress can alter the appearance of a person even to the point of ridiculousness, so excessive indulgence in loud or casual dressing of letterforms is often the cause of failure. Redundant decorative additions or obvious unusual dressing of letterforms are not creative enhancements of a typeface. The expressive means a designer has at his disposal in the designing of a typeface must not burden its legibility, nor can it disturb the healthy reserve of the forms nor call attention to themselves by their novelty.

The 1940s and 1950s were busy and productive decades in Menhart's life. In 1942–43 he designed a roman, italic, and bold for The Intertype Corporation of Brooklyn, New York, of which some trials were cut in 1947, but the face was never completed. In 1943–44, Manuscript was designed (cut in 1949) and an italic for it was designed in 1946 (cut in 1951). This highly unusual and idiosyncratic design derived directly from Menhart's experiments with the spring pen, and it is a spirited, jovial, unaffected type with a rustic, peasant-like quality. It is unfortunate that the type is so little known in North America and Western Europe. Max Caflisch writes of it: "This type is of a strong cut and of the highest individuality and exclusive character and [yet] of fine-flowing composition. Manuscript has no type design counterpart either contemporary or historic. Slowly evolved from Menhart's handwriting, its strokes show the energy, sureness, and self-consciousness of its writer. . . . The accents and punctuation form an organic whole with the letterforms. In spite of all the freedom of the stroke formation, the type is extraordinarily readable in large text areas. It produces calm and decidedly effective pages of a uniformly satisfying color."[6]

During 1949 Menhart handled the typographic design of Victor Hugo's poem "Satyr" which was decorated by a series of lithographic illustrations by Max Švabinský.[7] He lettered the title in a lightly shaded set of open caps, somewhat like a freely drawn Cochin Open. His friends prevailed upon him to consider producing the design as a typeface. He undertook the design work later that year and completed it in 1950. The design had undergone a marked development; the serifs were now more blunted, but maintained a hand-hewn quality which lends great visual excitement. Named Monument, the face was cut in 20, 28, 36, and 48-point Didot sizes by the Prague typefoundry. One size was re-cut in this country some years ago to fit on a 24-point Pica system body, and it shows up occasionally in American fine press books, usually in conjunction with Bembo or Palatino.

In 1950 Menhart was asked by the Czech government to produce a type design to be used in the printing of their constitution, a unique design which would be destroyed after the single use. For this unusual assignment he designed Parlament, which was cut in 24 point only. It was a beautiful, powerful, calligraphic roman which managed to evoke a sense of both peasantry and elegance.

The character of printing from each country is first of all determined by the type faces used there. The graphic appearance of our printing will be a reflection of what typefaces we have and with what sensitivity the typographer uses them.

Other types followed: Triga and Italic for linecasting matrices 1954–55; Standard (with its italic) (which was named for his friend and fellow calligrapher, Paul Standard of New York) was designed in 1959 and cut in 1966; Grazdank, a font of Cyrillic characters to match Manuscript, was designed in 1952 and cut in 1953–55.

Menhart, as a practicing calligrapher, had long studied the early uncial forms, and he had used them in a number of variations on diplomas and resolutions. Around the end of World War II he finished his drawings for a type of this form, and by April of 1949 he was able to show a proof of the 12-point size, cut by the State Printing Office. The larger sizes were cut in 1953 by Grafotekna, the collective typefoundry in Prague. In a privately printed brochure about the type, Menhart wrote: "The uncial letterform occupies, in modern type design, a special though not highly significant position. . . . It was with this form, held between only two guide lines, that the heritage of the Latin alphabet showed its greatest elasticity."[8] He notes the problems of a calligraphic design transmogrified into a metal type when he writes: ". . . because the uncial has historically known no display device other than color (i.e., no capitals), it can only be used for the most uncomplicated kinds of text. Perhaps this explains the fact that in the last fifty years only four attempts at reviving this form have been made: one each in Germany, France, Holland, and America." He was referring to the Hammer Unziale cut in 1921, the Peignot face designed by A. M. Cassandre in 1937 (a surprising candidate, since it is a rather mannered, modernized design and does have a full set of standard capitals), Libra designed by S. H. DeRoos and issued by Typefoundry Amsterdam in 1938, and Friar, issued by F. W. Goudy in 1937. It is unlikely that he was aware of some other rather obscure fonts, such as Hammer Uncial, Samson, Pindar, or Andromaque.

Menhart had worked on sketches for an uncial since 1922, tracing the many variations and national adaptations of this letterform. The study had lasted twenty-six years, ending in the casting of his design by the State Printing Office. There was now "a

fifth uncial form," he wrote, "this time of Czech origin."[9]

A typeface can only be judged correctly as a whole in the pages of a book or in similarly encompassing printed form. A designer must be aware of this and if he realizes that the details and little games which he considered his personal touches become redundant or even deleterious baggage, he should not hesitate to give them up for the sake of the whole. Where he does not abide by this basic rule, he errs.

In 1958 this accomplished designer and calligrapher gave a lecture in which he summed up much of his philosophy of the half century during which he had made such significant contributions to the graphic arts: "No 'Master' ever just fell out of the skies. That is, no letter-artist was born . . . but rather he arises through the accumulation of experience and through study and practical work. Thus does one learn to distinguish between good and bad type, ordinary and significant solutions. The creation of a typographic letterform is the most laborious task in this field, and it demands patience and discipline, for one is simply not allowed to get lost in the ways of error or failure."[10]

It is, however, critical that the good which progress brings man, by way of immense speeding up and cheapening of the work once done by hand, not be purchased too dearly with the destruction of cultural values which are the outcome of dedicated and enlightened work of prior generations.

In the 1960s, during the period of his declining health, prior to his terminal illness, Menhart wrote to a friend: "The days are murky and the light so weak that I can hardly see to draw. It is an odd feeling when, after thirty years, a person is sending in his last new type design. When a musician goes deaf, as happened to Smetana or Beethoven, he can still compose, but when a designer loses his sight, he can no longer do anything."[11]

On an occasion honoring Menhart near the end of his life, the poet Jan Noha said: "Your Manuscript is becoming to the written word what the national folk melodies are to song." To this Menhart replied: "I wrote the music, but without the musicians, engravers, foundry workers, typesetters and printers of the whole orchestra, which must be coordinated with the greatest sensitivity, there wouldn't be a song . . . and my typefaces would not exist."[12]

NOTES

1. Letter formerly in the archives of the Bauer type foundry; quoted in *Oldřich Menhart: 1897 bis 1962*. Hamburg: Hans Christians Verlag, 1968, p. 12. The author is grateful to Kurt Christians and the Hans Christians Verlag for permission to quote from this publication.

2. *Ibid.*

3. "Jak vznikalo moje písmo" (How my types are made), *Vitrinka*, Vol. 9, 1932, pp. 5–13.

4. *Ibid.*

5. Vojtech Preissig, 1873–1944, was a gifted designer whose ideal was to found a workshop in the tradition of William Morris. He designed one typeface by cutting the characters on the faces of quads with a pocket knife. The resulting design

avoided all rounded strokes, using a series of short straight strokes instead. There is some of his influence to be seen in Menhart's Figural Italic.

6. Max Caflisch: "Die Druckschriften von Oldřich Menhart" in *Oldřich Menhart: 1897 bis 1962*, p. 34.

7. *Ibid.*

8. Oldřich Menhart: "Die tschechische Unziale im zeitgenössischen typographischen Schriftschaffen" in *Oldřich Menhart: 1897 bis 1962*, p. 42.

9. *Ibid.*

10. Oldřich Menhart in his lecture, "Type Creation and Book Design" quoted in *Oldřich Menhart: 1897 bis 1962*, p. 48.

11. Memorial reprint of two letters from Oldřich Menhart to Miloslav Bohatec, Prague, 1963, p. 7.

12. Quoted in a pamphlet honoring an exhibition of Menhart's work in the Castle Zdar. Oldřich Menhart died, following a long illness, on February 11, 1962 and was buried in a section of the Prague cemetery reserved for artists, poets, and musicians.

BIBLIOGRAPHY

Babler, Otto F.: "Oldřich Menhart. Czech Printer, Type-Designer Penman." *De Gulden Passer*, Antwerp, 1950.

Bohatec, Miloslav: *Un Labeur Courageux. Über den künstlerischen Charakter Oldřich Menharts. Gutenberg-Jahrbuch*, 1962, pp. 76–81.

Hurm, Otto: "Der Grafiker Oldřich Menhart." *Exlibris, Mitteilungen der österreichischen Exlibris-Gesellschaft*, New Series, June, 1962.

Kaláb, Method: "Die moderne tschechische Buchtypographie." *Gutenberg-Jahrbuch*, 1942–43. pp. 378–89.

————. "Die Schriftkunst des Graphikers Oldřich Menhart." *Gutenberg-Jahrbuch*, 1939, pp. 303–09.

Menhart, Oldřich: *Česká unciála v soudobém typografickém písmarství* (The Czech uncial in contemporary letter creation). Prague, 1950.

————. *Nauka o písmu* (Letter instruction). Prague, 1954.

————. *Tvorba písma a grafická úprava knihy* (The creation of types and the graphic design of books). Brno, 1958.

————. *Výbor z díla písmaře a úpravce knihy* (Selections from the work of this type and book designer). Prague, 1956.

Schwanecke, Erich: "Der Buchgestalter Menhart." *Typographie.* Leipzig, 1960. Volume 9, pp. 17–22.

Standard, Paul: "Oldřich Menhart." *The American Printer.* Vol. 134, Nos. 10, 11, 12. (October, November, December), 1953.

A Rejoinder and Extension to Herbert Johnson's "Notes On Frederic Warde and the True Story of his Arrighi Type"

JOHN DREYFUS

ERBERT JOHNSON has done less than justice to my dead friends Stanley Morison and Beatrice Warde in his "Notes on Frederic Warde and the True Story of His Arrighi Type" (*Fine Print*, July 1986). He has also left out some important data about Frederic Warde's role in re-creating two different versions of Arrighi's types. I never met Frederic Warde, but as I share Johnson's high regard for his talents, I am grateful to the editor for an opportunity to present a number of facts to supplement Johnson's "notes," and also to correct what I know to be some of Johnson's errors of fact, as well as what I believe to be his occasional errors of interpretation.

In the article we are told, without supporting evidence, that Morison "studiously cultivated the Wardes' friendship while in America," but this suggestion is contradicted by surviving correspondence between the Wardes and Morison. Even before Morison made his first visit to the United States in August 1924, he had received what he described as "a huge letter of four quarto pp. in 10 point" from an unknown correspondent—Frederic Warde.[1] Morison had also heard from Beatrice on 14 May 1924 (copy in Columbia University libraries):

Dear Mr Morison:

Mr Bullen [Librarian of the American Type Founders Company in Jersey City] tells me that you are planning to visit our Library next September. I need not assure you of the cordial welcome that awaits you here; I am writing only to remind you that any form of assistance I can render will be at your disposal. If you need secretarial help during your stay here, or if you'd like to have someone arrange appointments, etc., let me know at any time. . . .

My husband, Mr Frederique Warde, joins me in asking you to be our guest in Princeton [where he worked as Director of Printing at the University Press] whenever you find it convenient to come down. I go back and forth by train every day, so I could bring you

down any evening; or we could motor down with B.R. [Bruce Rogers]: we have taken a whole house for the summer and there are loads of guest rooms! Then you could visit the Princeton University Press [where Frederic worked] and spend the rest of the day motoring —for it's going to be pretty hot around the first of September."

Readers should also be cautious about accepting Johnson's allegation that "in later years, Beatrice often 'confided,' *sotto voce* and not for publication, that she wrote the *Fleuron* article [on the work of Bruce Rogers] for Frederic, but Warde's notebook seems to indicate otherwise." The only source given in support of this allegation is a footnote reference to an interview given by Beatrice on 4 June 1965 to the late Paul Bennett while he was gathering material for a biography of Frederic. When Bennett died in 1966, this commissioned biography was still unfinished, but his notes are preserved in New York at the Grolier Club, by whom I am permitted to reproduce two paragraphs in Bennett's handwriting which are relevant to Johnson's allegation:

NOT FOR PUBLICATION. B wrote the essay on BR: Designer of Books which Frederic took credit for. He did the compilation and checked the bibliographical detail. Also got BR to check it.
B wrote other pieces F took credit for. Didn't take any stand on that sort of thing. I could write easily, perhaps better than he. So I helped as I could.

As Johnson has ignored the first three words, it seems fair to give the precise words used in Paul Bennett's notes. It also seems relevant to quote a passage from a letter Frederic Warde wrote on 2 June 1927 to William A. Kittredge: ". . . when I begin to write anything, I am always overwhelmed with the feeling that I should not dare to make the attempt but go back to school and learn how to construct sentences properly." It consequently appears less than surprising that Frederic accepted willingly given help with his prose from his wife, who had inherited some of her mother's great literary talent.

The Wardes became such close friends of Morison that he

1. See Stanley Morison & D. B. Updike, *Selected Correspondence* edited by David McKitterick. New York: Moretus Press, 1979, p. 75.

went to meet them in Cherbourg when they landed in Europe on 7 January 1925. Johnson describes the Wardes "as gentle as doves" but "not as wise as 'the Serpent,' which was Beatrice's nickname for Morison at the time." In fact Frederic was more worldly wise than Johnson's metaphor suggests, as can be discovered from a letter Frederic wrote to Henry Lewis Bullen from London on 22 January 1925 (the original is in Columbia University libraries):

> I want [you] to know that I was very glad to receive your letter. It came yesterday, and it confirms, in many respects, my own opinions about Morison. I have as yet not made any definite plans. I do not intend to make any plans until I have carefully surveyed the field; and one thing is certain, I shall not in any way depend on Morison. I was firmly convinced about Morison before I purchased our steamer tickets to sail. Do not think that I have come over in the paramount interest of Morison or any of his 'kidney.' I have been planning to visit Europe for some time, and long before I ever heard of Morison. If Morison has any work which I *wish* to do, and which he will leave *entirely to me*, and pay well for my time, I may consider such work entirely upon—caution and contract—as you have suggested.
>
> This is a rather mean sounding letter. I will write again soon.

Despite his wariness of working with Morison, Warde shared an office with him at 41 Bedford Square shortly after he and Beatrice arrived in London. Their office was in a building leased by Charles W. Hobson for his Fanfare Press, managed by Ernest Ingham (1885–1976). Hobson had previously owned the Cloister Press near Manchester where Morison had worked for him.

In the Fall, before the Wardes arrived in London, an article had appeared in *The Fleuron*, No. 3 on "The Chancery Types of Italy and France," written by A. F. Johnson and Stanley Morison. The first of its illustrations was captioned: "AR-RIGHI'S FIRST ITALIC: Blodius Palladius' *Coryciana* (Impressum Rome apud Ludovicum Vicentinum et Lautitium Perusinum, 1524)." Morison owned a copy of the *Coryciana*, which he allowed Warde to take over to Paris in order to have the Arrighi italic fount copied by a French punchcutter.

The earliest "mention" of Warde's Arrighi type discovered by Herbert Johnson is in a letter sent by Warde to Bruce Rogers on 29 May 1925. What seems to have been ignored by Johnson is the likelihood of two men sharing an office *discussing* their plans for a type which was to make its first appearance in Robert Bridges's poem *The Tapestry*, printed at the Fanfare Press. The colophon of this edition states that 150 copies were "printed with Arrighi type by F.W. and S.M. at 41 Bedford Square London November Mcmxxv." Facing the colophon was a "Printers' Note" which ended with the following comment:

> The design of the type used is based upon that of Lodovico degli Arrighi, born at Vicenza, who worked as a calligrapher and printer in Rome, where he was known as Lodovico Vicentino. Our punches were cut by hand.

The use of the plural in the heading and in the last sentence is significant. Warde thereby tacitly acknowledged that Mori-

son had played a role in the scheme to have Arrighi's types recut.

Curious to know more about the division of responsibilities between the two men, I was in touch several years ago with Ernest Ingham (already mentioned as manager of the Fanfare Press, and employed by Charles W. Hobson, for whose Cloister Press in Manchester both Morison and Ingham had previously worked). In a letter sent to me on 17 March 1970, Ingham wrote:

> It was Morison's idea to have the writing alphabet "translated into type." The "design" had existed for hundreds of years. The cutting was a reasonably faithful "derivation." Morison gave to F.W. the task of directing its technical creation, from the cutting of punches to the delivery of the type.

In the summer of 1953, John Ryder (then working in the production office of Phoenix House) asked Morison about the location and origins of the Arrighi types and its variants called Vicenza. As the complete texts of these letters show that Morison was aware of and acknowledged the unreliability of his memory in 1953,[2] I reproduce them now for the first time (by permission of the executors of Stanley Morison's estate and with John Ryder's consent, and with typing errors left uncorrected):

54 FETTER LANE, LONDON EC4
4th August 1953

Dear Sir,
> To the best of my belief, some of the type does still exist at Officina Bodoni.
>
> The punches were cut by Charles Malin in Paris at my instigation, and the type was first used for a small collection of poems by Robert Bridges, *The Tapestry*, about 1923 or so.
>
> Officina Bodoni printed the text *Ovid*, but I do not remember the date.
>
> If you wrote to Officina Bodoni at Verona, I do not doubt you could get more accurate and complete particulars than I can provide.
>
> I can say, however, that only one size was cut.
> Yours faithfully,
Stanley Morison

In reply to a further question from John Ryder, Morison wrote in terms far more tentative and unsure of his facts than subsequent writers on the subject have conveyed:

54 FETTER LANE, LONDON EC4
28th September 1953

Dear Sir,
> You ask a very puzzling question. I think I was solely responsible for the negotiations, and began the discussions with Malin about the Vicenza types, and handed the matter over to Frederick Warde when he later arrived in this country. This was because I found

2. Harry Carter in his entry on Morison in *The Dictionary of National Biography 1961–1970* (Oxford, 1981) remarked on p. 765 that as a scholar Morison "was quick to grasp essentials but inaccurate in details. . . ."

Above: Part of a sheet of drawings in the Newberry Library, Chicago, for Monotype Series 252 (Arrighi Italic). The method used by Frederic Warde for the preparation of these drawings was to work over reversed photographic enlargements of the original fount of Arrighi type, cut by hand under Warde's supervision by Georges Plumet.

A good deal of process white was used, partly to obscure unwanted areas of type metal which had photographed as black, and partly to improve the sharpness of Warde's line edges drawn in black ink. These drawings show the difficulty Warde encountered in making accurate drawings. Notice, for example, the weak handling of curves in the letter *c*, and the irregular weight and edges of the downstroke of the *d*.

Partly because of Warde's weakness as a draughtsman, many characters cut for Monotype Arrighi had to be recut during the course of its manufacture at the Monotype Works in England. Other modifications were needed to suit the design to its new role of acting as an accompanying italic to Bruce Rogers's Centaur Roman (also designated Series 252).

Below: Four of the characters drawn anew by Frederic Warde for the Monotype version of Arrighi. As the handcut version had not included ligatures or lining numerals, nor the £ or $ signs, Warde provided drawings for these characters in the same size as the drawings shown above.

On the three sheets of drawings at the Monotype Works (from which the four characters at left have been reproduced), Warde again made extensive use of process white to retouch his drawings, sharpening them to present a more accurate impression of the forms which he had in mind for these characters.

he knew more about these matters than I did, had more time and, finally, it made me happy to disengage myself. But the thing happened so long ago that my recollection may be as faulty about it as it is of other affairs of the kind and of the time.

However, I will still cudgel my memory and ask anybody I know who might conceivably have some information on the point. You might also write to Will Carter. Somebody recently told me that he had the, or a set of the, matrices. He may know about the punches. It is news to me that they are still in the Metropolitan Museum, though Frederick Warde may have told me.

I quite understand your being astonished that there is so little information available. But really, you know, this was a long while ago, and the people who were involved at the time had no idea that they were doing anything of use, importance, or curiosity. It certainly never occurred to me that the revival of Arrighi would reach the dimensions it now has.

Yours,

Stanley Morison

Had Morison been as determined as Johnson suggests to exaggerate his own role in the recutting of the Arrighi types, he would hardly have made so many admissions about the fallibility of his memory. Nor is it surprising that Morison confused Charles Malin with Georges Plumet, because it was Malin with whom Morison had repeated dealings in 1926 after Morison commissioned Malin to cut a trial set of punches by hand from Eric Gill's drawings for Perpetua. Moreover, Malin had played a part in the making of the Arrighi types by cutting a smaller set of roman capitals to the order of Giovanni Mardersteig, who used them for his edition of Ovid's *Amores* in 1932. (See Giovanni Mardersteig, *The Officina Bodoni, an Account of the Work of a Hand Press 1923–1977,* Verona 1980, p. 49, where he refers to the work's having been done by "Charles Malin, Plumet's successor".)

I endorse Herbert Johnson's view that "claims written by Morison about his career should not be accepted without documentation or independent collaboration": the same holds good for claims put forward by his critics, particularly when they are expressed in terms as general as Johnson's phrase "Morison frequently took credit for the work of others, that he constantly revised dates to demonstrate that he had seen, heard, thought, wrote, or acquired something before his colleagues had." Some similar allegations made by James Moran were refuted by Brooke Crutchley in his introduction to the new edition of Morison's *A Tally of Types,* Cambridge 1973. And from my own knowledge as typographical adviser to the Monotype Corporation 1955–82, I can state that there is not a shred of evidence to support Johnson's hypothesis that "Morison continued to overstate his influence and achievement perhaps in an attempt to keep the publicity mill churning at Monotype Corporation."

On the other hand, the immense contribution made by Warde to the success of the handcut and machine-cut versions of the Arrighi types has yet to be recorded, and I hope it will later be covered by Herbert Johnson in his "larger work on Frederic Warde" concerning which we have so far been given details only of the intended dedicatees.

Warde's memorialist Will Ransom observed (in *Print* vol. II, no. 1, May–June 1941) how fortunate it was that

> his translation of Arrighi's letter forms into type was interpretation rather than design, in the sense that design means adaptation or rearrangement of basic elements. His greatest service in this essay was failing, or refusing, to "improve on" the model. Instead he converted the free qualities of written letters into the rigid vocabulary of metal types but retained their grace, thereby showing a respect for origins regrettably absent from many type revivals.

No doubt this was intended by Ransom as high praise, but in fact Warde performed a far more delicate and difficult task than Ransom's remarks suggest. The scale of Warde's achievement becomes obvious when a direct comparison is made between the type used in the *Coryciana* and the so-called translation created by Warde. To help readers of *Fine Print* judge for themselves, Will Carter kindly set one line from the *Coryciana* in the Rampant Lions Press fount of Warde's Arrighi, cast from the matrices made in 1925.

Non placet hoc; nostri pietas laudanda Coryti est;

N *on placet hoc ; nostri pietas laudanda Coryti est ;*

A line from Arrighi's *Coryciana* as reproduced in the July, 1939 issue of *Signature.* The line below is set in the handcut Arrighi fount owned by Will Carter and kindly supplied by him.

Greatly to Warde's credit, he managed to create a more regular and consistent fount than Arrighi's, and has managed to make it even more graceful than the original. The bowls of the letters *d* and *p* are more in harmony with each other in Warde's version, and he has made the stems and terminals of the letter *d* and *l* both more elegant and more consistent than Arrighi's cuttings. Improvements in alignment can be seen in the word "laudanda." Moreover, Warde managed to overcome the problems of design in such a way that it was possible to cast founts of type which were capable of withstanding the strain of letterpress printing, provided they were carefully composed and locked up, despite the many kerning letters which involved overhangs of an inherently delicate character.

Arrighi's design could not have been successfully adapted by anyone without Warde's deep understanding of calligraphy. His interest in this subject was considerably heightened by his close association with Morison, which continued after their joint publication of *The Tapestry.* They joined forces again in a complete facsimile of *The Calligraphic Models of Ludovico degli Arrighi surnamed Vicentino* printed in March 1926, for which Morison wrote a lengthy introduction. The colophon explained that the edition had been printed "for and under the direction of Frederic Warde and with his Arrighi types," while Morison stated that the text of his introduction had been composed in a revived fount based on the type of the *Coryciana.* Morison also drew attention to the earliest use of another calligraphic letter in Arrighi's "Il Modo de Temperare le Penne" included in the 1926 facsimile. The precise sequence and dating of Arrighi's various founts is still a matter of debate among scholars, but it is evident that Warde was thoroughly familiar with these founts, and also with Arrighi's manuals on handwriting. It was this depth of understanding that made it possible for him to depart so far from the model of the *Coryciana* while still retaining the essence of Arrighi's calligraphic style.

How much the success of Warde's Arrighi was due to Plumet's skill and experience is impossible to quantify, but we do know what an advantage Warde found it to work in Paris, as he explained to his close friend William A. Kittredge on 6 March 1926:

> In all Europe I have found Paris to be the one place I find anything if that one thing is ever known to have existed, and I daresay even if it has never existed, one could find it in Paris. I mean this in regard to research, or in having a punch-cutter at my elbow who will cut any sort of punch for me, and strike the matrices and take them to the founder for me, and see to the details of having the characters cast for me. 'My' punch-cutter is a regular sixteenth century fellow in his metier, and at the same time thoroughly up-to-date. (Original in the Newberry Library, Chicago.)

Working with such an excellent punchcutter at his elbow, and with a copy of *Coryciana*, which passed between Plumet and the Parisian typefounders, P. Ribadeau Dumas, Warde did not need to make a complete set of drawings for the handcut version of Arrighi, though he did so for the later version cut by the Monotype Corporation. But before I describe his part in that enterprise, I want to draw attention to the fact that Warde had shown an interest in the technique of typefounding as early as August 1922, when he was in touch with Henry Lewis Bullen. Even earlier, in February 1922, he had worked on a *Monotype Bulletin* for the Philadelphia Lanston Monotype Machine Company. Curiously enough, Herbert Johnson asserts that "there was nothing in Warde's background to suggest that he knew more about cutting punches by hand than Morison did," although Johnson also mentions that Warde had corresponded in 1924 with the Sheffield typefounders, Stephenson Blake & Co, about the cutting of "a new roman type which he had designed (it was never cut)." And in a letter introducing Warde to Giovanni Mardersteig, on whose presses at the Officina Bodoni the 1926 facsimile of the *Calligraphic Models* was later printed, Morison wrote of Warde: "he is the practical man and I only an archaeologist."

During his stay in Paris, Warde (as he told Kittredge on 6 March 1926) had made "many experiments in having letters cut, and I now have three working alphabets in type. Soon I shall start a fourth alphabet which I can use with the other three." This information is all the more tantalizing when read in conjunction with remarks made earlier in his letters to Henry Watson Kent: ". . . I am seriously considering the roman lower-case face which I shall have cut" (27 October 1925), followed later by the news: "Punches are being cut of the roman lowercase, and I hope type cast by February" (10 December 1925). Though I cannot supply any other details about these projects, the extracts I have quoted from Warde's correspondence show that his interest in type design continued after the handcut version of his Arrighi types was finished.

The version of Arrighi which Warde drew for the Monotype Corporation in England was made at the request of Warde's friend Bruce Rogers. Working in much the same spirit as Warde to derive a new type from a Renaissance model, Rogers had derived his Montaigne/Centaur design from a type used by the fifteenth-century Venetian printer Nicolas Jenson. As Rogers explained in a note he wrote for the first piece of printing done in Monotype Centaur,[3] "being incapable of devising a suitable Italic letter I induced Mr. Frederic Warde to make a modified version of his beautiful Arrighi Italic to accompany my Roman characters." The task involved Warde in a great deal of work, because he had to alter the x-height, alignment, and color of the handcut version to make it satisfactory as an accompanying italic in the complete range of sizes cut for Monotype Centaur from 6 point to 36 point.

Warde supplied two different kinds of drawings for the Monotype version of Arrighi. For the lower case he used enlarged photostats of the handcut type, inking over the face of the type and at the same time considerably shortening the ascenders and descenders, and altering the finials to the shapes cut by Plumet for Vicenza. As roman capitals had been used with the handcut fount, he had to make new drawings for Monotype Arrighi capitals. The bulk of these drawings are now in the Newberry Library at Chicago with Bruce Rogers's designs for Monotype Centaur. There are some copies in the Warde archive in the Grolier Club, New York, and at the Monotype Works in England there are three sheets of Warde's drawings for a set of italic lining numerals, for the $ and £ signs, and for the ligatures æ and œ in capitals and lower case.

The reproductions on p. 73 of parts of the sheets at the Monotype Works show that Warde could not make such impeccable type drawings as Jan van Krimpen or Hermann Zapf, but his drawings demonstrate unmistakably what a deep and sensitive understanding he had of calligraphy and typography. The final production of Monotype Centaur also gained from detailed criticisms made by Rogers, as well as the expertise of the Type Drawing Office in Salfords which made many of the design modifications required to produce a harmonious range of sizes. Small wonder then that Rogers ended his printer's note by calling Monotype Arrighi "one of the finest and most legible cursive letters ever produced."

3. Alfred W. Pollard, *The Trained Printer and the Amateur and the Pleasure of Small Books*. London: Lanston Monotype Corporation, Ltd., 1929.

Designing a New Greek Type

KRIS HOLMES

THE LUCIDA FAMILY of typeface designs, designed especially for laser printing, is based on our study of traditional scribal hands. The roman forms are derived from the Humanistic scripts of the fifteenth century, and the italics from the later Chancery cursive hands. To provide another level of graphic differentiation, we also designed sans serif versions of these typefaces, a concept first realized by Jan van Krimpen in his Romulus family, designed in the 1930s. Lucida Greek is an extension of the family into non-Latin alphabetic forms, designed in harmony with the basic proportions, weights, and styles of the Lucida Latin characters.

Early Greek book hands were closely modeled on inscriptional letterforms, but by the third century AD they began to show rounding of sharp angles and other traits that characterize the uncial script. At the peak of its development, the Greek uncial served as the basis for the alphabet used in Slavonic languages.

By the eighth century, a new cursive minuscule form of Greek had developed, although its formative period is not well understood because few manuscripts have survived. The joining of characters in this cursive appears to follow rather strict rules, much as in the Arabic scripts, where certain characters may join in specific combinations, while others may not join at all. The early versions of this hand, those written between 800 and 950 AD, seemed to us to be the most vigorous, and these we studied and copied as part of our research for Lucida Greek.

Calligraphy by Kris Holmes based on a manuscript from about 862 AD written in Greek minuscules

Some of the character shapes (including beta and kappa) of this early Greek minuscule would be nearly illegible to modern readers of Greek, and in general its forms are both cursive and wide, with small, enclosed loops and a small x-height. None of these features is suitable for a typeface that must endure digital reproduction at 300 dots per inch on a laser printer.

For these reasons, after studying these traditional forms, we developed a calligraphic version of Greek minuscule to be written with a broad-edged pen. We kept the letter shapes simple and without small enclosed areas, while trying to maintain the liveliness of the historical minuscule. These original calligraphic forms were redrawn with their weights and alignments harmonized with the parameters of the Lucida types. The early proofs were sent to Greek scholars and linguists for critiques, and then corrections were made.

Ἀκρίδι ταῖ κατ' ἄρουραν ἀηδόνι, καὶ δρυοκοίται
τέττιγι ξυνὸν τύμβον ἔτευξε Μυρώ,
παρθένιον στάξασα κόρα δάκρυ· δισσὰ γὰρ αὐτᾶς
παίγνι' ὁ δυσπειθὴς ὤιχετ' ἔχων Ἀίδας.

Greek broad-edged pen calligraphy

When the design and production of a typeface is finished, the design must still be protected against plagiarism and piracy. Unfortunately, typeface copyright is not available in the United States, but the Lucida Greek design was sent off to Germany for registration under a special West German typeface copyright law, and similar design protections were applied for in other countries. It is regrettable that the United States permits innovative typographic hardware to be patented and typographic software to be copyrighted, but discourages the copyrighting of new typefaces. This regulatory bias disregards the fact that the design of a new family of types can require as much time and effort as the development of computer hardware and software for a new publishing system.

ἦν γάρ ποτε χρόνος ὅτε θεοὶ μὲν ἦσαν,
θνητὰ δὲ γένη οὐκ ἦν. ἐπειδὴ δὲ καὶ
τούτοις χρόνος ἦλθεν εἱμαρμένος

Lucida Greek

Bitwitched, Bothered, and Bewildered: Type 1987

SANDRA KIRSHENBAUM

Computer scientists believe that if you can't measure it, it doesn't exist. Therefore, it is not enough that we typographers know that legibility exists, we have to be able to prove it.
Richard Southall, Typographic Consultant
Xerox

Of all the arts and crafts, none lives more in the dirty tepid bathwater of the past than does typography.
Colin Banks, Type Designer
Banks and Miles, London

I sometimes like things that are not entirely legible; I like to read psychedelic posters. I like books that are set pretty tight; sometimes they're a little hard to read, they stick together in a certain way, but it looks nice to me. It's not always economical to put a lot of space between the lines, but that looks nice too.
Steve Bialer, Art Director
Chicago Times

Old typefaces never die, they just never die.
Steve Byers, Director of Typography
Linotype

The art of type design lies in getting rid of your "great ideas."
Kris Holmes, Type Designer
Bigelow & Holmes

We've had five hundred years of movable type; now we have mutable type.
Matthew Carter, Vice-President of Design
Bitstream

THERE IS INDEED A GRAND LOBBY in the Grand Hyatt Hotel in New York: tall gray marble columns glow darkly, and sleek brass-trimmed escalators bear visitors silently past glistening sheets of water spilling over the smooth walls of a two-story indoor fountain. But during the weekend of October 9–12, 1987, many of those riding the escalators and taking in the vast architectural symmetry had come to focus on something of a much smaller scale, invisible to most people, yet in its way, more grand in terms of harmony and function: type. The occasion was the Type Directors Club international conference on type design and design with type. The presiding genius of the affair was Roger Black, who is renowned for his design work on *Rolling Stone*, the *New York Times*, and *Newsweek*. Black modeled this conference after one organized by Charles Bigelow for ATypI in 1983 (see *Fine Print*, January 1984), mixing moss-backed traditionalists with headlong high-techies and coming up with a scintillating program of lectures, workshops, and seminars.

And so, at Type 1987, we had Stan Nelson, printing historian at the Smithsonian Institution, peering from behind magnifying goggles at a shaft of steel he was filing into the letter P, as he performed the ancient art of punchcutting; meanwhile, the technicians of URW were sitting in front of their glowing screens demonstrating how to use the Ikarus program to digitize letterforms. The way the conference was laid out was different and refreshing. Hardware, systems, and salesmanship were largely relegated to workshops in the upstairs rooms, while downstairs, the lectures and seminars focused on the quality, the aesthetics, and the history of the ultimate product—type—generated by whatever system, with intent amateur or professional.

The new world of digital type: new tools, new means of generating letterforms—so what?—such changes have happened many times before, perhaps the first time in 3000 BC when the Sumerians abandoned the pointed stick in favor of a wedge-shaped one. As became evident at Type 1987, digital type is revolutionary in two aspects which are both challenging and frightening. First, the new computer tools allow type forms to be elaborated, altered, and distorted with unprecedented ease. Each type manufacturing company (indeed, each individual, with a little determination, a personal computer, and a font design program) can scan any type design, alter its outline or bitmap, and print it out by laser printer without manual redrawing.

Second, because it is now in the form of a readily transmissible digital code, type has suddenly become widely accessible and affordable; it is output in hundreds of thousands of desktop laser printers beyond the control of the professional publishing channels that have tightly regulated its nature and form for half a millenium. Said one printer/typographer, "Now we know what the scribes felt like in the fifteenth century when faced with the rampant spread of printing." This may be the penultimate extension of Gutenberg's invention: his movable type made possible wide *access* to text; now digital type democratizes *generation* of text. (The ultimate extension will occur when text is freed of its paper bonds and *dissemination* of text becomes easy for all.)

Now all those sacred kabbalistic activities that only the typographer engaged in—spec-ing type, laying out pages, integrating graphics—are suddenly the province of Every-man. No longer is the type sophistication of John/Jane Q. Public limited to making the gut-wrenching choice between *script style* and BLOCK LETTERS on their rubber-stamp orders. All can be initiated into the mysteries of leading, x-height, letterspacing (which some computer programs call "track-ing"), and kerning (by which some programs mean letter-spacing). As we can see, the opportunities for confusion over terminology alone are myriad. At one of the master classes at Type 1987, where type designers discussed how they designed type, Ed Benguiat described his consternation when observing the digitizing of his type: "I've been to the companies that do this, and usually you will see the person there, a twenty-one- or twenty-two-year-old, massaging your alphabet and calling your serifs 'pipes'."

In this maelstrom of technological change, it is not sur-prising that, as in previous revolutions (scroll to codex, manuscript to print), the new order does not seem to want to bury the old order, but to carry it along for awhile in some state of preservation, rather like embalming the ancestors. Thus at Type 1987 lead was not dead at all, but made a lively presence in the form of Stan Nelson, Harold Berliner, a prac-ticing metal typefounder from Nevada City, California, and E. H. Taylor, who demonstrated typecasting at his Out-of-Sorts foundry in Mamaroneck, New York. The letterpress printing workshop, held at the Center for Book Arts, was over-subscribed for every session, and in discussions, principles of metal type design and composition were held up repeatedly as standards. As Paula Scher, a New York designer, com-plained, "The problem that seems to hurt working designers is how do we hold on to those things that existed before and not lose them in the new technology? The letters change shape; we lose things like small caps. . . ." Paul Duensing, type critic, emphasized that it is still consistency of forms that determines a good type design, "a visual belief that the weights are the same, that each curve belongs to the same family, that serifs act the same way in meeting stems, that question marks are not the upper half of the numeral 2, that 6's are not turned upside down to make 9's."

In creating digital type the principles should be the same, though the tools are very different and, once mastered, much quicker to use. Matthew Carter: "I spent about a year work-ing at punchcutting every day and by the end of that year I could just about create a punch which represented accurately an idea that I had. In other words, my manual facility was up to a point where I could express myself, more or less. I found that the students at Yale, who had some but not a great deal of prior knowledge, were producing decent [digital] letter-forms, some within a day, but most within two days."

It may be instructive at this point to consider exactly how most digital type is created. A drawing or sketch of the letter is entered into the computer using a scanner or a digitizing tablet, then, with a special program, of which the most widely used is Ikarus, points are selected along the outline of the character from which the computer calculates a smooth contour line. The character is changed and refined by moving the points and letting the computer "redraw" the lines. For digital typesetters and printers, the outline letterform is next translated by the computer into a pattern of bits (a bit is a single unit of on–off information in computer memory). The

pattern or map of bits in each character is called a bitmap. When digital type is composed, every curve and line is ac-tually made up of an arrangement of tiny picture elements (pixels); the simplest kinds of pixels are the bits of a bitmap. The greater the number of elements used to render a char-acter, the finer the resolution of the form. To appear in print, the bitmap must ultimately be scanned out onto film, paper, or display screens, either by electron beam, laser, or other techniques.

Though there seemed to be plenty of Ikarus-whiz-kids at the conference who spoke of "working" on some secret type of unimaginable originality, the consensus of weathered type designers like Carter, Zapf, Stone, and Holmes seemed to be: you want to design type? Be prepared to spend a few hundred hours at your drawing board.

Perhaps to assuage their feelings of insecurity and to assert that there really *is* a body of knowledge and skills to be mas-tered—that you can't just sit down at your PC, run in a few fonts, and call yourself a typographer—the participants of Type 1987 were happy to lionize those most basic of creative geniuses: the type designers. And stellar among them were two, who by themselves constitute a pantheon of the alpha-bet in the latter twentieth century, Adrian Frutiger and Hermann Zapf.

Frutiger, creator of Univers type, which has become a world-standard sans serif, was awarded the Type Directors' Club Medal for 1987. His other types, including Méridien, Frutiger, and Centennial are seen on everything from airport signage to fine book pages. Frutiger has dealt successfully with every new technology for over thirty years, although he ad-mitted at one seminar that "often I was frustrated; when I first saw my type, Méridien, on the CRT [cathode ray tube] with its distortions, my reaction was to want to make charac-ters that would support the new technique. After all," he said ruefully, "you cannot destroy the machine."

The final lecture of the conference was given by Hermann Zapf, who was there with his wife, type designer Gudrun Zapf von Hesse. Zapf is surely the most celebrated of type designers in a field of usually baffling anonymity. (At one master class, the panel of type designers laughed about the "dreaded moment at cocktail parties" when the inevitable question was, "what do you do for a living?" "Just say you're a brain surgeon," suggested Matthew Carter.)

Zapf seems to be the stern patriarch of type design, ex-horting practitioners to maintain standards and integrity in a field pulled by the limitations of technology on one side and the demands of the marketplace on the other. Lamenting the lack of copyright protection for typefaces, Zapf pointed out that the right to use a photograph is protected beginning the moment the camera clicks; yet with that same click of the camera, a person can reproduce and use a typeface, like Optima, which took Zapf eight years of experimentation and research to perfect. At its worst, this system fosters the crea-tion of unauthorized, bastardized versions of type, "a lot of Palatinellos around." Zapf portrayed this very vividly by putting up on the screen blow-ups of a brochure produced by the Grand Hyatt itself that was set in a pirated version of his Palatino italic: it exhibited unseemly width, too-short descenders, and bad gaps between letters.

Zapf expressed the hope that letterpress printing be kept

alive, for he feels that only metal type can provide a standard of comparison and a true connection with our great typographic heritage. He suggested that Stanley Morison's *First Principles of Typography* be printed in every desktop-publishing handbook. He does not recommend the transfer of existing alphabets into low-resolution systems, for the compromises will be too apparent; rather, he urged, let the new systems provide fresh opportunities for young designers.

Theoretically, such opportunities should abound, as new tools like the Ikarus program, Fontographer, and Metafont facilitate the creation of custom typefaces for individual firms and special uses. In order to overcome the copyright problems of their product, the industry has developed a rather labyrinthine system of agreements and evasions which still allows them to make money from type. Sumner Stone, Design Director at Adobe Systems, explained the situation at one seminar. "Type is a strange business. Until very recently the design, development, and manufacture of typefaces was done by people who manufacture typesetting machines. The reason typefaces were made was to sell machines. However, conditions have been changing. It was Aaron Burns who, greatly to his credit, figured out a way to make a business out of doing type design."

What Stone was referring to is the system of licensing developed by Aaron Burns at the ubiquitous ITC, International Typeface Corporation. Burns figured out that even though a typeface design could not be copyrighted, a trademark for the NAME could be acquired; then the right to use the name could be licensed, accompanied by master images of the typeface. This scheme gave some assurance that one was getting the real thing—although for some traditional faces actually what one got was ITC's revised versions of them. Nonetheless, the company sponsored quite a few new designs and did much to increase type awareness in the hinterlands through its house organ, *U&lc*. Though frequently only semi-legible, it is fresh and sassy and is found, it seems, on the tables of every design office in the land.

The phenomenal success of ITC marked the rise of the independent type house, of which there are now several. But at the same time, the refusal of some large firms to license their proprietary designs fostered the rampant growth of a pernicious industry, the plagiarism of typefaces and the reflagging of their names. Thus Bembo becomes Bem and, in a recent offering, Ambo (you've seen the movie, now buy the type!). Obviously, this only encourages the bastardization of original designs. More deleterious yet is the confusion it causes in the public mind. How can the type industry complain about rejection of typeface copyright when it is their

abcdefghijklmnopqrstuvwxyz
ABCDEFGHIJKLMNOPQRSTUVWXYZ
& ÆÐŁŒØÞ åæçðèfiflíijłñœøßüþð
1234567890 £$¢ƒ%
.,:;-"!?«»()[]*†‡§

Amerigo, designed by Gerard Unger.

name games which obfuscate the fact that a type design is an original work of art?

Despite these problems, the old-line manufacturers, Berthold, Linotype, Monotype are digitizing the huge type libraries they have developed over the years at a dizzying rate. They are commissioning a few new faces, as are "digital type-foundries" like Bitstream, Digital Type Systems, Bigelow & Holmes, and Adobe Systems. Several new typefaces were shown at the conference, some of them enlarged and displayed on festive twenty-foot banners in the foyer: Bigelow & Holmes' Lucida (Imagen and Adobe), Matthew Carter's Charter (Bitstream), Sumner Stone's Stone (Adobe), Gerard Unger's Amerigo (Bitstream), and Gudrun Zapf von Hesse's Nofret (Berthold) and Carmina (Bitstream).

abcdefghijklmnopqrstuvwxyz
ABCDEFGHIJKLMNOPQRSTUVWXYZ
1234567890&£$¢%.,:;-"!?()[]*†‡§
ÆÐŁŒØåæçðèfiflíłñœøßü

Carmina Light, designed by Gudrun Zapf von Hesse.

The most glamorous attractions at Type 1987 were personal-computer applications like Bitstream's Fontware. Having purchased a Fontware installation kit, the PC owner can endow his/her VDT and printer with machine fonts, the aforementioned Bitstream faces, plus Futura, and Carter's own Galliard, among others. Bitstream did play a bit to popular tastes by adding facile favorites like Souvenir. Fortunately, Bitstream was careful to place some of the more eccentric faces in a separately labeled "Headline" package, so that we may, one hopes, be spared brain damage inflicted by reading an entire text set in University Roman or Broadway. One wonders why Bitstream feels compelled to provide two monospace typewriter faces, Prestige 12-pitch and Courier 10-pitch. Yes, we know, they're comfy and familiar, but did Henry Ford provide two free buggywhips with every Model A?

One inclusion in Adobe's publicity kit for the conference was spare but telling: a four-page keepsake designed by Jack Stauffacher for the Book Club of California. Three rustic woodcuts from the crude early nineteenth-century street ballads of Jemmy Catnach provided an interesting foil for the debut of the new Stone typeface, designed by Sumner Stone. Said Stauffacher modestly of his first effort at computer typography, "I'm a very slow worker with these computers;

✦✦ abcdefghijklmnopqrstuvwxyz
ABCDEFGHIJKLMNOPQRSTUVWXYZ&
ABCDEFGHIJKLMNOPQRSTUVWXYZ
& ÆÐŁŒØÞ åæçðèfiflíijłñœøßüþð
1234567890 1234567890 £$¢ƒ%
.,:;-"!?«»()[]{}*†‡§ ✦✦

Charter, designed by Matthew Carter.

you can do instant sketches, smaller, larger, explore typographic problems. I want to keep my own aesthetic, not let the machine dictate to me."

This was a fine showcase in which to debut an elegant new typeface, and would seem to demonstrate vividly what a master typographer can do with an Adobe PC system. However, the brochure was ultimately output on a Linotype Linotronic 300 at 1270 dpi (dots per inch), not exactly your average Postscript-equipped desktop printer (300 dpi). The accompanying specimen sheets of Stone were closer to what the average PC owner can hope to achieve without the aid of a professional typesetter: in the large sizes, you can see the jaggies if you look closely, nonetheless the type holds up very well under lower resolution devices, just as Sumner Stone intended.

A mathematician and a calligrapher by training and practice, Sumner Stone has brought a humanistic quality to the Adobe-Postscript environment. Postscript is the language which allows the computer to speak to the printer, allowing it to describe graphic images and type characters as abstract outlines and to fill them in for printing in the form of bitmaps. The Stone family of types—"a clan, really"—consists of three different groupings of typefaces: serif, sans serif, and informal, altogether eighteen different faces in three different weights. The informal is Stone's innovation on the old medieval scribes' idea of using different scripts to indicate different purposes (e.g., Carolingian minuscule combined with uncial). He came to Adobe three years ago, when they were developing the Laserwriter, and quickly realized that many people would want to use the machine more informally, for letterwriting, memos, etc. They would need a type that would serve the same purpose as a typewriter face, but with more grace, and have the ability to blend fully in weight and color with the more formal versions of the typeface.

Stone Informal Medium ABCDEFGHIJKLMNOPQ RSTUVWXYZ abcdefghijklmnopqrstu vwxyz 1234567890&

Stone Informal, designed by Sumner Stone.

Two pioneers in democratizing typography, in making real types available on affordable, low-resolution printing devices, are Charles Bigelow and Kris Holmes, who, as early as 1981 predicted the need for a typeface specially designed for the revolution in publishing. What was needed was a multiresolutional typeface which would hold up well over a broad range of printing devices. Lucida, by Bigelow and Holmes, was the first original typeface designed for laser printing (see *Fine Print*, July 1985). The type has a large x-height and serifs made to be slightly trapezoidal, with no right angles; at low resolution they are seen as simple slab serifs, but at high resolution the full detail of the bracketing is captured.

Speaking at Type 1987, Kris Holmes explained how Lucida was adapted to the redesign of *Scientific American*. Adrian Fruti-ger commented on how rare it is to see a project in which the type designer works so closely with the art director of a publication. Finding the original Lucida very readable but just a trifle too heavy for the open quality of layout desired by *Scientific American*, Holmes designed a lighter and longer serif, and, with the magic of the Ikarus program, she was able to apply the new serifs to all the characters with just a few keystrokes, something that in earlier eras would have taken hours of redrawing. She also thinned the hairlines and tightened letterfitting. Pick up the new *Scientific American* at the newsstand, note the harmonious use of the Lucida family in

Can myopia, or nearsightedness, be caused by too much reading? A long history of observations suggests that it can—including a reported increase in myopia among Eskimos after the advent of compulso-

Lucida, redesigned for *Scientific American*, by Bigelow & Holmes.

roman, italic, and bold and the newly designed modern-style titling in the tradition of Didot and Bodoni. If you can, compare its fresh-faced readability with earlier issues, and doubt not the importance of encouraging this kind of original *custom* type design, something the new systems may make affordable and practical for more than a few businesses and organizations, if not hampered by lack of copyright protection.

While type designers seemed to be riding high at Type 1987, type users seemed to be wallowing in a slough of discontent. Even though type resources are at an all-time high, with literally thousands of display and text faces available for their palette, graphic designers and type directors voiced again and again their disappointment with the type offered by the average typesetter. They are frustrated with the difficulty of getting authentic versions of the classic types they specified. And very often, the type is set too close ("but all the agencies are doing it") with uneven letterspacing. Hearing the complaints, Gerald Lange, a fine letterpress printer now working at University of California, Los Angeles, said, "This certainly makes letterpress printing look like a clean, safe, well-lighted place."

Nonetheless, most people have to work in dirty, risky, murky places. They want more grounding, more guidance from type manufacturers, more detailed specimen books, which show how the designer intended the type to be used. The link between type designer and type manufacturer seems relatively healthy, given the contortions of the licensing system, but in the communications between type manufacturer, typesetter, and type specifier, a serious disconformity exists. People don't know what they're getting and don't know how to use what they've got.

The new facile type mutability brings our alphabetic heritage into a parlous state. Up to now we could count on the fact that those who shaped our letters and gave form to the printed page would have absorbed a certain minimum body of practice, would share certain aesthetic principles. Said Colin Banks, quoting Frederic Goudy, "The man who would space lowercase italic would steal sheep." No longer.

But at Type 1987, at least, the heritage and the aesthetic were reaffirmed. James Mosley traced the origins of sans serif types, linking them to influences arising from the English enthusiasm for Roman antiquity in the early nineteenth century, and demonstrating how type design can be, perhaps not a bellwether, but certainly a weathervane of cultural trends. And in one of the most inspiring lectures, John Dreyfus examined the work of five giants of typography, Stanley Morison, Edward Johnston, Jan van Krimpen, Giovanni Mardersteig, and Roger Excoffon, showing how those working in typography today are "standing on their shoulders."

Said Dreyfus, "Tradition becomes a force only when used in a new age that transforms it." The trouble is that for many new practitioners who won't know where they are standing, it will be all too easy to fall off. The critical task of all typographers and typophiles in the years ahead will be one of education and communication, lest we all topple together.

This article was reported with the assistance of E. M. Ginger; also Charles Bigelow, Margery Cantor, Paul H. Duensing, and Michael Sheridan.

The Stone Family of Typefaces: New Voices for the Electronic Age

AaBbCcDdEeFfGgHhIiJjKkLlMmNnOoPpQqRrSsTtUuVvWwXxYyZz

AaBbCcDdEeFfGgHhIiJjKkLlMmNnOoPpQqRrSsTtUuVvWwXxYyZz

AaBbCcDdEeFfGgHhIiJjKkLlMmNnOoPpQqRrSsTtUuVvWwXxYyZz

AaBbCcDdEeFfGgHhIiJjKkLlMmNnOoPpQqRrSsTtUuVvWwXxYyZz

AaBbCcDdEeFfGgHhIiJjKkLlMmNnOoPpQqRrSsTtUuVvWwXxYyZz

AaBbCcDdEeFfGgHhIiJjKkLlMmNnOoPpQqRrSsTtUuVvWwXxYyZz

It is a common practice to use different alphabet styles together in one text. In fact, the use of roman capitals with lower case is so ingrained, we think of them as being part of a single style, even though the invention of the capital alphabet is separated from that of the lower case by more than 1,000 years.

Different alphabet designs used together serve many functions: to punctuate the text, i.e., to give visual expression to the structure of its meaning; and to serve as the visual equivalent of different voices. One might say that the feeling or character of a particular alphabet design is equal to a tone of voice:

Hands off, she shouted. *Yes ma'am*, he whispered.

In the early history of Roman manuscripts only one style is used in a given manuscript. A manuscript from the fourth century, for example, would be written with only uncial letterforms although the letters which started a sentence were sometimes written in a larger size. However, the convention of using different historical scripts for different functions in the text is not new. During the period in which Carolingian minuscule was the main text script (roughly the eighth through eleventh centuries), the roman forms that had previously been employed for text were in use in a secondary capacity. A document written with the

Carolingian manuscript with minuscule and uncial letterforms, A.D. 860.

Carolingian minuscule for the main text, for example, might also contain uncial, rustic, and square capital letters for emphasis of various kinds such as initial letters, headings, and for setting off of certain parts of the text. The scribes who produced these documents created compatability in differing letterforms by using the same pen, same letter heights, and sometimes even the same form for some of the letters.

When different writing systems or scripts are first combined, they may have very different characteristics, but as these typographic experiments become conventions, the inclination of the type designer is to think of the collection of scripts as being related by use and to design them accordingly. Thus, when the first italic typefaces were developed for Aldus Manutius in fifteenth-century Venice, they were intended to stand as the sole type style for the text of a book. When printers began to use the italic as a secondary typeface accompanying the roman, the two

Auguſtin Romein
Illi nihilominus contra, qui magis ſobr e
ratiocinati ſunt, agnoverunt in ipſo etian
gentiliſmo, ubi nullum ſupernaturale lᴎ-
Auguſtin Curs
Illi nihilominus contr a, qui magis ſobrie ratio-
cinati ſunt, agnoverunt in ipſo etiam gentilis
mo, ubi nullum ſupernaturale ſplenduit lumen
quod univerſum hoc ſuum aliquando habuerit

From a specimen of the types of Nicolas Kis, 1686.

styles came to be designed together, with global characteristics such as uniform character heights and equivalent weights as seen in the example from Nicolas Kis. This integration process is what yields a typeface *family* rather than just a collection of alphabet designs used together.

The type designer's approach to creating compatibility among different styles is similar to that of the Carolingian scribes. The letterforms are designed with similar weights, letter heights, and proportions in order to create textures which are not too dissimilar. Of course, it is also important to preserve some of the essential differences which motivated the simultaneous use of different styles in the first place.

The phenomenon of the type family is not restricted to Western writing systems. The Japanese routinely combine three different writing systems – the Chinese ideographs, called *kanji* in Japan, and two different syllabic systems called *kana*. One syllabic system, the *hiragana*, is used to inflect *kanji* (and thus bridges the gap between the mono-

の阿部が富士通に持参したい
その時項目１の回答とJIS-83コ
ングとRyumin-Lightフォント

Kanji are the most complex characters. Katakana are simpler, but still angular and formal. The most cursive and rounded forms are the hiragana.

syllabic basis of the Chinese writing system and the poly-syllabic requirements of Japanese grammar). A second syllabic system, the *katakana,* is used among other things, to transliterate foreign words. Both the *hiragana* and the *katakana* evolved from the *kanji*, just as Latin minuscule letters evolved from the roman capitals. A designer of Japanese type confronts the task of harmonizing all three systems – *kanji, katakana,* and the more cursive *hiragana,* much as a Western designer must harmonize capitals, roman lower case, and italic.

According to our current notion for using Latin scripts, a typeface family comprises capitals and lower case characters for an upright or roman typeface and accompanying italics, plus bold versions of each, and sometimes other weights as well. In recent years, designers have elaborated the concept of a typeface family considerably by adding more weights as well as condensed and expanded versions. The most systematic example of this is the Univers series designed by Adrian Frutiger, which consists of 21 versions.

Since the beginning of the nineteenth century, there have been many new variations in alphabet design. Several of these styles are now commonly used together in order to solve complex typographic problems. One of the most common type mixtures we find in texts today is that of serif and sans serif typefaces, but in general these types have not been designed to be part of the same typographic family. The idea of designing a serif and sans serif typeface as part of the same family seems to have originated with Jan van Krimpen, who designed a sans serif version of Romulus in the 1920s. Although preliminary cuttings were made, the sans serif was never issued. Gerard Unger, a contemporary Dutch designer, created Demos and Praxis, a related serif and sans serif set of families for Hell Digiset in the 1970s. Ed Benguiat extended this idea outside the realm of traditional text typefaces and into display faces with ITC Benguiat and ITC Benguiat Gothic (1979). Charles Bigelow and Kris Holmes included serif and sans serif versions as part of their family of types called Lucida, the first designed specifically for laser printers, released in 1985.

The collection of eighteen typefaces that I have designed over a period of three years and which now immodestly bear my name, represent an even further extension of our common notion of a typeface family. The Stone family might actually be thought of as a type clan with three different branches on the family tree. There is a serif, a sans, and a new kind of design which I have called "informal." Each design has three weights with matching italics for a total of eighteen typefaces.

Producing eighteen typefaces is a major undertaking. Bob Ishi, a book designer and my assistant on this project, did a great deal of the detailed work necessary to produce such a large family in an integrated and systematic way – including the editing of bitmap screen fonts – a total of 20,000 characters. Type designer Matthew Carter has remarked that in designing typefaces, the hardest part is coming up with a name. I mulled over many names, including a vast array of trilogies. The deciding factor was a flashcard for learning Japanese, which Bob Ishi left on my desk one morning. Ishi means "stone" in Japanese – the coincidence was just too great to ignore.

The Stone typefaces are to a certain extent based on a common underlying model; they have the same cap heights, the same lower case x-heights, and the same stem weights. Each design is a manifestation of an underlying skeletal set of letterforms. Thus, though there are numerous differences, each typeface has many characteristics in common with the others. However, to do their jobs properly the typefaces needed to be distinct from one another. In the design process several nuances in the basic forms were introduced. For example, the lower case a has similar forms in the Serif and Sans, and a different form in the Informal. The lower case g has similar forms in the Sans and Informal, and a different form for the Serif. These variant

a a a
g g g
Serif   *Sans*   *Informal*

forms are appropriate to the function of each style, and they help distinguish the styles when used together.

Stone Informal is intended to be used in much the same way in which monospace typewriter typefaces have been in the past, as, for example, correspondence. I began thinking about the need for such a design when I started working at Adobe Systems about four years ago. I noticed that I was frequently receiving letters and memos printed out in Times Roman on the laser printer. I had the feeling that these messages were probably not for me, or if they were, that they had come from the IRS. I realized that as laser printing technology became more commonplace, there would be an increasing need for typefaces suited to personal communications generated by computer.

There was no historical model for these Informal designs, but I had several basic ideas to start with. I thought first that they should be related in some way to handwriting and that they should have a more dynamic, rhythmical character than formal text typefaces. The branching used in the lower case letters **abdgpqhmn** is one such cursive characteristic. The **a** and **g**, as shown earlier, are based on cursive rather than formal models. At the same time, I

bbbbbbb

This sequence demonstrates how the medium lower case b was transformed into the bold b. The points that are indicated on the contours of the characters were moved in an interactive drawing process on the screen of a computer. The medium b contour on the left shows all the bezier spline points that are used to define the character. The contours which follow to the right display in each case only the points that were moved in order to create that variation.

thought that they should have some formal typographic characteristics that would make them readable in fairly long passages of text. The serif structure, which underwent many changes during the design process, is intended to provide some of this formality.

It also seemed a good idea for the letters to have some relationship to their only legitimate predecessors, typewriter types. Therefore they are low contrast (little difference in weight between thick and thin strokes), and have somewhat rounded shapes and stroke endings.

During the summer of 1987 two graduate students from

Stone Extra Informal

the graphic design program at Yale, Min Wang and Brian Wu, were interns at Adobe. Their assignment was to create a variety of graphic material using the Stone typefaces. Their arrival coincided with the beginning of "Stone" jokes. In the mornings I frequently found interesting things taped to my door or lying on my chair. The lower case "r" from Stone Extra Informal is one of them – the rest of the font never appeared.

The design of Stone began with a well-known method – letter drawings for a "test word" in the form of rough pencil sketches. Next, a finished pencil drawing based on a capital height of about six inches was made for digitization. Digitization, in this case, means plotting selected points along the contour of the character on an electronic tablet connected to a computer; this produces a mathematically defined outline representation of the character. This kind of mathematical description is known as a "spline." Splines are parametric representations of curves described by polynomial equations. The particular splines used in this case were bezier splines, invented by the French mathematician, Pierre Bezier.

Traditional letter drawing was used at several stages in the design process. After digitizing, editing, and in some cases, redrawing on the computer, some of the roman letters (along with guidelines) were printed on the laser printer. These proofs were then used as drawing paper for the italic, so that sketches of the italic forms could be made next to the roman type.

In a few cases the digitized character was printed at large size and then used as a template for creating variations. Most of the design work, however, was done by drawing with a computer; only about 100 out of the 4,000 drawings were made on paper. The process of drawing with a computer program is difficult to describe without being able to demonstrate. The points defining the spline outline can be pulled and pushed by the designer in a fashion which seems more like sculpture than drawing; this creates new shapes, or subtly modifies the existing shape. It is possible to use a letterform as raw material for creating another form. For example, all the bold characters were created from the medium characters.

To design the semibold weights, I used a computer program that does interpolation. Here interpolation means "averaging" the light and the bold outlines of a character to produce an outline of intermediate weight. This is a fairly simple mathematical operation in which the coordinates of the points which define the splines are averaged. The process has been used very successfully in designing letterforms for some time. By the same means, it is possible to make very subtle adjustments to the weights of the medium and bold, which is extremely useful in fine tuning the relationships between the designs.

The Stone typefaces were designed for cultural reasons, not technological ones. They were, however, designed for use in the present technological environment, the main component of which is the PostScript® page description language invented and implemented by Adobe Systems of Mountain View, California.

In designing typefaces for PostScript machines, a large range of resolutions and imaging technologies have to be considered. Since new PostScript devices are being created all the time, it is not possible to know what the universe of imaging devices is going to be. There are already 300, 400, and 600 dpi (dots per inch) laser printers, typesetters which function at 635, 1270, and 2540 dpi, dot matrix printers,

nanbncndnenfngnh
nanbncndnenfngnh

1270 dot per inch typesetter output on top, 300 dpi laser printer output on the bottom.

ink jet printers, LED (light emitting diode) printers, and thermographic color printers, as well as the many CRT (cathode ray tube) displays of computer terminals that will be used for Display PostScript™, with many more to come. Type designers have long had to design type for many different printing processes executed on many different kinds of surfaces by printers with varying levels of skill. The advantage in designing typefaces for PostScript machines is that output from many of these devices is readily available for examination during the design process. For example, a proof output from a 300 dpi laser printer shows a completely different quality of sharpness when compared to that from a 1270 dpi laser typesetter.

The design process was clearly affected by the ability to view the type in many of its manifestations. In both a conscious and unconscious process I was drawn toward forms that would work well in varied environments. All of the Stone letterforms are fairly sturdy, avoiding attenuated thin parts and features that create obvious problems at low resolution, such as lines which are not quite horizontal or vertical.

The PostScript environment also is capable of creating the same letterform in a very large range of sizes. This has been a design consideration since the advent of phototypesetting with its facility to photographically enlarge and reduce the same font. As the type will be used both for text and display, the forms have to be functional and legible for text, but have to retain some elegance in large sizes.

My training as a designer started when I was a calligraphy student of Lloyd Reynolds at Reed College in Portland, Oregon. In my early days as a calligrapher, I had a tendency to think of the invention of movable type as a major force in the degradation of letterforms. Technological revolutions in letter making have frequently been viewed in this light, and it is true that letterform design is always affected by the medium that is used. I am not now convinced, however, that it has ever been the major influence: look at the amazing variety of letters created with the edged pen.

Creating typefaces by computer has advantages and disadvantages. I have been focusing on the advantages and the new opportunities created by this technology. In the process of creating the Stone types I used the computer as a design tool because it was the best tool I had at hand. Some of the advantages are dramatic. For the first time since the punchcutter used smoke proofs it is possible to get an almost immediate proof of your letterforms. In fact, these proofs are in some ways better than smoke proofs since they are the actual finished product created by the same machine(s) that will generate the type when the design is finished. The immediate feedback, the chance for many iterations of the design, and the capacity to organize and proof many typefaces, enabled me to design eighteen typefaces as a single family in what now seems like the short period of three years.

Another notable feature of the new technology is its accessibility. Anyone who can purchase a personal computer and a laser printer has the means to produce typefaces. It seems very likely that we will see a new flowering of type design activity.

A common query I hear is whether we really need more type designs – the implication being that perhaps we have too many already. This idea seems so obviously silly to me, that I have had trouble in the past in responding to it. Think for a minute about how many different kinds of spoons you own, yet have you ever heard anyone say that there are too many kinds of spoons? The reasons for having so many are precisely the same as those for having a large variety of typefaces.

The design of a new typeface, like the invention of a long-handled spoon for stirring sugar into iced tea or the making of a beautiful hand-carved wooden spoon, is a sign of a lively, growing society. Typefaces are both functional and aesthetic objects, and the invention of new variations may be motivated by either need or beauty, or some combination of the two.

Part of the reason that new type designs might seem superfluous may be that we, as a culture, are out of touch with our alphabet, even though we are surrounded by letterforms. How many people, even well-educated people, know anything about where the alphabet comes from or why letters look the way the do?

The fact that so many people now have type making and typesetting tools within their grasp already seems to be stimulating a new interest in letterforms. I certainly believe that those of us who are engaged in producing type for the new technology have a responsibility to promote letterform education. Perhaps this new technology will help breathe new life into the letter making arts.

Sumner Stone

*These four pages of **Fine Print** are set in Stone type and produced entirely with PostScript software and compatible application programs. The design is by Jack W. Stauffacher of the Greenwood Press, San Francisco; he used an Apple Macintosh computer to do the page composition and an Apple Laserwriter to proof the pages. The pages were set at 1270 dots per inch on a Linotronic 300 typesetter at Adobe Systems by Fred Brady.*

Philosophies of Form
in Seriffed Typefaces of Adrian Frutiger

Charles Bigelow

IN COMPARISON to modern fine arts, typeface design seems at first glance to be lacking in self-expression. The canons of acceptable alphabet shape and proportion have been so established through centuries of precedence that deviations from the norm can vitiate the utility of a typeface. Hence, the contemporary text type designer cannot break with tradition as readily as a painter or sculptor.

Yet, deeper study of the art of type design reveals, beneath a superficially arid canopy, a world lush with diversity. Within the traditional confines of typography – abstraction, achromaticity, and utility – the interplay of created forms can reveal the personal style of an original designer, if not as an unvarying theme, then as a pattern of family resemblances.

Such a pattern is readily evident in the work of Adrian Frutiger. Over the past thirty years he has produced a series of text typefaces which, despite their external differences, appear to be related when examined closely. Just as individual members of the human species may differ in musculature, proportion, clothing, and complexion, but are alike in possessing a similarly articulated skeleton, so the type designs of Frutiger often share a similar internal architecture.

The textural quality of a typeface is like the timbre of a musical instrument, and the individual letters are like musical notes. A text composed in one typeface can look very different when composed in another because a complex visual sensation emerges from the repetition and interaction of nearly subliminal design features of the type. Frutiger's exploration of manifold type forms delights the eye with textural variations and deepens the understanding with abstract forms that express their distinctive meanings.

A typeface design is a system of variations. The particular features and combination of form elements in a given face create an effect that has meaning – not phonic or verbal, like that signified by the letter shapes themselves – but graphic. Most readers understand at least a small set of graphic meanings based on variations within a typeface family or between families: italic versus roman; bold versus normal weight; seriffed versus sans serif; but Frutiger leads us further into a realm of varied halftones, delicate patterns, and subtle textures, all built up from simple form elements. His work is an exploration of a realm where one thinks not *about* forms but *with* forms, and his typeface designs are philosophies expressed not in a language of words but in a language of images. The look of a type in text is a complex graphic expression that is not the content of the text; rather it is an ephemeral yet necessary accompaniment, a visual sensation that is forgotten once the text has been read, as a

wrapping is discarded after the gift has been opened, or a glass set aside after the wine has been drunk.

Though Frutiger's most popular designs have been the sans serifs Univers and Frutiger, his seriffed faces constitute an equally significant and useful body of work. Here we review three seriffed families, Iridium, Icone, and Breughel, designed by Frutiger for photographic and digital composition. But to begin, a brief look at his recent sans serif may help to introduce Frutiger's approach to type design.

FRUTIGER

By the 1970s, the grotesque style sans serifs of the 1950s Univers, Helvetica, and Folio began to look dated, and typographers searching for a fresh look in the post-modern period were presented with a new sans by Frutiger. Originally designed for the signage of the Charles de Gaulle airport at Roissy, the new family was adopted for photocomposition in 1976 by Linotype, and eponymously christened Frutiger.

The Roissy-Frutiger face shows Frutiger's second thoughts about the nature of sans serif. It is not a grotesque, but a humanist style of sans, like Edward Johnston's London Under-

ABCDEFGHIJKLMNOPQ
RSTUVWXYZ
abcdefghijklmnopqrs
tuvwxyz   1234567890

ground lettering, Eric Gill's Sans, or Hans Meier's Syntax. In its inner lines, Frutiger echos the old-style forms of the renaissance more than the constructive symmetries of nineteenth-century industrialism. The counters of a, c, e, g and s are more open than in the grotesque style, differentiating the letters for easier discrimination. The shapes of the counters, though different from those of Univers, also show sensitive sculpting and refined simplicity. The capitals are old style in form and proportion, closer to roman inscriptional majuscules than to nineteenth-century upper case.

Compared to grotesque faces, the pattern of Frutiger in text is more lively because the letter forms are not subordinated to the strict grotesque principle that calls for equaliza-

Each section in this article discusses a different Frutiger typeface and is set in that face. The introduction, however, is set in Méridien, originally a hot metal face produced by Deberny & Peignot in 1957.

tion of widths, especially in capitals, and assimilation of lower case forms in which round letters like c and e tend to be closed, resembling o, and slightly condensed, thus resembling straight letters like n. Frutiger produces more distinctive word images because the widths of letters are more variable; it is less linear in emphasis because the terminals of curved strokes end with vertical rather than horizontal cuts, and more liberated in feeling, because the letter shapes are more varied.

IRIDIUM

Iridium is a seriffed design in the modern or neo-classical style, produced by Linotype in 1972 for photographic typesetting technology. Frutiger used the photocomposition medium to experiment not only with the shapes of the letters, but with the basic features of the design style. A style comprises many characteristics, some essential, some not. An essential characteristic of the neo-classical style is its chiaroscuro, strong dark stems contrast with thin, delicate hairlines and serifs. Other important features are an emphasis on bilateral symmetry, a vertical axis in shading or stress (orientation of thick and thin), and a sculptural rather than calligraphic treatment of joins, terminals, and similar details. A less important characteristic, but one emphasized in most revivals of modern faces, like ATF Bodoni, is rigid rectangularity of unbracketed stems and serifs, aligned in strictly vertical and horizontal directions.

ABCDEFGHIJKLMNOPQ
RSTUVWXYZ
abcdefghijklmnopqrs
tuvwxyz   1234567890

In Iridium, Frutiger separates the essential from the non-essential. He retains the thick-thin contrast of the modern style, its symmetric structure, and sculpted treatment, including bulbous terminals of curves in such letters as a, c, f, g, j, and r. Frutiger repudiates the monotonous rectangularity by fashioning stems and serifs that flare* gently toward their extremes, and he softens their intersections with slight bracketings. In the lower case, the ascender and x-line serifs are not strictly horizontal, but angled slightly, a feature associated more with transitional than modern faces. The resulting face has the expected glittery brilliance of a modern, but also exhibits an unusual liveliness. Where a pedestrian modern like ATF Bodoni is stiff, static, and predictable, Iridium is supple, dynamic, and refreshing.

Iridium Italic is a true cursive, rather than a slanted roman. Like the italics of Bodoni or Didot, the lower case has near horizontal entrance serifs at the ascender and x lines, and curved exit serifs at the base line. Bulb terminals appear on *s, k, v, w, x, y,* and *z,* in addition to those also found in the roman. Rounded vertices on the *v* and *w,* familiar in round-hand script, soften a potentially pointy appearance.

In all typefaces, it is not just the contrast between thick and thin, but the distribution of weight, the arrangement of dark

*The slight flaring of serifs noticeable in the photocomposition original of this face are not apparent in the digital rendering of Iridium in this article.

and light, that determines the pattern presented to the eye of the reader. In traditional moderns like Didot, as well as most revivals of the style, the vertical stems and curved bowls are often assimilated into an excessively vertical, monotonous pattern. In Iridium, a reverse entasis is created by thickening the stems at their terminals and arches and thinning them in the middle; this differentiates the straight stems from the curved bowls where weight accumulates in the middle of the stroke. Iridium thus replaces the picket-fence pattern of tradi-

ABCDEFGHIJKLMNOPQ
RSTUVWXYZ
abcdefghijklmnopqrs
tuvwxyz   1234567890

tional moderns with a softer, more complex texture, in which weight is distributed along the base line, x line, ascender line, and capital line.

Bodoni, like all type designers before the end of the nineteenth century, cut his own punches in steel by hand. Frutiger, who throughout his lettering career has shown himself to be handy with a knife and graver, cut the final, master designs for Iridium by hand in a photo-mask film. Although it is

nave

difficult to say how much the small personal touches of Frutiger's hand-cutting would affect the printed image of a letter passed through several photographic processes on its way to a page of paper, his technique shows that even in an industrial era far from the days of William Morris, the artist can involve himself in the craft.

Although Iridium is a radical departure from most plodding revivals of the modern style, an examination of Bodoni's faces shows that the maestro himself was not as rigid and doctrinaire as his imitators. Many of Bodoni's own cuttings exhibit slightly flared serifs, subtle bracketing, and delicate deviations from a strictly constructive technique. Bodoni himself had his eye on the total effect more than a particular technique when he wrote that the modern style should show "regularity, neatness and polish, good taste, and grace." Certainly these qualities are also evident in Iridium.

ICONE

On all sides in the modern world, we are confronted by the tyranny of the rectangle. The wall, the ceiling, the floor, the window, the newspaper, the book, the magazine, the photograph, the painting, the sidewalk, the street, the building, the cabinet, the box, the crate, etc. The opposition between the rectangle, a conceptual, cultural artifact, and the freely complex curves of nature is more than a pythagorean abstraction.

The economic and political battle between environmentalists and lumber companies, for example, is in part a struggle between the geometry of the free form and that of the rectangle. When a tree is "saved," it remains a living organism with an intricately complex geometry. When it is lost, it becomes a bunch of rectangles – boards, panelling, shingles, and even sheets of paper. In the aesthetic politics of contemporary graphic design, the sans serif face, whose rectangular, constructed forms suggest modernism, technocracy, and commerce, is often opposed to the old style seriffed face, whose cursive, curving forms derived from handwritten origins, suggest classicism, calligraphy, and humanism.

The rise of digital typographic technology initially appeared to be a victory for the side of the rectangles. The beautiful, free-form curves of classical faces were mutilated on the procrustean grid of digital rasters, chopped into rectangular bits like french-fried potatoes in a fast-food franchise. In opposition to this trend, Frutiger designed a face almost wholly comprised of complex curves, Icone, released by Linotype in 1980 for photographic and digital typesetters.

The stems of Icone flare emphatically toward their terminals, and the flares are asymmetric, stronger at the upper left

nave

entrances and lower right exits of strokes, echoing the ductus of a carolingian or humanist hand. The only straight lines in the lower case are brief horizontal terminations of strokes at the base line, ascender line, cap line, and x line, occasional crossbars, and brief vertical terminations of curves in letters like c and s. In the capitals, straights appear only in the horizontal arms and crossbars of letters like E and H, and in the middle sections of vertical stems. Icone remains a challenge to digital technology, but today (1988) there are high resolution digital typesetters that can render it crisply and faithfully.

The style of Icone is difficult to classify. Its name comes from the Greek word for a likeness or image, though like all alphabets descended from the Greek, its letters are abstract and symbolic. If Icone is an image, its representation can only be at a rarefied level of abstraction, an evocation of patterns seen in the leaves of a tree against the sky, in the trails of insects skittering across the surface of a pond, or in seeds sprouting in a spring garden.

Linotype lumps Icone together with Decorative and Display faces in its recent type catalog, but the face clearly does not belong together with such aberrations as Souvenir and Korinna, those bizarre products of fevered pre-World War I delusions, which have lately come back from oblivion to trouble our reading lives.* Icone more obviously derives from a classical

*Today's popular ITC Souvenir is a 1970 reworking of Morris Fuller Benton's ATF Souvenir of 1914, which itself was an American semi-plagiarism (a reworking with some design changes) of Schelter Antiqua and Kursiv produced c. 1912 by the Leipzig foundry of Schelter and Giesecke. In *Asymmetric Typography* (Reinhold, 1967 [the English translation of *Typographische Gestaltung*, 1935]), Jan Tschichold, chief proponent of the modern movement in typography, shows a page from the German printing magazine *Deutscher Buch- und Steindrucker*, and writes, "Example of German typography (1922) before the advent of Jan Tschichold's *New Typography*. Disgust with such degenerate type faces and arrangements led the author to attempt to eradicate them entirely." The majority of faces on that page are Schelter Antiqua and Kursiv.

lettering tradition – its pen-written ductus is clear – but the puzzle is to identify the kind of pen writing, for the face is just as obviously not a direct interpretation of any actual historical hand. Accumulation of weight at terminals and asymmetric flarings are reminiscent both of rustic and gothic scripts with their variable but usually steep pen angles, but the horizontal terminals with flat base line and x line recall the uncial, with its flat pen angle.

Both the capitals and lower case of Icone are generously wide, and the pattern of the alphabet in text is, despite its

ABCDEFGHIJKLMNOPQ
RSTUVWXYZ
abcdefghijklmnopqrs
tuvwxyz   1234567890

unfamiliarity, charmingly legible. A quality that contributes to legibility at small sizes, but which is discernible only at larger sizes, is the distinctive sculpting of internal counters, a technique found in all of Frutiger's faces. The light and normal weights (45 and 55) are appropriate for text composition, and the bold and extra black weights (65 and 85) for display. Each weight has a companion italic that is an oblique rendering of the roman. Lining figures are provided for use with capitals, and old-style figures for lower case.

Icone has been used with taste and sensitivity in publications and posters for French national museums by Bruno Pfäffli, a Swiss-trained typographer who has been Frutiger's studio partner for many years. The Icone family would find greater acceptance among American typographers if Linotype and Frutiger provided in addition to the chancery-style lower case g, an alternative, humanist (two-looped) g for the romans, thus neutralizing the objection that Icone is not a serious text face because its g is like that of most sans serifs.

BREUGHEL

Like Icone, Breughel is a challenge to typographic taxonomy and technology, and an invitation to the innovative typographer to explore new textures on the printed page. Linotype, which produced the family in 1982, classes it with the renaissance faces, Venetians and old-styles like Centaur, Bembo, and Garamond. But where Centaur is erratic in its asymmetry, Breughel is purposeful. Where Bembo is polished, Breughel is rough-hewn. Where Garamond is delicate, Breughel is strong.

nave

The incunabular punchcutters Jenson and Griffo diverted the cutting of roman types away from the pen-written ductus, and their techniques were refined by Garamond. Base-line serifs of lower case – asymmetric in humanist script – were assimilated to those of capitals, made more symmetrical, and refined. In contrast, the base-line serifs of Breughel are asymmetrical. Strong parallelograms, heavier than the hairlines, are short and bracketed on the left, long and un-bracketed on the right. Serifs at the x line and ascender line are similar horizontal parallelograms, long, bracketed, and

ABCDEFGHIJKLMNOPQ
RSTUVWXYZ
abcdefghijklmnopqrs
tuvwxyz 1234567890

extending to the left, rather than the triangular shapes common to renaissance types.

The pen angle used to write the humanist minuscule was approximately 30 degrees, which gives a backward tilt to the elliptical counters of curved letters like o, as well as an oblique distribution of weight that is also found, to a lesser extent, in arched letters like n. As the roman typeface evolved, this virtual angle was flattened and the weights made more balanced. But in Breughel, the tilted counters and obliquely weighted curves and arches indicate letterforms written with a broad-edged pen.

The stems of renaissance types, cut rather than written, were straighter and more regular than scribal pen strokes, but the stems of Breughel are emphatically curved and bracketed on their left. Thus, while the old-style faces evolved toward equilibrium, the forms of Breughel have been set in motion along the line of the scribe's hurrying hand. The capitals are classical and well formed in their structure, but share the asymmetrical flared stems and parallelogram serifs of the lower case, emphasizing the dynamic pattern of the face.

Breughel Italic is a true cursive, but does not follow renaissance models. It is neither the humanist cursive that Griffo cut for Aldus in Venice, nor the formal chancery developed by Arrighi and used by Blado in Rome, nor the Basle italic perfected and standardized by Granjon in Lyon, Paris, and Antwerp. Its most striking feature is that its base-line serifs are not curved upward but flat. They are the same parallelogram shapes as the roman serifs, but extend only toward the right, with a pronounced bracket.

nave

Like Icone, Breughel has lining figures that align with the capitals as well as old-style figures that ascend and descend, for composition with the lower case.

Culminating in the work of Garamond, the renaissance punchcutters progressively sought lightness and refinement. But Frutiger has given Breughel a strong color, even in the lightest of its three weights, decimal 55. The bolder weights, 65 and 75, are primarily for display.

In its strength, its oblique distribution of weight, its asymmetry, and its rough-hewn forms, Breughel is closer to a humanist writing hand than a renaissance typeface. Yet,

though the ductus and features of Breughel seem to have bypassed the renaissance punchcutters and come to us directly from a pen-written past, it cannot have been our own scribal past. Though Breughel en masse has textural affinities with manuscripts written by humanist scribes like Antonio di Mario or Gherardo del Ciriagio, neither its roman letters nor its italic could have been written by those humanist hands. The precision of the shapes is closer to engraving than to writing. The repeated features are more rational and regular than in humanist hands derived from an arbitrary combination of inscriptional capital and carolingian minuscule. The complex stem shapes would require a wearying twisting of the pen instead of the quick rhythmic strokes favored by the professional scribe. It would seem that the forms of Breughel stem from some alternate humanist past, a probability world that did not quite exist until Frutiger discovered it.

ABCDEFGHIJKLMNOPQ
RSTUVWXYZ
abcdefghijklmnopqrs
tuvwxyz 1234567890

And indeed, our world today, the world of laser printers and typesetters, bitmap CRT display screens, and digital type, is not the world of the humanist scribes, and the letterforms of one may not live in the other. Like the head of Janus, Breughel faces in both directions. The leading edge of its stems is straight and clear, adapted to the digital grid, but the trailing edge is strongly curved, remembering the articulation of the scribe's hand. Its serifs are thick and flat, aligned with the low-resolution raster, but their shapes are elongate parallelograms, miming the movement and angle of the pen that might have made them. The contours of its counters are composed of almost natural curves, but interrupted by straight, mechanical cuts, like a flower petal sliced by a knife edge.

As with Icone, Frutiger's studio partner, Bruno Pfäffli, has used Breughel to advantage in publications and posters for French museums, but in America the face still awaits designers of perception and skill to exploit it fully. Perhaps they will arrive with the new generation entering typography armed with personal computers, laser printers, and enthusiasm. Newcomers with wide open eyes could find in the faces of Frutiger a deep well of inspiration, and use the manifold forms of his designs in ways that we who were raised in a sterner school might never imagine, blinkered as we are by the glint of type metal and distracted by reflections off the crystal goblet.

FURTHER READING

Frutiger, Adrian. *Type Sign Symbol*, with contributions by Maurice Besset, Emil Ruder, and Hans Rudolf Schneebeli. Zurich: ABC Editions, 1980.

_____. *Der Mensch und seine Zeichen*. Edited by Horst Heiderhoff. Echzell, West Germany: Horst Heiderhoff Verlag; 3 vols., 1978-81. French edition, *Des signe et des hommes*. Denges (Lausanne): Editions Delta & Spes, 1983.

LinoType Collection; Mergenthaler Type Library, Typeface Handbook. Eschborn, West Germany (Postfach 5660, D-6236), 1988.

Index

Type Designers

Type Specimens

Punchcutters

Authors

Charles Bigelow is associate professor of digital typography at Stanford University. His typeface designs, created in collaboration with Kris Holmes, include Lucida, the first typeface designed for laser printers; and Pellucida, a related font family used on computer screens and artificial intelligence workstations. He was editor of the "On Type" column from 1980 to 1984.

Max Caflisch, graphic design consultant, was for twenty years the managing director and professor of typography at the School of Arts and Crafts in Zurich. More than a hundred of his book designs have received awards worldwide, and he is the designer of the Columna typeface.

D. Steven Corey is the special collections librarian, Richard A. Gleeson Library, University of San Francisco. He is the editor-in-chief of *The Book Club of California Quarterly News-Letter* and is one of the four founding editors of *Fine Print*.

Donald Day is a calligrapher and designer of electronic graphic systems; he teaches at the California College of Arts and Crafts in Oakland, California.

John Dreyfus is a printing historian and book designer. He is honorary president of the Association Typographique Internationale and formerly typographical advisor to Cambridge University Press and the Monotype Corporation.

Paul Hayden Duensing was trained in languages, music, and the graphic arts. He is the designer of thirteen typefaces (most of which he would like to disavow) and operates a private press and typefoundry from his home near Vicksburg, Michigan. He has been typographic editor for *Fine Print* since 1985.

David Farrell is associate dean for collection management and development in the Indiana University libraries. He is the author of "John Baskerville" in the *Encyclopedia of Library and Information Science* and of *Collegiate Book Art Presses*. He recently compiled the bibliography of The Stinehour Press.

Linnea Gentry is art director and production manager of Harbinger House, trade book publishers in Tuscon, Arizona. She was one of the four founding editors of *Fine Print,* and the first editor of the "On Type" column, from 1977 to 1979.

The late **Horst Heiderhoff** was professor of graphic design at the Hochschule Hanover, as well as typographic consultant to the D. Stempel foundry in Frankfurt, West Germany.

Kris Holmes is the co-designer, with Charles Bigelow, of Lucida, the first original family of typefaces for laser printers. She designed Isadora, a family of script types, and Sierra, a family of calligraphic types for the high resolution typesetting systems of Dr.-Ing Rudolph Hell of West Germany. Most recently she has created a new modern typeface called Galileo for use in the redesign of *Scientific American*.

Herbert H. Johnson is an associate professor in the School of Printing, Rochester Institute of Technology, Rochester, New York. He is writing a bibliography of the work of Bruce Rogers.

Sandra Kirshenbaum is founding editor and publisher of *Fine Print*.

Mark Livingston, a native of Virginia and onetime associate in Mason Hill Press, Pownal, Vermont, now lives in Berkeley, California, where he works in the University library. An amateur handletterer, he studied fitfully with an estimable teacher, Florence Brooks, then of Lenox, Massachusetts. His academic training is in the humanities.

James Mosley, noted printing historian, is librarian of the St Bride Printing Library in London.

Stan Nelson is museum specialist in the Division of Graphic Arts at the Smithsonian Institution, where he demonstrates the arts of printing and typefounding. He is known worldwide as an expert in the cutting of letterforms on steel punches, which are used for striking type matrices.

The late **G. W. Ovink** was professor emeritus of the history and aesthetics of printing and related graphic techniques at the University of Amsterdam. In 1983, in the last few months of his life, he organized an exhibition entitled "Five Times Sixty-Five" featuring the work of Fernand Baudin, Max Caflisch, John Dreyfus, Huib van Krimpen, and Hermann Zapf, all of whom turned sixty-five that year.

Stephen O. Saxe is a former scenic designer for stage and television, turned book designer (Harcourt Brace), turned printing historian. He has been on the board of the American Printing History Association since its founding in 1976, and is now the editor of its bimonthly newsletter. He is currently writing a book about American and English iron hand presses.

Paul Shaw is a calligrapher and graphic designer in New York City. In 1981 he was awarded a Smithsonian Fellowship to study Morris Fuller Benton, and a Newberry Library Fellowship to study George Salter. When not running his design studio, he is at work on a Ph.D. dissertation on W. A. Dwiggins.

Donald E. Stanford is alumni professor emeritus of English at Louisiana State University and editor emeritus and consulting editor of *The Southern Review*. His publications include *The Selected Letters of Robert Bridges; In the Classic Mode; The Achievement of Robert Bridges;* and *The Selected Poems of Robert Bridges*.

Sumner Stone, designer of the Stone family of digital typefaces, is currently director of typography at Adobe Systems, Mountain View, California. He trained as a calligrapher with Lloyd Reynolds.

Walter Tracy was for many years on the staff of the British Linotype companies, in charge of typeface development. He has designed a number of newspaper text types, and some Arabic display faces. The essays on Van Krimpen's types are now included in *Letters of Credit* (David R. Godine, 1987).

This book is created from reproductions of the actual pages of *Fine Print* magazine in which these essays first appeared. Because each issue in the first four years was designed by a different designer, the earlier essays display considerable typographic variation. Beginning in the fifth year, the format was standardized: most of the articles are set in Jan van Krimpen's Monotype Spectrum by Mackenzie-Harris Corp. of San Francisco; the others are set in the typefaces under discussion in the particular essay.

Typographic design of the front matter by Jack W. Stauffacher in Stone Sans designed by Sumner Stone. The type was composed by Fred Brady at Adobe Systems.

Typographic elements of the cover design:
Plato's Phaedrus, first Greek printing by Aldus Manutius 1513; illustrated initial 'H' from Aristotle's *The Politics*, printed by Lorenzo Torrentino, Florence 1559; fragment of a type specimen of Nicholas Kis, Amsterdam, 1686; 'A' construction from *Champ Fleury* by Geofroy Tory, 1529; early twentieth-century wooden poster type; hand set in Adrian Frutiger's Univers. Originally designed and letterpressed by Jack W. Stauffacher at the Greenwood Press, San Francisco.

Printing and binding by Malloy Lithographing, Inc. of Ann Arbor, Michigan.